NUTC.

HUMAN RIGHTS

AUSTRALIA
Law Book Co.
Sydney

CANADA and USA
Carswell
Toronto

HONG KONG
Sweet & Maxwell Asia

NEW ZEALAND
Brookers
Wellington

SINGAPORE and MALAYSIA
Sweet & Maxwell Asia
Singapore and Kuala Lumpur

NUTCASES

HUMAN RIGHTS

SECOND EDITION

by

MAUREEN SPENCER
Principal Lecturer in Law, Middlesex University

and

JOHN SPENCER
Barrister

London • Sweet & Maxwell • 2005

Published in 2005 by
Sweet & Maxwell Limited of
100 Avenue Road, London, NW3 3PF
(http://www.sweetandmaxwell.co.uk)
Typeset by LBJ Typesetting Ltd of Kingsclere
Printed in Great Britain by Creative Print and Design
(Wales) Ebbw Vale

No natural forests were destroyed to make
this product; only farmed timber
was used and replanted

A CIP Catalogue record for this book
is available from the British Library

ISBN 0–421–890509

©
Sweet & Maxwell
2005

CONTENTS

CONTENTS

TABLE OF CASES

1. SOURCES OF HUMAN RIGHTS LAW

ECHR and Responsibility of the State

Key Principle: **Article 1 of the European Convention on Human Rights: "The High Contracting Parties shall secure to everyone within their jurisdiction the rights and freedoms defined in Section 1 of this Convention"**

Key Principle: **A state must provide a legal framework to protect Convention rights effectively.**

Young, James and Webster v UK

British Rail and three trade unions had agreed a "closed shop" condition whereby membership of one of the unions became a condition of employment with British Rail. The three applicants had been working for British Rail before the date of the agreement. They refused to join one of the unions on political and conscientious grounds. They could not claim protection on the sole ground of exemption from union membership, namely religious belief. They alleged breaches of Articles 9, 10, 11 and 13.

Held: (ECtHR) The state was responsible for allowing the violations since Article 1 requires each contracting state to secure Convention rights for those within its jurisdiction. (1981) 4 E.H.R.R. 38

Commentary

The court considered that it was not material to the case that British Rail was a public body. The obligation would have applied if a private body had been the employer, since "it was the domestic law in force at the relevant time that made lawful the treatment of which the applicants complained. The responsibility of the Respondent State for any resultant breach of the Convention is thus engaged". Article 1 has not been incorporated under the Human Rights Act 1998 (HRA). This is arguably understandable since the Government has assumed the responsibility referred to in the Article by passing the Act. On the other hand the omission has implications for the obligation to uphold Convention rights in the private law sphere. The European Court of Human Rights, as this case indicates, imposed a responsibility on states for violations by private bodies by citing Article 1. (See pp.41–43 for more recent cases on the obligations of private bodies).

Key principle: **Statutes should be interpreted so as observe constitutional principles including the rule of law.**

Anufrijeva, R (on the application of) v Secretary of State for the Home Department
The claimant sought asylum and was awarded income support. An internal decision was taken in the Home Office to reject her asylum application in November 1999. Relying on the terms of statutory instrument, the social security department forthwith stopped her benefit even though she had not been informed of the outcome of her asylum application. She was not told the result of her application until April 2000 and sought judicial review of the withdrawal of her benefit.

Held: (HL) Constitutional principle required that a matter such as this should not be treated as having been determined until the claimant had been notified of the result, so that she could challenge it in the courts if she wished. [2003] UKHL 36

Commentary
Lord Steyn stated that the "Constitutional principle requires that a constitutional state must accord to individuals the right to know of a decision before their rights can be adversely affected. The antithesis of such a state was described by Kafka: a state where the rights of individuals are overridden by hole in the corner decisions or knocks on doors in the early hours. That is not our system." *R. v Secretary of State for the Home Department Ex p. Salem* [1999] Q.B. 805, holding that an uncommunicated administrative decision could bind an individual, was wrongly decided.

Judicial Reasoning

Key Principle: **Articles 8, 9, 10 and 11 of the European Convention on Human Rights allow limitations that are, *inter alia*, prescribed by law.**

Hashman and Harrup v UK

The applicants, hunt saboteurs, had blown a horn with the intention of disrupting a hunt. This was not an unlawful act, there was no threat of violence and no breach of the peace. It was likely that behaviour would have been reported. They were bound over to be of good behaviour under the Justices of the Peace Act 1361. They claimed breaches of Articles 10, 11 and 5. The Commission declared admissibility under Articles 10 and 11.

Held: (ECtHR) The applicants' behaviour was an expression of opinion within the meaning of Article 10. The measures taken interfered with their right to freedom of expression and the interference was not "prescribed by law" within the meaning of Article 10(2). Conduct *contra bonos mores* was defined in English law as behaviour which was "wrong rather than right in the judgement of the majority of contemporary fellow citizens". This definition did not give sufficiently clear guidance, and was too imprecise and unpredictable in its operation to satisfy Article 10(2). (2000) 30 E.H.R.R. 241

Steel v UK

The applicants were arrested and detained as a consequence of being engaged in various forms of public protest. They were charged with conduct likely to cause a breach of the peace. The first applicant walked in front of a member of a grouse shoot as he lifted his shotgun and was committed to prison for 28 days when she refused to be bound over to keep the peace following a finding that the case against her was proved. She was convicted of breach of the peace and an offence contrary to s.5 of the Public Order Act 1994. In respect of the former offence the magistrates did not specify what behaviour justified the conclusion. The second applicant was arrested after protesting against the extension of a motorway. She stood under a digger, was arrested for conduct likely to cause a breach of the peace and was committed to prison for seven days after refusing to be bound over. The other three applicants were detained by police for seven hours after attending a "Fighter Helicopter 11" conference to protest against the sale of fighter helicopters. They had held up banners saying "Work for Peace not War". They were taken into custody where the custody record stated the "circumstances" as being that they were acting in breach of the peace. They were detained for seven hours. The proceedings against them were dropped when the prosecution decided not to call any evidence. They all complained that their arrest and detention had not been "prescribed by law" as set out in Article 5(1) since the concept of breach of the peace and the power to bind over were not sufficiently clearly defined. There were breaches, they alleged, of Article 5(5) because of the magistrates' immunity from civil proceedings. They stated that because of the uncertainty inherent in the concept of breach of the peace and the power to bind over and the fact that their detention was a disproportionate response that their rights under Articles 10 and 11 were infringed.

Held: (ECtHR) The concept of breach of the peace was sufficiently clarified by the English courts to satisfy the requirement of "prescribed by law" under Article 10(2) and was formulated with sufficient precision to satisfy Article 5(1)(a). There was no breach of Articles 5(1) or 10 in respect of the first two applicants. There had been violations of Article 10 in respect of the third, fourth and fifth applicants since the arrests and detention were not "prescribed by law" in that they were disproportionate to the aim of preventing disorder or protecting the rights of others. There were no breaches of Article 5(5). (1998) 28 E.H.R.R. 603

Commentary

In *Steel*, the court considered that the law in relation to breach of the peace was sufficiently precise and with foreseeable legal consequences to satisfy Article 5(1) and thus appeared to give the member state some scope for interpretation although the judgment itself does not refer to margin of appreciation. However the term *contra bonos mores*, meaning contrary to a good way of life, set out in the Justices of the Peace Act 1361, was too imprecise as the *Harrup* decision stated. In *McLeod v UK* (1999) 27 E.H.R.R. 493 the European Court of Human Rights also found that the breach of the peace doctrine was in accordance with the law under Article 8 although the police response was disproportionate. The key factors in defining legal basis are certainty and accessibility. The principle of legality is upheld also in the alternative phrasing "in accordance with law". In *Silver v UK* (1983) 5 E.H.R.R. 347 the court accepted that lawfulness may be based on the exercise of judicial discretion but there must be sufficient indication of the circumstances in which the discretion will be exercised. In *Malone v UK* (1985) 7 E.H.R.R. 14 the court held that any restriction must be certain and reasonably foreseeable, but also commented that "the requirements of foreseeability cannot mean that an individual should be enabled to foresee when the authorities are likely to intercept his communications so that he can adapt his conduct accordingly".

Key Principle: **Permissible restrictions of Convention rights must be proportionate.**

R. v Lambert

The appellant was convicted of the offence of possessing a controlled drug of class A with intent to supply, contrary to s.5(3) of the Misuse of Drugs Act 1971. His trial had taken place before the HRA came into force. In his defence he had relied on s.28(3)(b)(1) of that Act asserting that he did not believe or have reason to suspect that the bag which he carried contained a controlled drug. The judge had directed the jury to the effect that the prosecutors had to prove (1) that he had the bag in his possession; (2) that he knew that he had the bag in his possession and (3) that the bag contained a controlled drug. To establish a defence under the section the defendant had to prove on the balance of probabilities that he did not know the bag contained a controlled drug. Such was the accepted law at the time. The appeal was on the grounds that the requirement to prove the defence on the balance of probabilities was contrary to the presumption of innocence guaranteed under Article 6 of the European Convention on Human Rights. The Court of Appeal dismissed the appeal. There was an appeal to the House of Lords. The court also certified as a point of law whether a defendant whose trial took place before ss.6 and 7(1)(b) of the HRA were in force was entitled once they were in force to rely on an alleged breach of his Convention rights by the trial court or prosecuting authority. The appellant contended that he was so entitled and also that s.6 of the HRA meant that the House of Lords as a public authority sitting in judgment once the Act was in force could not affirm convictions obtained in breach of such rights before October 2, 2000.

Held: (HL) It was not justifiable or a proportionate response to the problem of illegal drugs to transfer the legal burden on the accused and require him to prove on the balance of probabilities that he did not know the bag contained a controlled drug. It was however possible using s.3 of the HRA to interpret s.28 as imposing an evidential burden only. Such a requirement was not a violation of the Convention. If the trial judge had given the direction to the jury that the accused had only the evidential burden the jury would have reached the same conclusion. The conviction should therefore stand. Furthermore the HRA was not available to the applicant since his conviction predated its coming into force. [2001] 3 W.L.R. 206

Commentary

The word proportionate does not appear in the text of the Convention. It relates to the application of the requirements for restrictions in rights to be "necessary in a democratic society", implying the existence of a "pressing social need" (see *Handyside v UK* (1976) 1 E.H.R.R. 737). The concept is most often applied in considering the restrictions of rights under Articles 8–11 but also applies to Article 6, as here, Articles 5 and 12, and Article 1 of the First Protocol. The differing decisions of the Court of Appeal and the House of Lords illustrate contradictory views on the extent to which the state should be allowed to undermine the rights of defendants in the interests of protecting society against the dangers of drug dealing.

Key Principle: **States should be allowed some measure of freedom, or a margin of appreciation in applying the Convention.**

Handyside v UK

The applicant was convicted under the Obscene Publications Acts 1959 and 1964. He was the owner of a publishers which published a book, *The Little Red Schoolbook*, which included a section on sex, covering topics such as masturbation, menstruation and pornography. He claimed a violation of Article 10.

Held: (ECtHR) There was no uniform European concept of morals and state authorities were in a better position to assess the situation than international judges. There was no violation of

Article 10 since the interference with the applicant's freedom of expression was necessary in a democratic society, "for the protection of morals". The United Kingdom had acted in good faith within the limits of the margin of appreciation allowed. [1976] 1 E.H.R.R. 737

Commentary

The book had been published in Denmark in 1969 and then in a number of other countries including Belgium, France, Greece, Iceland, Italy, Norway and Sweden. There had been no criminal proceedings anywhere else. The close connection between the concepts of proportionality and margin of appreciation is illustrated also in *Gay News and Lemon v UK* (1983) 5 E.H.R.R. 123 where the Commission considered the application of the law of blasphemous libel. In finding that there was no violation of Article 10 in a private prosecution against a publisher and editor for vilifying Christ, the Commission stated "it is in principle left to the legislature of the state concerned how it wishes to define the offence, provided that the principle of proportionality which is inherent in the exception clause of Article 10(2) is being respected". In *R. v DPP Ex p. Kebilene* (see also pp.36, 98) Lord Hope stated that "by conceding a margin of appreciation to each national system the court has recognised that the Convention, as a living system, doesn't need to be applied uniformly by all states but may vary in its application according to local needs and conditions. This technique is not available to the national courts when they are considering Convention issues arising within their own countries". As Lord Hope's statement indicates, national courts are not required to consider the doctrine of margin of appreciation in applying the Convention. In domestic law the doctrine of proportionality is sufficient to allow an assessment of the appropriateness of a policy decision by the executive.

Smith and Grady v UK

United Kingdom Government policy was that homosexuality was incompatible with service in the armed forces and that personnel known to be homosexual or engaging in homosexual activity would be administratively discharged. The applicants were serving members of the armed forces who had been administratively discharged because of their homosexuality. The Court of Appeal had dismissed their applications for judicial review of the decision to discharge. They claimed violations of Articles 8 and 3.

Held: (ECtHR) The discharges were in violation of Articles 8 and 13. The Court of Appeal's application of the test of irrationality placed the threshold so high as to preclude consideration of proportionality and whether pressing social need existed for the ban on homosexuals. [2000] 29 E.H.R.R. 493

Commentary

The Court of Appeal had been ready to apply a lower threshold of unreasonableness in a case such as this involving human rights but on the facts had found against the applicants. By contrast the European Court of Human Rights although recognising that in pursuing the aim of national security the state was entitled to a broader margin of appreciation, emphasised that when a state infringes "a most intimate aspect of an individual's private life particularly serious reasons by way of justification [are] required".

Key principle: **The principles upon which the courts allocate discretionary decision-making powers to public authorities are principles of law.**

R. (Prolife Alliance) v BBC

An anti-abortion organization stood candidates in Wales in the 2002 general election and prepared an election broadcast showing footage of an abortion and images of aborted foetuses. The BBC refused to transmit the broadcasts on grounds of taste and decency, maintaining that to do otherwise would contravene an agreement with the government and breach s.6(1)(a) of the Broadcasting Act 1990. An application by the organization for judicial review was refused at first instance but granted on appeal by the Court of Appeal. The BBC appealed.

Held: (HL) The appeal would be allowed. It was common ground that party political broadcasts were subject to the same restrictions on the transmission of offensive material as other programmes. There was no ground to interfere with the BBC's decision that, applying the statutory standards, the election broadcast should not be transmitted. The BBC's decision was not a discriminatory, arbitrary or unreasonable denial of the right under Article 10(2) of the European Convention to freedom of expression. [2003] UKHL 23; [2004] 1 A.C. 185

Commentary

The judgment included a discussion on the concept of judicial deference. Lord Hoffman stated that the allocation by the courts of its decision-making powers to another branch of government was not a matter of deference or courtesy. The allocation of these decision-making responsibilities is based upon recognised legal principles. One example of such a principle was the recognition that the independence of the courts is necessary for a proper decision of disputed legal rights or claims of violation of human rights. Another was that majority approval is necessary for a proper decision on policy or allocation of resources. Lord Hoffman stated that when a court decides that a decision is within the proper competence of the legislature or executive, it is not showing deference. It is deciding the law. See also *R. (on the application of Bloggs 61) v Secretary of State for the Home Department* [2003] 1 W.L.R. 2724 where it was held that the prison service and police were best placed to assess the risk to life of a prisoner whose protected witness status had been removed. These cases show that while the courts have rejected the Strasbourg concept of the margin of appreciation in practice they adopt a similar approach in deciding the area of discretionary judgment of public authorities.

Key Principle: **The Convention is a living instrument and must be interpreted in the light of present day conditions.**

Tyrer v UK
The 15-year-old applicant had been sentenced to three strokes of the birch in the Isle of Man for unlawful assault. This was administered in a police station. He was held down by two policemen while a third birched him. He claimed a violation of Article 3 of European Convention on Human Rights. The Government relied on Article 63(3) of the Convention and argued that since public opinion in the Isle of Man supported birching it was a "local requirement".

Held: (ECtHR) Judicial corporal punishment was degrading within the meaning of Article 3. The task of the European Court of Human Rights was to develop the rules instituted by the Convention which must be regarded as a living instrument. The Convention should not be interpreted as it would have been by those who drafted it but "must be interpreted in the light of present day conditions". (1978) 2 E.H.R.R. 1

Commentary
This principle allows the meaning attached to articles to change over time but old cases do not have to be specifically overruled.

There is no doctrine of precedent under the Convention although the court will usually follow its previous decisions. However, older decisions may be disregarded in the light of new conditions. For example, in a case involving the rights of transsexuals (*Sheffield and Horsham v UK* (1999) 5 B.H.R.C. 83) the European Convention on Human Rights noted the changing attitudes in this area compared to a situation involving a previous case (*Cossey v UK* (1990) 13 E.H.R.R. 622). There was now "an increased social acceptance of transsexuals" and "the Court reiterated that this area needs to be kept under review by the contracting state". See also p.165.

Derogations and Terrorism

Key Principle: **Article 15(1) of the European Convention on Human Rights: "In time of war or other public emergency threatening the life of the nation any High Contracting Party may take measures derogating from its obligations under this Convention to the extent strictly required by the exigencies of the situation, provided that such measures are not inconsistent with its other obligations under international law."**

Brannigan and McBride v UK

The applicants had been arrested and detained in Northern Ireland under the provisions of the Prevention of Terrorism (Temporary Provisions) Act 1984 (PTA). Brannigan was detained for six days, 14 hours and 30 minutes and McBride for four days, six hours and 25 minutes. Both were interrogated, denied access to reading and writing materials and access to a solicitor was delayed for 48 hours. The applicants relied on the *Brogan* case (see p.59), the Government relied on its derogation under Article 15 which purported to authorise further detention of suspected terrorists for questioning without charge.

Held: (ECtHR) There was a breach of Article 5, para.3, but the derogation lodged by the United Kingdom satisfied the requirements of Article 15. [1994] 17 E.H.R.R. 539

Commentary

The European Court of Human Rights noted that the remedy of habeas corpus was available to test the lawfulness of the original arrest and detention and that the detainees had an absolute and legally enforceable right to consult a solicitor after 48 hours from the time of arrest. It considered that the Government had not exceeded its margin of appreciation in deciding for executive rather than judicial control of the extension of the period of detention. The United Kingdom entered the derogation after the case of *Brogan v UK* (1988) 11 E.H.R.R. 117 in which the court held that the detention of the applicants under the PTA for more than four days without charge was a breach of Article 5(3). The introduction of judicial authorisation for extended detentions in the Terrorism Act 2000 allowed the derogation to be withdrawn in February 2001.

Key Principle: **An order for derogation must observe the United Kingdom's treaty obligations to afford equality before the law and protect the human rights of all individuals within its territory.**

A v Secretary of State for the Home Department

The Anti-Terrorism, Crime and Security Act 2001 provided for the indefinite imprisonment without trial of foreign nationals suspected of terrorism who could not lawfully be deported to their country of origin. In order to bring in the measure the government declared that the terrorist threat constituted a public emergency threatening the life of the nation which entitled it to derogate from its obligations Article 5(1) of the European Convention on Human Rights, which enshrines the right to liberty and security of person. The applicants, who were imprisoned pursuant to the provision, were nationals of various North African countries and Jordan, whose personal safety might be at risk if they had been deported. They appealed to the Special Immigration Appeals Commission, which held that although the terrorist outrages of September 11, 2001 in New York and Washington had created a public emergency threatening the life of the nation, s.23 unlawfully discriminated against those imprisoned on grounds of nationality, since the government had no power to imprison British terrorist suspects without trial. Such discrimination violated Article 14 of the Convention. The SIAC decision was overturned by the Court of Appeal and the applicants appealed to the House of Lords.

Held: (HL) It was pre-eminently a matter for parliament and the executive whether there was a public emergency threatening the life of the nation within Article 15 of the European Convention. On the evidence, SIAC had reached a view which was open to it on that issue and there were no grounds for displacing its conclusion that there was such a public emergency. However the right to personal liberty was among the most fundamental protected by the Convention and the courts were obliged to scrutinise closely inroads into that right. Section 23 did not stand up to scrutiny because of its discriminatory nature and the fact that it could apply to persons who did not pose a terrorist threat. Accordingly it did not rationally address the threat to security and was inconsistent with the UK's treaty obligations to afford equality before the law and protect the human rights of all individuals within its territory. Their Lordships quashed the derogation order and made a declaration that s.23 was incompatible with Articles 5 and 14. [2004] UKHL 56; [2005] 2 W.L.R. 87

Commentary

The Anti-Terrorism Crime and Security Act 2001 passed through Parliament in the aftermath of the September 11 atrocities in the United States. It widens the powers of the authorities to act against terrorism and introduces internment for foreign nationals suspected of terrorist involvement, where human rights considerations do not permit their deportation. This provision involves an explicit derogation from Article 5 of the European Human Rights Convention, which would otherwise have the effect of limiting the time under which a person facing deportation could be held and would not allow further detention without charge or trial where a deportation was no longer being pursued. Under s.14(5) HRA the Secretary of State may amend s.3 of the Act to extend existing derogations and add any new ones. This decision of the House of Lords was a notable setback for the government. It included an impassioned dissenting speech by Lord Hoffman, who said: "Terrorist violence, serious as it is, does not threaten our institutions of government or our existence as a civil community. . . . The real threat to the life of the nation, in the sense of a people living in accordance with its traditional laws and political values, comes not from terrorism but from laws such as these." The House of Lords' judgment coincided with the resignation of Home Secretary David Blunkett, the author of s.23. The new Home Secretary Charles Clarke did not immediately release the detainees but proposed to modify the legislation so as to allow the house arrest of suspects, including British nationals. Under Clarke's proposals, suspects could be subjected to civil court orders prohibiting their free movement and banning them from using telephones and computers. Human rights groups urged the government to allow the use in criminal trials of electronic intercept evidence, so that the allegations against suspects could be tested in the courts.

The interaction between human rights and terrorism has become an important legal question. The Terrorism Act 2000 Act defines terrorism in broad terms as the use or threat of action anywhere in the world involving serious personal violence, serious damage to property, endangering of life or creating serious risk to health and safety or designed seriously to interfere with or seriously to disrupt an electronic system. The act must be designed to influence a government or to intimidate the public or a section of the public anywhere, and its use or threat must be made for the purpose of advancing a political, religious or ideological cause.

A number of groups considered to come within this definition are specifically proscribed by the Act. Three of the original proscribed organizations sought judicial review of their proscription in *R. (on the application of the Kurdistan Workers Party) v Secretary of State for the Home Department* [2002] EWHC 644 (Admin). Judicial review was not the appropriate route, the Divisional Court decided. The proper route was an application to the Home Secretary to deproscribe, followed if necessary by an appeal to the Proscribed Organisations Appeal Commission.

In 1999 SIAC had upheld the appeal of a Pakistani national refused indefinite leave to remain in the UK because he was believed to be a danger to national security. It considered the expression "national security" had been drawn too widely. The Court of Appeal and the House of Lords upheld the Home Secretary's appeal. Lord Slynn of Hadley stated that the Home Secretary was "undoubtedly in the best position to judge what national security requires". However in a later case the Court of Appeal supported SIAC's decision. In *Secretary of State for the Home Department v M* [2004] EWCA Civ 324, the Court of Appeal upheld a Tribunal decision quashing the detention of a Libyan national under the Home Secretary's new powers. The Home Secretary was refused permission to appeal. The 2001 Act also gives the police powers to freeze terrorist assets on suspicion. Both Acts are subject to special review procedures. The workings of the 2000 Act are reviewed annually by an independent reviewer, Lord Carlile of Berriew QC, who also reviews the internment provisions of the 2001 Act. A committee of Privy Councillors, headed by Lord Newton of Braintree, is reviewing the whole of the Anti-Terrorism Crime and Security Act 2001. The British Institute of Human Rights has condemned the 2001 Act as introducing disproportionate restrictions on fundamental human rights and basic civil liberties. The

Institute has complained that it is an abuse of the right of derogation under international law and subverts the purpose of human rights treaties to introduce emergency measures without first demonstrating the necessity of such derogation, and observes that such deviations from human rights standards are invariably applied in a discriminatory way. (In July 2003, Protocol 13, ratified by the United Kingdom, came into force. This abolishes the death penalty in all circumstances, unlike Protocol 6 which allowed the death penalty in respect of acts committed in time of war or imminent threat of war. No derogations or reservations are allowed in respect of these Protocols.)

During the hearing before the Court of Appeal the issue arose whether the Secretary of State was entitled in considering whether to intern terrorism suspects to take account of evidence obtained overseas by torture. The Court held there was no violation of Article 3 in making use of such evidence unless it had been directly procured by UK agents or with their connivance. Neuberger L.J. dissented, on the basis that there was an international consensus against torture and all such evidence was tainted. At the time of writing an appeal to the House of Lords was pending.

Other International Obligations

Key Principle: **The UK has treaty obligations to change the law so as to comply with human rights obligations under the European Convention on Human Rights.**

The Sunday Times v UK
The Sunday Times brought an action before the European Commission on Human Rights claiming that the injunction upheld by the House of Lords [1974] A.C. 273 infringed their right to freedom of expression guaranteed by Article 10 of the European Convention on Human Rights. The Commission referred the case to the Court of Human Rights.

Held: (ECtHR) The interference with the applicant's freedom of expression was not justified under Article 10(2) which permitted such restrictions "as are prescribed by law and are necessary in a democratic society. . .for maintaining the authority and impartiality of the judiciary". There was no "pressing social need" for the injunction. [1979] 2 E.H.R.R. 245

Commentary
This is one example where the United Kingdom introduced legislation to implement the court's decisions. The judgment led to the Contempt of Court Act 1981.

Key Principle: **International treaty obligations may provide guidance when a court is called upon to interpret an ambiguous statute.**

R. v Secretary of State for Home Department Ex p. Brind

The Secretary of State made orders under the Broadcasting Act 1981 banning television and radio stations from broadcasting the words spoken by spokesmen of organisations proscribed under anti-terrorism legislation. Broadcasters sought judicial review of the orders as being outside the Secretary of State's powers because the ban was disproportionate to its ostensible object of preventing intimidation by the organisations concerned and also because he should have regard to the European Convention on Human Rights. The application was dismissed by the Divisional Court and by the Court of Appeal. The broadcasters appealed.

Held: (HL) The presumption that Parliament had intended to legislate in conformity with the European Convention might be resorted to in order to resolve ambiguities in a statute, but in the present case there was no ambiguity and no presumption that the Secretary of State had to exercise his discretion under the Act in accordance with the Convention. [1991] 1 A.C. 696

Commentary

Lord Ackner said that since there was no ambiguity in the relevant section of the statute there was no need here to have recourse to the Convention. He said that the limits placed upon discretion were that the power should be used for the purpose for which it was granted and that it must be exercised reasonably in the *Wednesbury* sense (*Associated Provincial Picture Houses Ltd v Wednesbury Corp.* [1948] 1 K.B. 223). He also referred to Lord Denning's judgment in *R. v Chief Immigration Officer, Ex p. Salamat Bibi* [1976] 1 W.L.R. 979 where he said: "the position as I understand it is that if there is any ambiguity in our statutes, or uncertainty in our law, then this Court can look to the Convention as an aid to clear up the ambiguity and uncertainty." The status of the European Convention in United Kingdom law has been changed as a result of the HRA. From October 2000 the courts must "take into account" the judgments of the Court of Human Rights and the opinions of the former European Commission on Human Rights. This on its wording has a stronger meaning than calling on the Convention as an aid to interpretation in cases of ambiguity. The status of the other treaty obligations is unchanged by the HRA but in practice they are far less often at issue. In *Brind v UK* (1994) 77-A D.R. 42 the Commission rejected the journalists' contention that there was a violation of Article 10. The ban was proportionate in view of the need to combat terrorism. A number of commentators are critical of the position that international treaties can only be relied on as sources of law where legislation is ambiguous. For example Murray Hunt has argued:

> "in short, English courts have been asking the wrong question. Instead of asking, 'Is the domestic law ambiguous?' they should have been asking 'Can the domestic law be read in a way which avoids a conflict with international law?' To answer that question properly, it will always be necessary for the domestic court to have regard to the terms of those obligations, without first having to undertake the wholly artificial exercise of construing domestic law in isolation to determine whether it is 'ambiguous'."

(Murray Hunt, *Using Human Rights Law in English Courts*, Hart Publishing 1998, p.39). The United Kingdom is signatory to a number of international human rights treaties apart from the European Convention on Human Rights. These include the Universal Declaration of Human Rights, the International Covenant on Civil and Political Rights and the International Covenant on Economic Social and Cultural Rights. In *R. v Secretary of State for the Environment, Ex p. NALGO* (1992) 5 Admin. L.R. 785 the court stated that human rights treaties may be used where the relevant rules of common law or equity are uncertain. Along with *Brind* this is a controversial principle since it appears to state that administrative decision makers are only obliged to take account of international human rights treaties if the common law or statute is unclear. However on a more positive note Neill L.J. stated that human rights treaties "may be used when the court is considering how a discretion is to be exercised", for example in deciding whether to grant an interlocutory injunction.

Key Principle: **There is a body of customary international law which is part of the common law.**

R. v Bow Street Metropolitan Stipendiary Magistrate, Ex p. Pinochet Ugarte (No. 3)
For facts see p.62.

Held: (HL) Though a former head of state had immunity from the criminal jurisdiction of the United Kingdom for acts done in his official capacity as head of state, torture was an international crime against humanity and there was a universal jurisdiction to extradite or punish a public official for torture. That principle extended to heads of state because the state parties who had created the international jurisdiction by the International Convention against Torture, Inhuman or Degrading Treatment could not have intended to create an immunity for a head of state who was a torturer. *Per* Lords Millett and Phillips the systematic use of torture was an international crime against humanity for which there could be no immunity even before the International Convention came into effect, consequently there was no immunity under customary international law for the offences relating to torture alleged against the applicant. [1999] 2 W.L.R. 827

Commentary
This case demonstrates how increasingly English judges are drawing on human rights cases from other jurisdictions in their judgments. Similarly in *R. v Lambert* Lord Steyn cited Canadian and South African human rights cases; see p.5.

2. HUMAN RIGHTS ACT 1998

Interpretation

Key Principle: **Section 3 of the HRA—Interpretation of legislation:**

"(1) So far as it is possible to do so, primary legislation and subordinate legislation must be read and given effect in a way which is compatible with the Convention rights.

(2) This section—

   (a) applies to primary legislation and subordinate legislation whenever enacted;

   (b) does not affect the validity, continuing operation or enforcement of any incompatible subordinate legislation if (disregarding any possibility of revocation)

primary legislation prevents removal of the
incompatibility."

Key Principle: **Courts must adopt a purposive approach to
interpretation of legislation to ensure compliance with the
ECHR.**

Ghaidan v Godin-Mendoza

For nearly 30 years before his death, the defendant had been the
homosexual partner of a protected tenant in a flat owned by the
claimant. When the tenant died the claimant brought possession
proceedings and obtained a declaration that the defendant could
not succeed to the tenancy as the tenant's surviving spouse in
accordance with para.2 of Sch.1 to the Rent Act 1977. The judge
held that he was nonetheless entitled to an assured tenancy of
the flat by succession as a member of the original tenant's family
within para.3(1) of the Schedule. The Court of Appeal held on
the defendant's appeal that his rights under Articles 8 and 14 of
the European convention were infringed by the 1977 Act since
he was in a less secure position than he would have been had he
been the original tenant's wife. The court decided that the word
"spouse" in the relevant paragraph of the Schedule should be
read so as to include persons in the same position as the
defendant and admitted him to the tenancy. The claimant
appealed to the House of Lords.

Held: (HL) The appeal would be dismissed. There was no
rational or fair ground for treating survivors of homosexual
partnerships less favourably than survivors of heterosexual
partnerships. The provision as read literally infringed Articles 8
and 14 of the Convention and by s.3 of the Human Rights Act
1998 must if possible be read so as to comply with the
Convention. This could be done in the manner proposed by the
Court of Appeal without contradicting any cardinal principle of
the 1977 Act. [2004] UKHL 30; [2004] 2 A.C. 557

Commentary

In the judgment their Lordships set out clearly the principles which
should apply in interpreting legislation under s.3. Lord Steyn
rejected a linguistic approach stating that it was necessary to
concentrate on the fundamental rights which were involved. He

reviewed the issuing of declarations of incompatibility by the courts and pointed out that these must be exceptional. The preferred approach was to apply s.3 as the principal remedial measure. Lord Nichols stated that by applying s.3 courts could modify the meaning and effect of primary and secondary legislation, being bound only by what was possible. The case emphasises that the courts are required to identify possible meanings of the statute in order to avoid a breach of Convention rights.

Key Principle: **In applying a statutory provision in the light of the ECHR it may sometimes be necessary to adopt an interpretation which may appear to be linguistically strained.**

R. v A (No. 2)

The defendant had been charged with rape. He had claimed that sexual intercourse with the complainant had been by consent and that they had had a prior sexual relationship for about three weeks. At a pre-trial hearing the judge, relying on s.41 of the Youth Justice and Criminal Evidence Act 1999, had ruled that the complainant could not be cross-examined and that evidence could not be led about her alleged sexual relationship with the defendant. The defendant appealed against the decision. The Court of Appeal allowed the appeal and conveyed the following question to the House of Lords: "May a sexual relationship between a defendant and complainant be relevant to the issue of consent so as to render its exclusion under section 41 Youth Justice and Criminal Evidence Act 1999 a contravention of the defendant's right to a fair trial?"

Held: (HL) Section 41 of the 1999 Act should be read in accordance with s.3 of the HRA 1998 and given effect in a way that was compatible with the fair trial guaranteed under Article 6 ECHR. [2001] 2 W.L.R. 1546

Commentary

This case illustrates the new interpretative technique introduced by the HRA. The House of Lords considered that the defendant's prior relations with the complainant, although they may be relevant, could not be admitted under normal canons of statutory interpretation under s.41 of the Youth Justice and Criminal Evidence Act. The House avoided making a declaration of incompatibility by interpreting the section in a manner compatible with the demands of Article 6 of the Convention. Lord Steyn (at para. 44) made it clear that the courts should not imply the word "reasonable" into s.3. In other words they should find a possible not necessarily a reasonable interpretation according to the wording. It is arguable however that the kind of creative juridical reasoning adopted here flouts the will of Parliament. The courts are in these cases developing an approach to demarcate between s.3 interpretive technique and incompatibility under s.4. In *Donoghue v Poplar Housing and Regeneration Association* [2001] 3 W.L.R. 183 (see p.41) Lord Woolf stated that "Section 3 does not enable the courts to legislate; its task is still one of interpretation but interpretation in conjunction with the direction contained in section 3". In *R. v A* Lord Steyn's liberal interpretation of s.3(1) of the HRA was in part based on the desirability of avoiding making a declaration of incompatibility. He said that such a declaration would only occur if "a clear limitation on Convention rights is stated in terms. . ." The position Lord Steyn is putting forward suggests that he would only make a declaration of incompatibility if the statute stated expressly that it was limiting Convention rights. Such an occurrence would be very rare.

Key Principle: **Article 3 should not be applied in such a way as to alter the effect of the statutory scheme.**

Bellinger v Bellinger

A transsexual who had been born male but subsequently had undergone gender reassignment surgery went through a marriage ceremony with a man. The couple were refused a declaration that the marriage was valid and subsisting. The judge held the marriage to be invalid on the basis of s.11(c) of the Matrimonial Causes Act 1973: "A marriage . . . shall be void on the following grounds only, that is to say . . . that the parties are not respectively male and female . . .". An appeal to the Court of Appeal was dismissed and the couple appealed to the House of Lords.

Held: (HL) The words "male" and "female" in s.11(c) of the 1973 Act had their ordinary meaning and referred to a person's biological gender as determined at birth. A person born with one sex, even after undergoing reassignment surgery, could not marry as a person of the opposite sex. To interpret the section any differently would make a major change in the law, which would upset the traditional concept of marriage. Such a change ought to be decided by Parliament, not the courts. However, s.11(c) did interfere with the claimant's right to respect for her private life under Article 8 of the Convention and with her right to marry under Article 12. A declaration would be granted to that effect. [2003] UKHL 21; [2003] 2 A.C. 467

Commentary
The national courts have had a wide margin of appreciation in dealing with cases of this sort, and the Strasbourg jurisprudence has been uncertain. *Goodwin v UK* [2002] 35 E.H.R.R. 18 shows that the courts can no longer rely solely on biological sex to deny legal recognition to the changed status of a transsexual. (See also p.165)

Key Principle: **Section 2 of the HRA—Interpretation of Convention rights:**

"(1) A court or tribunal determining a question which has arisen in connection with a Convention right must take into account any—

  (a) judgment, decision, declaration or advisory opinion of the European Court of Human Rights;
  (b) opinion of the Commission given in a report adopted under Article 31 of the Convention;
  (c) decision of the Commission in connection with Article 26 or 27(2) of the Convention; or
  (d) decision of the Committee of Ministers taken under Article 46 of the Convention,

whenever made or given, so far as, in the opinion of the court or tribunal, it is relevant to the proceedings in which that question has arisen.

(2) Evidence of any judgment, decision, declaration or opinion of which account may have to be taken under this section is to be given in proceedings before any court or tribunal in such a manner as may be provided by the rules.

(3) In this section 'rules' means rules of court or, in the case of proceedings before a tribunal, rules made for the purposes of this section—

(a) by the Lord Chancellor or the Secretary of State, in relation to any proceedings outside Scotland;
(b) by the Secretary of State, in relation to proceedings in Scotland; or
(c) by a Northern Ireland department, in relation to proceedings before a tribunal in Northern Ireland—

    (i) which deals with transferred matters; and
    (ii) for which no rules made under paragraph (a) are in force."

Key Principle: **When scrutinising executive decisions that interfere with human rights the courts must take into account the European jurisprudence in accordance with s.2 of the 1998 Act.**

R. (Mahmood) v Secretary of State for the Home Department
The applicant was an illegal immigrant married to a British citizen who had had his asylum claim refused. He applied for leave to remain on the basis of his marriage. This was refused. The applicant applied for judicial review of the Secretary of State's decisions.

Held: (CA) Appeal dismissed. The case should be approached as if the Act had been in force when the Secretary of State reached his decision since it involved fundamental rights including the right to family life under Article 8. In considering the test of necessity in this context the court must take into account the European jurisprudence. There were reasonable grounds for concluding that the applicant's deportation was necessary in the interests of an orderly and fair control of immigration and that his right to family life was not violated. [2001] 1 W.L.R. 840

Commentary
Under s.21 of the HRA Strasbourg jurisprudence is persuasive but not legally binding. In *R. (Alconbury Developments Ltd) v Secretary of State for the Environment, Transport and the Regions* (see p.124) Lord Hoffman stated: "The House is not bound by the decisions of the European Court and, if I thought that the Divisional Court was right (it was not) to hold that they compelled a conclusion fundamentally at odds with the distribution of powers under the British constitution I would have considerable doubt as to whether

they should be followed." In practice the United Kingdom courts have followed the interpretation of the ECHR at Strasbourg. Of course the Strasbourg decisions can be interpreted differently or there may be no Strasbourg decision on the case in point (see *R. (DPP) v Havering Magistrates* [2001] 1 W.L.R. 805, pp.79–80). One issue in that case was whether the provisions of Article 5 include a requirement that underlying facts relevant to detention are to be proved to the criminal standard of proof. Latham L.J. stated:

> "It is true that the European Court of Human Rights on occasion refers to the need for evidence; but that is used in contradistinction to a mere assertion. It does not seem to me that any of the authorities to which we have been referred assist in determining the nature of that 'evidence'. Bearing in mind the differences in the rules for admissibility of evidence in their different jurisdictions of the Member States, it is perhaps not surprising that the court appears to have left resolution of that question to domestic law".

He drew on authorities from English law in this case.

Key Principle: **The Human Rights Act has extra-territorial application but successful reliance on Articles other than Article 3 requires a very strong case.**

R. (Ullah) v Special Adjudicator

Two asylum seekers, one an Ahmadi preacher from Pakistan, the other a Vietnamese Catholic, entered the UK claiming fear of religious persecution and were refused asylum. They each appealed to immigration adjudicators on the basis that even if they had failed to demonstrate a well-founded fear of persecution, their rights to practice their religion on their return to their countries of origin would be so restricted as to constitute an infringement of their right to freedom of religion under Article 9 of the European Convention. In the first case the adjudicator found that there was no credible evidence that the claimant's exercise of his religious rights would be seriously interfered with, since he has been able to practice his religion without serious problems in the past. In making the removal order the Secretary of State was acting in pursuit of a legitimate aim of immigration control. His application for judicial review was dismissed. The appeal of the Vietnamese asylum-seeker was also dismissed, both by the adjudicator and by the Immigration

Appeal Tribunal. These decisions were upheld on appeal to the Court of Appeal. The asylum-seekers appealed to the House of Lords.

Held: (HL) The appeals were dismissed. English courts were obliged to take account of the Strasbourg case law of the European Court of Human Rights and should follow it, save in special circumstances. Strasbourg case law made it unlawful to remove a person to country where he would face torture or inhuman or degrading treatment and a person might rely on Articles other than Article 3 to resist a decision to remove him to a state where the anticipated treatment might infringe the Convention. However to rely on Articles other than Article 3 of the Convention the claimant would need to show that the actual or threatened treatment would amount to a flagrant denial or gross violation of the relevant right, and this the claimants had failed to do.

Commentary

The House of Lords reversed the decision of the Court of Appeal on the question of extra-territoriality. The Court of Appeal had held that Article 9 was not engaged by the decision to expel the applicants. It held that only Article 3 might be engaged in such situations. The House of Lords held that, having regard to the jurisprudence of the European court, while a contracting state would, in the context of Article 3, incur liability under the Convention for removing a person to a country where he was foreseeably at real risk of proscribed ill-treatment, the court's case law did not exclude the possibility that issues might exceptionally be raised where the anticipated ill-treatment would infringe other articles of the Convention, in particular, Articles 2, 5, 6, and 8, and did not rule out such a possibility in respect of Article 9. A person might rely on Articles other than Article 3 to resist a decision to remove him to a state where the anticipated treatment would or might infringe the Convention; but that reliance on such Articles required presentation of an exceptionally strong case such that the actual or threatened treatment would amount to a flagrant denial or gross violation of the relevant right. The facts relied on by the claimants fell far short of supporting such a claim and that, accordingly, they could not rely on Article 9 to resist their expulsion from the United Kingdom. [2004] UKHL 26; [2004] 2 A.C. 323

Declarations of Incompatibility

Key Principle: **Section 4 of the HRA—Declaration of incompatibility:**

"(1) Subsection (2) applies in any proceedings in which a court determines whether a provision of primary legislation is compatible with a Convention right.

(2) If the court is satisfied that the provision is incompatible with a Convention right, it may make a declaration of that incompatibility.

(3) Subsection (4) applies in any proceedings in which a court determines whether a provision of subordinate legislation, made in the exercise of a power conferred by primary legislation, is compatible with a Convention right.

(4) If the court is satisfied—

(a) that the provision is incompatible with a Convention right, and

(b) that (disregarding any possibility of revocation) the primary legislation concerned prevents removal of the incompatibility,

it may make a declaration of that incompatibility.

(5) In this section 'court' means—

(a) the House of Lords;
(b) the Judicial Committee of the Privy Council;
(c) the Courts-Martial Appeal Court;
(d) in Scotland, the High Court of Justiciary sitting otherwise than as a trial court or the Court of Session;
(e) in England and Wales or Northern Ireland, the High Court or the Court of Appeal.

(6) A declaration under this section ('a declaration of incompatibility')—

(a) does not affect the validity, continuing operation or enforcement of the provision in respect of which it is given; and

(b) is not binding on the parties to the proceedings in which it is made."

Key principle: **A declaration of incompatibility may be made if the express words of the statute prevent an interpretation under s.3 HRA which would safeguard Convention rights.**

R. (Anderson) v Secretary of State for the Home Department
Two claimants serving life sentences for murder challenged the tariff or minimum sentence period fixed for them by the Home Secretary, in accordance with s.29 of the Crime (Sentences) Act 1997. The Home Secretary had taken advice from the Lord Chief Justice and departmental officials before fixing the tariff which was the minimum period necessary to satisfy the requirements of retribution and deterrence before the prisoner could be considered for parole. In the case of the first prisoner the recommended tariff was 15 years, but the Home Secretary set it at 20. In the second, where the L.C.J. and officials had recommended 16 the Home Secretary originally set a 30-year tariff, later reduced to 22 years. The claimants challenged the Home Secretary's exercise of his statutory power on the basis that they were entitled under Article 6(1) of the Convention to a fair hearing by an independent and impartial tribunal to determine their tariff. Discretionary life prisoners had already established that their tariffs should be determined judicially. The claims failed before the Divisional Court and Court of Appeal, but subsequently the Strasbourg court decided there was no material distinction between mandatory and discretionary life prisoners to justify the different treatment of the two categories. The claimants appealed to the House of Lords.

Held: (HL) That in determining the tariff the Secretary of State was performing a sentencing function such as was regularly undertaken by the judiciary. Though the Strasbourg decision did not bind the English court, it was based on an accurate understanding of the process and would be followed. Imposition of sentence was part of trial for the purposes of Article 6(1) and tariff-fixing was legally indistinguishable from sentence. The Secretary of State was not independent of the executive and was not a tribunal and so should play no part in the fixing process. However there was no way of reading the statute so as to make it Convention-compatible, and the only appropriate relief was a declaration that it was incompatible with the Convention. [2002] UKHL 46; [2003] 1 A.C. 837

Commentary
Lord Bingham said that to apply s.3 to the statute would be judicial vandalism not judicial interpretation.

International Transport Roth GmbH v Secretary of State for the Home Department

Under s.32 of the Immigration and Asylum Act 1999 carriers were liable to a fixed penalty of £2,000 for every clandestine entrant found concealed in a vehicle. The penalty could be enforced by impounding the vehicle and applied even where the driver had detected the illegal entrants and informed the police. The judge held that the penalty scheme was incompatible with Article 6 of the European Convention and that it infringed Articles 28 and 49 of the EC Treaty relating to the free movement of goods and the right to provide haulage services. The Home Secretary appealed.

Held: (CA) The penalty scheme was a criminal rather than a civil scheme and consequently the fair trial provisions in Article 6 of the Convention applied. The scale and inflexibility of the penalty, which was not determined by an independent tribunal, made the scheme unfair. It imposed excessive burdens on carriers, including strict liability and reversal of the burden of proof, which were disproportionate to the objective of deterring dishonesty and carelessness in the transport of clandestine entrants to the UK, and so breached Article 1 of the first protocol. However the effects of the scheme were too insignificant and remote to amount to an unjust restriction on the movement of goods and services contrary to European law. [2003] Q.B. 728

Commentary

As a result of this decision the statutory scheme was changed by the Immigration, Asylum and Nationality Act 2002.

R. (H) v Mental Health Tribunal North and East London Region

Section 73 of the Mental Health Act 1983 states that a restricted patient should be discharged if the tribunal is satisfied that certain conditions apply and it is not appropriate to continue with treatment. The conditions include that he is not suffering from mental illness and it is not necessary for him to receive treatment either for his benefit or for the safety of others. The question was on whom was the burden of proof that the conditions were satisfied. If the patient was not to be discharged unless the tribunal was satisfied as to the conditions this arguably would reverse the burden of proof and be a breach of Article 5 whereby a person could only be detained in accordance with the law.

Held: (CA) Section 73 of the 1983 Act was incompatible with the HRA. The Convention required that the discharge should be ordered unless the criteria were made out. Section 73 did not provide this. [2001] 3 W.L.R. 42

Commentary
The House of Lords granted leave to appeal in *Wilson*. It is arguable that the courts will in future take a different approach to declarations of incompatibility in the light of the House of Lords decision of *R. v A* (see p.19). The Divisional Court in *R. (Alconbury Developments Ltd) v Secretary of State for the Environment, Transport and the Regions* made a declaration of incompatibility. The ruling was made in respect of four planning cases but the declaration was reversed by the House of Lords on the grounds that a close reading of the Convention case-law revealed that no incompatibility arose. The courts have generally been reluctant to make declarations of incompatibility and even where they have been made they have on occasion been reversed on appeal. In *R. (Uttley) v Secretary of State for the Home Department* [2004] 1 W.L.R. 2278 the House of Lords allowed the appeal by the Secretary of State in holding that it was not a breach of Article 7(1) when statutory changes to the law to provide that a prisoner serving a sentence of 12 years imprisonment for sexual offences including rape should be released on licence after serving two-thirds of his sentence, even though at the date when the offences were committed he would have been released, free from any licence conditions on the completion of his two-thirds sentence. The "applicable penalty" for the purposes of Article 7(1) was the maximum penalty which could have been imposed, namely life imprisonment.

Key Principle: **Resort to Hansard would rarely be appropriate in deciding whether a statute was compatible with HRA.**

Wilson v First County Trust Ltd
The claimant and a firm of pawnbrokers had made a credit agreement for a loan. A BMW car was proffered as security. There was a technical fault in agreement and as a result it was unenforceable by virtue of s.127 of the Consumer Credit Act 1974. The issue was whether the section was incompatible with the right to property in Protocol 1, Article 1. The Secretary of

State intervened arguing that the act complained of occurred before the HRA came into force and so the court should not consider the issue. The Court of Appeal made a declaration of incompatibility on the basis that the court had to act in a way which was compatible with the Convention. The Secretary of State appealed.

Held: (HL) The court was entitled in assessing compatibility to take account of relevant background material, including ministerial statements and explanatory departmental notes, but it was not proper to investigate or consider parliamentary debates. The courts should not treat ministerial statements as if they indicated parliament's objective intention, since it was a cardinal constitutional principle that the will of Parliament was expressed in the statutory language, and it was this that should be used to judge the proportionality of the legislation. The appeal would be allowed. [2003] 3 W.L.R. 568 HL

Commentary
Parliament was entitled to decide that the appropriate way of protecting the borrower under money-lending transactions was to deprive the lender of all rights under the agreement. This was a proportionate means of achieving the legitimate aim of consumer satisfaction. The House of Lords, reversing the Court of Appeal, took the view that the concept of proportionality should be restrictively applied and refused to grant a declaration of incompatibility. Lord Nicholls stressed that the courts had a "reviewing role". He stated "Parliament is charged with the primary responsibility for deciding whether the means chosen to deal with a social problem are both necessary and appropriate. Assessment of the advantages and disadvantages of the various legislative alternatives is primarily a matter for Parliament".

Key Principle: **A s.3 interpretation should not be applied if the effect would be to impliedly contradict the statute.**

In Re S (Minors) (Care Order: Implementation of Care Plan)
In two appeals by parents whose children had been taken into care, the Court of Appeal concluded that the existing regime for making final care orders under the Children Act 1989 was incompatible with the rights of parents and children under

Articles 6(1) and 8 of the European Convention. It declared that a new procedure "should be adopted in which a care plan would be drawn up by the court with its essential milestones "starred". A local authority which failed to reach a starred milestone within a reasonable time after the date set by the court would have to notify the child's guardian, who would have the right to seek new directions from the court. Judges should have a wider discretion to make an interim care order and put off the making of a final care order. The local authority in one case and the Secretary of State in the other appealed. The mother of one of the children cross-appealed, arguing that the starring system was essential to comply with her Convention rights.

Held: (HL) The appeals by the local authority and the Secretary of State would be allowed and the mother's appeal dismissed. The Court of Appeal had wrongly crossed the boundary between interpreting the 1989 Act and amending it, which was a function reserved for Parliament. It was a basic principle of the 1989 Act that the courts could not intervene in the way local authorities carried out their parental responsibility under final care orders. The Court of Appeal could not impose extra obligations on local authorities in the absence of any finding that they were acting unlawfully. Parents whose rights under Article 8 were breached could bring proceedings against the local authority under s.7 of the Human Rights Act 1998. A gap in a statute was not the same as a statutory incompatibility. The courts should not encroach on the local authority's statutory discretion. [2002] UKHL 10; [2002] 2 A.C. 291

Commentary
Lord Nicholls stated that the court would cross the boundary between interpretation and amendment if it gave a meaning which was substantially different from an Act of Parliament. The Court of Appeal had exceeded its role in making innovations in the construction and application of the provision of the 1989 Act.

Key Principle: **Section 5 of the HRA—Right of Crown to intervene:**

"(1) Where a court is considering whether to make a declaration of incompatibility, the Crown is entitled to notice in accordance with rules of court.

(2) In any case to which subsection (1) applies—

   (a) a Minister of the Crown (or a person nominated by him),
   (b) a member of the Scottish Executive,
   (c) a Northern Ireland Minister,
   (d) a Northern Ireland department,
      is entitled, on giving notice in accordance with rules of court, to be joined as a party to the proceedings.

(3) Notice under subsection (2) may be given at any time during the proceedings.

(4) A person who has been made a party to criminal proceedings (other than in Scotland) as the result of a notice under subsection (2) may, with leave, appeal to the House of Lords against any declaration of incompatibility made in the proceedings.

(5) In subsection (4)—

      'criminal proceedings' includes all proceedings before the Courts-Martial Appeal Court; and
      'leave' means leave granted by the Court making the declaration of incompatibility or by the House of Lords."

Key Principle: **The purpose of s.5 in conferring on a minister the right to be heard was to ensure that the relevant minister had the opportunity to participate in the hearing.**

R. v A (No. 1)
For background facts see p.19.

There was no proposal by the parties that during the course of the appeal the House should be asked to consider making a declaration of incompatibility. Accordingly the circumstances had not arisen for applying the proceedings prescribed by Directions 30.2 and 30.4 of the House of Lords Practice Directions and standing orders applicable to Criminal Appeals on the hearing of such an issue. The Home Secretary nevertheless petitioned for leave to intervene.

Held: (HL) Although as a general rule the effect on the fairness of a trial of the admission or exclusion of evidence was to be judged after its completion in the context of the proceedings as a whole, it was undesirable that the vulnerable witness, the complainant, should be exposed to the risk of having to give evidence again if the trial was found to be unfair. The issue of incompatibility was one of general public importance and it was in the best interests of all the parties that the issue should be determined in advance of the trial and without delay. The Secretary of State who had borne responsibility for the promotion of the Youth Justice and Criminal Evidence Act 1999 should be joined as a party to the proceedings. [2001] 1 W.L.R. 789

Commentary
The House considered that although the Crown was an appellant and represented by the Director his role as prosecutor was different from that of a minister with executive responsibilities.

Key Principle: **Section 19 of the HRA—Statements of compatibility:**

"(1) A Minister of the Crown in charge of a Bill in either House of Parliament must, before a Second Reading of the Bill—

   (a) make a statement to the effect that in his view the provisions of the Bill are compatible with the Convention rights ('a statement of compatibility'); or

   (b) make a statement to the effect that although he is unable to make a statement of compatibility the government nevertheless wishes the House to proceed with the Bill.

(2) The statement must be in writing and be published in such manner as the Minister making it considers appropriate."

Key Principle: **Statements of compatibility are not binding on the courts.**

R. v A
For facts and holding see p.19.

Commentary
Statements of compatibility are, according to Lord Hope, no more than expressions of opinion by the minister. Counsel for the Secretary of State did not rely on the statement in the course of argument.

Retrospectivity

Key Principle: **(1) Section 7 of the HRA—Proceedings:**

"(1) A person who claims that a public authority has acted (or proposes to act) in a way which is made unlawful by section 6(1) may—

    (a) bring proceedings against the authority under this Act in the appropriate court or tribunal; or

    (b) rely on the Convention right or rights concerned in any legal proceedings,

but only if he is (or would be) a victim of the unlawful act.

(2) In subsection (1)(a) 'appropriate court or tribunal' means such court or tribunal as may be determined in accordance with rules; and proceedings against an authority include a counter claim or similar proceeding.

(3) If the proceedings are brought on an application for judicial review, the applicant is to be taken to have a sufficient interest in relation to the unlawful act only if he is, or would be, a victim of that act.

(4) If the proceedings are made by way of a petition for judicial review in Scotland, the applicant shall be taken to have title and interest to sue in relation to the unlawful act only if he is, or would be, a victim of that act.

(5) Proceedings under subsection (1)(a) must be brought before the end of—

    (a) the period of one year beginning with the date on which the act complained of took place; or

    (b) such longer period as the court or tribunal considers equitable having regard to all the circumstances,

but that is subject to any rule imposing a stricter time limit in relation to the procedure in question.

(6) In subsection (1)(b) 'legal proceedings' includes—

    (a) proceedings brought by or at the instigation of a public authority; and

    (b) an appeal against the decision of a court or tribunal.

(7) For the purposes of this section, a person is a victim of an unlawful act only if he would be a victim for the purposes of Article 34 of the Convention if proceedings were brought in the European Court of Human Rights in respect of that act.

(8) Nothing in this Act creates a criminal offence.

(9) In this section 'rules' means—

    (a) in relation to proceedings before a court or tribunal outside Scotland, rules made by the Lord Chancellor or the Secretary of State for the purposes of this section or rules of court,

    (b) in relation to proceedings before a court or tribunal in Scotland, rules made by the Secretary of State for those purposes,

    (c) in relation to proceedings before a tribunal in Northern Ireland—

        (i) which deals with transferred matters; and

        (ii) for which no rules made under paragraph (a) are in force,

    rules made by a Northern Ireland Department for those purposes,

and includes provision made by order under section 1 of the Courts and Legal Services Act 1990.

(10) In making rules, regard must be had to section 9.

(11) The Minister who has power to make rules in relation to a particular tribunal may, to the extent he considers it necessary to ensure the tribunal can provide an appropriate remedy in relation to an act (or proposed act) of a public authority which is (or would be) unlawful as a result of section 6(1), by order add to—

    (a) the relief or remedies which the tribunal may grant; or

    (b) the grounds on which it may grant any of them.

(12) An order made under subsection (11) may contain such incidental, supplemental, consequential or transitional provision as the Minister making it considers appropriate.

(13) 'The Minister' includes the Northern Ireland department concerned."

(2) Section 22 of the HRA:

"(4) Paragraph (b) of subsection (1) of section 7 applies to proceedings brought by or at the instigation of a public authority whenever the act in question took place; but otherwise that subsection does not apply to an act taking place before the coming into force of that section."

Key Principle: **A defendant whose trial took place before the coming into force of the HRA 1998 was not entitled to rely in an appeal on an alleged breach of his Convention rights under s.22(4) of the HRA.**

R. v Lambert
For facts see p.5.

Held: (HL) Since the relevant provisions of the HRA were not in force at the date of the trial, the decision of the court could not be challenged on the ground that it had acted in a manner contrary to the European Convention on Human Rights. The House should still however consider whether the transfer of the burden of proof under s.28 of the Misuse of Drugs Act 1971 was contrary to the Convention. [2001] 3 W.L.R. 206

R. v Kansal (No. 2)
At his trial in 1992 for obtaining property by deception, the prosecution adduced against the defendant answers he had given under compulsion when he was examined under oath in bankruptcy proceedings. The trial judge admitted the answers despite a defence submission that it was unfair to do so. His appeal was dismissed on the basis that the Insolvency Act 1986 had abrogated his privilege against self-incrimination and made his answers admissible in any proceedings. In 2000 he appealed to the Court of Appeal which quashed his conviction on the basis that the 1998 Act had made the right to a fair trial retrospective. The Crown appealed.

Held: (HL) The House was bound by the decision of the majority in *R. v Lambert* [2001] 3 W.L.R. 206, that appeals were excluded from the retrospectivity provisions of the 1998 Act. *Lambert* had been decided after the Court of Appeal decision in the appellant's case and the House would not depart from it without a compelling reason to do so. In tendering the disputed evidence, the prosecutor had been acting in accordance with primary legislation which could not at the time have been read differently in accordance with s.6 of the 1998 Act. Accordingly there had been no ground for the Court of Appeal to declare the conviction unsafe and the conviction would be reinstated. [2001] 3 W.L.R. 1562

Commentary

A majority of the House in *Kansal* expressed doubt about the interpretation of retrospectivity in *Lambert*. The Court of Appeal in *Lambert* had also commented that judicial authorities were divided as to the retrospective nature of s.22(4) of the HRA. This states that the right to rely on Convention rights in s.7(1)(5) of the Act "applies to proceedings brought by or at the instigation of a public authority whenever the act in question took place". In the House of Lords decision in *Lambert*, the majority (Lord Steyn dissenting) held that an appeal brought by an unsuccessful defendant was not to be treated as proceedings brought by a public authority. (Despite this finding the court did consider the substantive issue of the reverse onus of proof). Lord Steyn considered that if there has been a breach of the Convention, whenever it occurred, it must be wrong to uphold the conviction, due to the requirements in s.6 of the HRA. In *R. v DPP Ex p. Kebilene* [2000] 2 A.C. 326 the majority had held that a criminal prosecution was "proceedings brought . . . by a public authority" (see also pp.7, 98). In *R. (Mahmood) v Secretary of State for the Home Department* [2001] 1 W.L.R. 840, an immigration decision case, the Court of Appeal stated that a court required to review an administrative decision made before the incorporation of the Convention was not obliged to consider Convention rights as having been incorporated into domestic law by the 1998 Act but that since the Secretary of State had stated that he had had regard to Article 8 of the Convention when giving his decision the court ought to approach the decision as if the 1998 Act had been in force. The approach in *Lambert* and *Kansal* was followed in *R. v Lyons* [2002] UKHL 44.

Public Authorities

Key Principle: **Section 6 of the HRA—Acts of public authorities:**

"(1) It is unlawful for a public authority to act in a way which is incompatible with a Convention right.

(2) Subsection (1) does not apply to an act if—

   (a) as the result of one or more provisions of primary legislation, the authority could not have acted differently; or

   (b) in the case of one or more provisions of, or made under, primary legislation which cannot be read or given effect in a way which is compatible with the Convention rights, the authority was acting so as to give effect to or enforce those provisions.

(3) In this section 'public authority' includes—

   (a) a court or tribunal, and

   (b) any person certain of whose functions are functions of a public nature,

but does not include either House of Parliament or a person exercising functions in connection with proceedings in Parliament.

(4) In subsection (3) 'Parliament' does not include the House of Lords in its judicial capacity.

(5) In relation to a particular act, a person is not a public authority by virtue only of subsection (3)(b) if the nature of the act is private.

(6) 'An act' includes a failure to act but does not include a failure to—

   (a) introduce in, or lay before, Parliament a proposal for legislation; or

   (b) make any primary legislation or remedial order."

Key Principle: **The Strasbourg jurisprudence may invoke proportionality as a new ground of judicial review.**

R. (Daly) v Secretary of State for the Home Department

The applicant, a prisoner, had stored in his cell correspondence with his solicitor. He was, like all prisoners in a closed prison, subject to standard cell searching without him being present. The applicant sought leave for judicial review of the decision to require examination of prisoners' legally privileged correspondence in his absence.

Held: (HL) A person sentenced to custodial order retained the right to communicate confidentially with a legal adviser under the seal of legal professional privilege. The current policy amounted to an interference with the applicant's rights under Article 8(1) to a greater extent than was necessary for the prevention of disorder and crime. The courts should adopt a test of proportionality in reviewing executive decisions. [2001] 2 A.C. 532

Commentary

In *R. v Secretary of State for the Environment Transport and the Regions Ex p. Holding and Barnes (Alconbury)* 2001 Lord Slynn stated (para.51):

> "I consider that even without reference to the Human Rights Act the time has come to recognise that this principle [of proportionality] is part of English administrative laws, not only when judges are dealing with Community acts but also when they are dealing with acts subject to domestic law. Trying to keep the *Wednesbury* principle and proportionality in separate compartments seems to me to be unnecessary and confusing."

Lord Steyn here indicated that the "heightened scrutiny test" which was developed for human rights inferences in *R. v Ministry of Defence Ex p. Smith* [1996] Q.B. 517 1995 may not necessarily be appropriate. The Strasbourg Court stated that the threshold at which the Court of Appeal could find the MoD policy irrational was "placed so high that it effectively excluded any consideration by the domestic courts of the question of whether the interference with the applicants' rights answered a pressing social need or was proportionate to the national security and public order aims pursued, principles which lie at the heart of the Court's analysis of complaints under Article 8 of the Convention". This test was applied in *Daly*, signalling in effect that proportionality is a new ground of review. Lord Steyn denied that this meant a shift to review on merits. The House of Lords declared in this case that it was following *Campbell v UK* (1993) 15 E.H.R.R. 137 as well as a number of English authorities including *R. v Secretary of State for the Home Department Ex p. Leech* [1994] Q.B. 198. The effect of ss.2 and 3 of the HRA will be that the Strasbourg method of judicial reasoning will have increasing impact in English courts. However, it should be noted that the duty is to take account of the Strasbourg case law, not necessarily to follow it. It may be that the English courts will surpass the Strasbourg jurisprudence in developing concepts of rights. The limits of the application of the principle of proportionality were shown in *R. (Association of British Civilian Internees: Far East Region) v Secretary of State for Defence* [2003] EWCA Civ 473, [2003] Q.B. 1397. There the claimants were British subjects who had been civilian internees in the Far East during World War II. They sought judicial review of an *ex gratia* compensation scheme which was confined only to internees who had been born in the UK or who had at least one British-born parent. This excluded some civilians who were British subjects when they were interned. Their association maintained that the birth criterion was disproportionate and irrational and defeated the legitimate expectations aroused in members by the original announcement suggesting that all interned British subjects would be eligible. Their claim was dismissed and they appealed. The Court of Appeal dismissed the appeal. Proportionality had not replaced the test of reasonableness traditionally applicable on judicial review claims which raised no human rights or European Community law issues. It was not irrational for the Secretary of State to limit the scheme as he had. The original announcement had not unequivocally promised a payment to all British internees. There was no abuse of power and the claim based on legitimate expectation was rejected.

Key Principle: **The HRA identifies two types of public authorities: standard (or pure) public authorities and hybrid authorities.**

Aston Cantlow and Wilmcote with Billesley Parochial Church Council v Wallbank

The claimant was a parochial church council whose thirteenth century chancel had fallen into disrepair. The council brought an action against the defendants to foot the bill for the repairs under the Chancel Repairs Act 1932. The defendants were the proprietors of glebe land and thus lay-rectors of the church. The liability of the proprietors to fund chancel repairs had arisen as a result of the enclosure of the land in 1742. They had bought the land in 1970 knowing that it was subject to the repair liability. They resisted the claim on the grounds only that it was unlawful as a result of s.6 of the Human Rights Act 1998 as an act of a public authority (the parochial church council) contravening their right to peaceful enjoyment of their possessions under Article 1 of the first protocol to the European Convention. The judge found them liable for the cost of the repairs, but the Court of Appeal held that the council was a public body levying an indiscriminate form of taxation and thus its claim was not lawful. The defendants appealed to the House of Lords.

Held: (HL) The appeal would be allowed. Although the Church of England was an established church and the council was a body through which the church functioned, its functions were primarily pastoral and administrative and so not wholly of a public nature, more particularly when it was enforcing what was essentially a private law liability. In addition the council was acting under primary legislation (the 1932 Act) and so was exempt from the effects of s.6 of the 1998 Act. The House of Lords also held that the Convention right to peaceful enjoyment of possessions did not relieve the defendants from civil law liabilities which they had knowingly taken on and which were not different from other liabilities which might run with the ownership of land. The defendants were not being discriminated against, nor were they being subjected to arbitrary taxation and their peaceful enjoyment of their possessions was not affected. [2003] UKHL 37

Commentary
This case sets limits to the effect of Article 1 of the first protocol and clarifies what is meant by a public body. The enforcement of purely private law rights by public bodies or bodies with some public and some private functions is not affected by the Human Rights Act. Here the House of Lords decided that a parochial church council was not a standard or core public authority and commented on how to analyse a "hybrid" body. Relevant factors in deciding what was a core public body included the possession of special powers, democratic accountability, public funding in whole or part, an obligation to act only in the public interest and establishment under statute. There was no universal test to define whether a body carried out a public function. Factors to be taken into account include the extent to which in carrying out the relevant function the body is publicly funded, or is exercising statutory powers, or is taking the place of central government or local authorities, or is providing a public service. The majority of

the House of Lords held that a PCC was a hybrid body but that its enforcement of the respondent's liability to repair the church's chancel was a private not a public act and so not covered by the HRA.

Key Principle: **Private bodies to which public authorities had delegated some of their functions might not be held accountable in public law.**

Donoghue v Poplar Housing and Regeneration Community Association Ltd

The appellant had been originally granted a tenancy by the local authority which later transferred it to Poplar Housing and Regeneration Community Association Ltd (Poplar). Poplar was a non-profit organisation created by the local authority to manage the housing stock. An order was made by the local authority for the possession of the appellant's property which was held under an assumed shorthold tenancy according to s.21 of the Housing Act 1988. The authority had determined that the appellant was intentionally homeless. The appellant appealed against the order for possession on the grounds that Poplar, being a public authority in terms of s.6 of the HRA was making a disproportionate interference under Article 8 right to respect for private life. A subsidiary issue was the procedure to be followed when the crown was notified that the court might be considering a declaration of incompatibility under s.4 of the HRA.

Held: (CA) Poplar was a public authority but there was no breach of Article 8. The transfer by the local authority to Poplar of their housing stock did not also transfer their public duties but only the means by which to enact them. Providing houses for rent was not a public duty. The court should defer to the will of Parliament which had given the courts limited intervention in the area of possession against people with low housing priority. (2001) U.K.H.R.R. 693

Commentary

The court gave extensive consideration to the factors which should be taken into account in deciding whether a body is a public authority. Many of these were derived from the pre-existing administrative law jurisprudence but some controversial new issues were raised. In *Costello-Roberts v UK* (1995) 19 E.H.R.R. 112 the Strasbourg Court stated that "the state cannot absolve itself from responsibility by delegating its obligations to private bodies or individuals". (See also p.136). However in *Donoghue* the Court of Appeal expressed the view that a local authority in privatising some functions would not automatically make the actions of the private company public in nature. More controversially it stated that providing houses for rent was not in itself a public duty, no matter which section of society the houses were for. In addition the fact that Poplar was a charity meant that the motivation of the organisation was more likely to be in the public good but that was not an indicator that it was a public body in terms of s.4 of the HRA. In the instant case Poplar was functioning as a public authority. Some commentators have pointed out that there are advantages in excluding a body from the designation of "public authority" since as a result it has potential standing as a victim to make a claim under the Act in appropriate circumstances. Professor Dawn Oliver for example argues that the interpretation of "public authority" under the Act should be restrictive. If this were not so a whole range of institutions which might wish to make claims under the Act would not be able to do so. She gives the universities, charities and the BBC as examples and expresses concern lest the Government restricted research, broadcasting and charitable campaigning without fear of counter challenge under Article 10 of ECHR. This line of argument suggests that amenability to judicial review should not necessarily be the determining factor in deciding whether a body was a "public authority" for the purposes of the HRA. Oliver comments, "the issues are different [in human rights cases] and in particular there is no reason why bodies which violate Convention rights when exercising public functions should benefit from the protection of Order 53, the existence of which may have influenced the court in developing the concept of public function for the purposes of that jurisdiction" ("The Frontiers of the State: Public Authorities and Public Functions under the Human Rights Act" (Autumn 2001) *Public Law* at 476).

R. (Heather) v Leonard Cheshire Foundation

Residents placed by their local authority or health authority in a long-term care home run by the defendant were refused judicial review of the defendant's decision to close the home and move them to smaller community-based homes nearby. They claimed that the defendant was exercising functions of a public nature within s.6(3)(l) of the Human Rights Act 1998 and were therefore required not to act in contravention of their rights under Article 8 of the European Convention. They claimed their Article 8 rights to a home had been infringed and that the defendant had reneged on promises made to them that they would remain in the home where they were originally placed.

Held: (CA) The appeal would be dismissed. The local or health authorities which had placed the residents in the home had not contracted out to the defendants their obligations to the residents under Article 8. The residents had contractual rights against the defendant. Had the residents been placed at the home after the coming into force of the 1998 Act they might have been able to insist that the contract between the authority and the care home should fully reflect their rights under Article 8. But the actual role being performed by the defendants had no public element and was indistinguishable from the role it played in caring for private patients. [2002] EWCA Civ 366: [2002] 2 All E.R. 936.

Commentary

This is another case on the boundaries between public and private functions under the Human Rights Act 1998. Lord Woolf C.J. applied the reasoning in *Donoghue* (see above) in holding that the defendant was not carrying out a public function. The fact that the residents' stay was being funded publicly did not give them extra rights against the owners of the care home. This was a controversial decision since the Foundation received public funding, was state regulated, and if it had not provided long stay residential care the state would have been obliged to do so. A contrasting case is *R. (on the application of A) v Partnerships in Care* [2002] 1 W.L.R. 2610. There the managers of a private psychiatric hospital were held to be a public authority. They were acting under statutory powers. Similarly in *Hampshire CC v Beer* [2004] W.L.R. 233 a non-profit making company which had been previously managed by a local authority was a public authority. The company exercised public functions which made it open to judicial review. On the other hand in *R. (on the application of West) v Lloyd's* [2004] All E.R. 251, the Court of Appeal decided that although it regulated its members' activities that did not make Lloyd's a governmental organization.

The Report of the Joint Parliamentary Committee on Human Rights on the Meaning of Public Authority has criticised the approach of the courts in a number of cases. It argued that "a narrow judicial view of the meaning of 'public authority' . . . means that many private and voluntary sector provides of public services are considered to fall outside the scope of the Act, with no obligation to comply with the rights and freedoms it incorporated into domestic law". It concluded that there was "a fundamental problem not with the design of the law, but with its inconsistent and restrictive application by the courts". However it praised the House of Lords decision in *Aston Cantlow* (see above) which balanced "a narrow category of 'pure' public authority against a generously wide and flexible category of 'functional' public authority". The Committee recommended that the lower courts should also be adopting such a clear "functional" approach. In the conclusion to its Report, it considered that it "would be unsatisfactory to leave this matter to the present sate of the case law." It urged the "Government to intervene in the public interest as a third party in cases where it can press the case for a broad, functional interpretation of the meaning of public authority under the Human Rights Act".

Key Principle: **In matters of general policy where opinions in a democratic society may differ the courts should give the role of the domestic policy maker special weight.**

Marcic v Thames Water Utilities Ltd

The claimant suffered repeated flooding of his house and garden by sewage overflowing from drains operated by the defendant, a public authority for human rights purposes. He brought proceedings for damage to his property caused by the flooding. The judge held as a preliminary issue that the defendant was not liable at common law for failing to carry out works to eliminate the nuisance, which had come about because third parties were connected as of right to the defendant's system. However, he also ruled that the stance of the water authority violated the claimant's right to respect for his home and private life under Article 8(1) and also his right under Article 1 of the First Protocol to peaceful enjoyment of his possessions and that the water authority was liable in nuisance. The decision was upheld by the Court of Appeal. The defendant appealed to the House of Lords.

Held: (HL) Appeal allowed. The Water Industry Act 1991 had established a detailed scheme of regulation, with an independent regulator whose decisions were subject to judicial review. The claimant's interest had to be balanced against those of other customers who would ultimately have to finance additional works to stop the flooding of the claimant's house. It was inconsistent with the statutory scheme to allow a cause of action in nuisance. The statutory scheme was compatible with the claimants Convention rights. [2003] UKHL 66; [2004] 2 A.C. 42

Commentary
In giving his decision at first instance Judge Richard Havery said: "In the absence of authority I would have thought that [Article 8 and Protocol 1, Article I] had nothing to do with the case. I would have been wrong". Havery's decision was initially hailed as creating a new constitutional tort under the HRA. The Court of Appeal however was anxious to bring the decision within the existing common law framework. The House of Lords followed the decision in *Hatton v UK* (2003) (see p.164) in that the Court there held that national authorities have direct democratic legitimation and were better equipped than the court to evaluate local needs. This approach was akin to the doctrine of the margin of appreciation.

3. KILLING, TORTURE, SLAVERY

Right to life

Key Principle: **Article 2 of the ECHR—Right to life:**

"1   Everyone's right to life shall be protected by law. No one shall be deprived of his life intentionally save in the execution of a sentence of a court following his conviction of a crime for which this penalty is provided by law.

2   Deprivation of life shall not be regarded as inflicted in contravention of this article when it results from the use of force which is no more than absolutely necessary:

  a in defence of any person from unlawful violence;
  b in order to effect a lawful arrest or to prevent the escape of a person lawfully detained;

    c in action lawfully taken for the purpose of quelling a
       riot or insurrection."

Key Principle: Article 2 of the ECHR is not concerned solely
with intentional killing but also covers situations where the
unintended outcome of the state's actions is the deprivation of
life.

Association X v UK

The Government had instituted a voluntary scheme for vaccination of children. Some of the children had suffered injury or
died. The Association of parents of these children complained
that the scheme was poorly administered and that proper steps
had not been taken to avoid the risk of serious injury or death.

Held: (Commission) On the facts there was no violation since
"there exists a general common knowledge that vaccination
schemes involve certain risks". The state had established a
system for control and supervision which was "sufficient to
comply with obligation to protect life under Article 2 of the
Convention". (1978) 14 D.R. 31

Commentary

It is implicit in the Commission's findings that without a proper
system of control and supervision there might have been a breach
of Article 2. It is also clear that the state is permitted to introduce
measures involving medical risks to individuals but which are for
the general good.

Key Principle: The scope of Article 2 does not cover prescrib-
ing how resources in a national health service should be
allocated.

Taylor v UK

Parents whose children had been unlawfully killed or injured in
hospital by nurse Beverley Allitt in violation of Article 2. Allitt
was convicted of murder of four children, the attempted murder
of three children and of causing grievous bodily harm to six
children. The parents had pressed for a public inquiry into the

tragedy but only an internal inquiry was held. The parents argued that financial and other shortcomings of the National Health Service had allowed an untrained and dangerous person to care for their children unsupervised. The internal inquiry report did not comment directly on the parents' claims that the hospital had been poorly funded and understaffed. The parents claimed on their own behalf and on that of their children. They alleged that they continued to be affected by the events which had arisen from government failings and which could be repeated in the future.

Held: (Commission) The organisation and the funding of the National Health service does not fall within the scope of Article 2. "Any doubts which may consequently arise as to the policies adopted in the field of public health are, in the Commission's opinion, matters for public and political debate which fall outside the scope of Article 2 and the other provisions of the Convention." [1994] 79–A D.R. 127

Commentary
This case leaves unanswered the question of how far the state has a positive duty to provide resources to preserve life. It is a particularly pertinent issue in relation to the state's responsibility to provide life-saving medical treatment. In *R. v Cambridgeshire Health Authority Ex p. B* [1995] 1 F.L.R. 1055 the Court of Appeal overturning the decision of the High Court held that the Health Authority was entitled to refuse to fund potential life-saving treatment for a young child since it was entitled to deploy its resources as best it could. It seems in the light of *Taylor v UK* that such a decision would not necessarily be resisted in the light of the HRA. However, it should be noted that Article 14 requires public authorities to safeguard Convention rights without discrimination on any ground. It might therefore be the case that if life saving treatment was withheld on the grounds of age, or youth or mental condition that such action was a breach of Article 14 taken together with Article 2.

Reasonableness Test

Key Principle: **The state's positive duty to protect life must be construed in the light of prevailing circumstances.**

Osman v UK

A teacher harassed and intimidated a pupil and his family. He eventually killed the pupil. The family argued that the police, who had been alerted to the situation, had not taken sufficient measures to protect the family.

Held: (ECtHR) There was no violation of Article 2 since none of the events leading up to the killing had appeared to be threatening the life of the boy. The court considered however that in order for there to be a breach of Article 2 it was not necessary to demonstrate that there had been "gross negligence or wilful disregard of the duty to protect life". It was "sufficient for an applicant to show that the authorities did not do all that could reasonably be expected of them to avoid a real and immediate risk to life of which they have or ought to have knowledge." It was also necessary on the other hand to ensure that the police acted in a way which respected due process and the guarantees in Articles 5 and 8. [1999] 1 F.L.R. 193 (see also p.50).

Keenan v UK

A mentally ill person committed suicide. The family argued that there was a violation of Article 2 in that the authorities had not taken sufficient care.

Held: (ECtHR) There was no violation of Article 2 since the prison authorities made a reasonable response to his conduct and had not omitted any step which should reasonably have been taken. (App. No. 27229/95) [2001] H.R. 178

Commentary

In *Guerra v Italy* (1998) 26 E.H.R.R. 357 the court also held that the authorities only had an obligation to inform local people about environmental dangers which posed a potential threat to health in "circumstances which forseeably and on substantial grounds present a real risk of danger": that was not so in that case. However, although the authorities might be able to argue in defence of an act under Article 2 that they had acted reasonably, the content of "reasonableness" is open to various interpretations. The common law has accepted the justification of the interests of the patient for the decision of doctors to turn off the life-support system of someone who is in a permanent vegetative state. In *Airedale NHS Trust v Bland* [1993] A.C. 789 Lord Mustill had considered an additional argument based on the best interests of the community as a whole. However although this was persuasive "in social terms" he did not consider that the House of Lords was qualified to make such an assessment.

Key Principle: **The obligation of a public authority under Article 2 may be to avoid making a decision exposing anyone to the real possibility of a risk to life in the future.**

R. v Lord Saville Ex p. (1) 28 Widgery Soldiers (2) 8 Inquiry Soldiers
This was a challenge by way of judicial review of a decision made by the Bloody Sunday Inquiry Tribunal which ruled that soldier witnesses who are to give oral evidence before the Tribunal over a period of six months should do so in the Londonderry Guildhall, where the Tribunal had for the most part sat, rather than in London or in some other part of Great Britain. The soldier witnesses who were due to give evidence claimed that they would be exposed to lethal danger. The tribunal ruled that they must nevertheless give evidence. They appealed first to the Divisional Court by way of judicial review and then to the Court of Appeal. It was common ground that the High Court had a reviewing jurisdiction in relation to decisions of the Tribunal but it was argued that the Tribunal did not fall within the ambit of s.6 of the HRA and so the HRA did not apply.

Held: (CA) The Tribunal has to comply with the HRA and so the High Court had jurisdiction to entertain the application. The Tribunal had misdirected itself in law by applying the wrong test when assessing the risk to the lives of the soldiers if they gave evidence in Londonderry. It was not open to the Tribunal to conclude that the soldiers had no reasonable fears for their own safety. The test of "real and immediate" danger to life was not the appropriate test to invoke in the present circumstances. The appropriate course was to consider the nature of the witnesses' fears, the extent to which they were objectively founded and then to consider the extent to which those fears would be reduced if the soldiers' evidence were taken elsewhere in the United Kingdom. That had to be balanced against the adverse consequences to the inquiry of taking the evidence outside Londonderry. The risk posed in Londonderry to the soldier witnesses was real and fairness required that their evidence be taken elsewhere. The Administrative Court was correct in concluding that the Bloody Sunday Inquiry's ruling on the venue of soldier—witness hearings did not comply with the requirements of Article 2. [2002] 1 W.L.R. 1249

Commentary
The Administrative Court compared the tests set out on the one hand in *Osman* (see p.48) and on the other in *R. v Governor of Pentonville Prison Ex p. Fernandez* (1971) 1 W.L.R. 987 and *R. v Lord Saville Ex p. A* (1999) 4 All E.R. 860. These tests were different. In *Osman* the European Court of Human Rights had limited the obligation of the state to intervene to protect against the activities of third parties in circumstances in which there is a real and immediate risk to life. It should have considered the tests in *Ex p. Fernandez* and *Ex p. A* where the obligation of a public authority was defined more broadly. The degree of risk set out in *Osman* was well above the threshold that would engage Article 2.

Absolutely Necessary Force

Key Principle: **Deprivation of life is not inflicted in contravention of Article 2 when it results from the use of force which is no more than absolutely necessary (1) in defence of any person from unlawful violence or (2) in order to effect a lawful arrest or to prevent the escape of a person lawfully detained or (3) action lawfully taken for the purpose of quelling a riot or insurrection.**

McCann v UK
Three Provisional IRA members were in Gibraltar to plant a car bomb. At the time, however, there was no bomb in Gibraltar; it was in fact in a long stay facility in Spain. Soldiers of the Special Air Service shot the three IRA members dead in the street. The soldiers claimed in each case that they had opened fire because they suspected that their targets were about to set off a bomb by remote control. A coroner's jury in Gibraltar found the killings lawful. Attempts by the families of the dead IRA members to bring judicial review proceedings failed.

Held: (ECtHR) In assessing whether the use of force had been "absolutely necessary", the court must subject the deprivation of life to the most careful scrutiny and take into account not only the actions of the state agents who used the force, but also all the surrounding circumstances. The test of "absolutely necessary" requires that "a stricter and more compelling test of necessity must be employed from that normally applicable when determining whether the state's action is 'necessary in a democratic society'". There was no violation of Article 2 in the actions of the soldiers who shot the terrorists but there was a violation as regards the control and organisation of the operation. The court refused to award damages, however, accepting that the men had been intending to plant a bomb. (1996) 21 E.H.R.R. 97

Stewart v UK

The applicant's son, a 13 year old boy, was killed by a soldier in Northern Ireland firing a plastic bullet into a rioting crowd. She had taken an unsuccessful case as administratrix of the child for assault, battery and trespass to the person. The appeal judge in the hearing had found that the firing was a reasonable and lawful use of force for the prevention of crime since the boy had been participating in a riot. The applicant claimed a violation of Article 2.

Held: (Commission) There was no violation of Article 2. Force was "absolutely necessary" if it was "strictly proportionate to the achievement of the permitted purpose". The court considered that Article 2(2) did cover unintentional as well as intentional killings. (1984) 39 D.R. 162

Commentary

The test of absolute necessity applied by the court and the Commission imposes a higher standard than that under English statutory law. A subjective test of reasonableness is applied in the Criminal Law Act 1967, s.3. The case illustrates that the court and Commission will take into account exceptional circumstances such as that in Northern Ireland which face states.

Investigation of Deaths

Key Principle: **Article 2 requires a proper investigation of suspicious deaths.**

Jordan v UK

Relatives of people killed by the security services in Northern Ireland complained that their right to life had been violated by the authorities' failure to conduct a proper investigation into the circumstances of their deaths. They also, in two of the cases, alleged violation of the right to a fair trial, and in all four cases discrimination and a breach of the right to an effective remedy.

Held: (ECtHR) Article 2 ranked as one of the most fundamental provisions in the Convention, and no derogation was permitted in peacetime. The circumstances in which deprivation of a life could be justified had to be strictly construed. The burden of proof rested on the authorities to provide a satisfactory and convincing explanation of the deaths or of persons or within their control in custody. The Article covered not only intentional killing but also all situations where it was permitted to use force which could result, as an unintended outcome, in the deprivation of life. It required by implication some form of effective official investigation on the authorities' own motion. In all cases the next of kin of the victim had to be involved in the procedure to the extent necessary to safeguard his or her legitimate interests. The court rejected the applicants' other complaints. (App. Nos 24746/94, 28883/95, 37715/97) [2001] H.R. 178

Key Principle: **Article 2 requires coroners to determine not only the means but also the circumstances in which a prison suicide occurred.**

R. (Middleton) v West Somerset Coroner

A prisoner hanged himself in his cell. His family maintained he should have been on suicide watch as a known suicide risk. At the inquest the coroner told the jury to determine the dead man's identity and make findings only on how, when and where he came by his death. The jury were forbidden to bring in a verdict of neglect, though they were allowed to hand a note to the coroner indicating that they considered the Prison Service had failed in its duty to the dead man. The family sought judicial review of the coroner's directions, seeking publication of the note. They succeeded at first instance, but the decision was partly overturned in the Court of Appeal. The Secretary of State appealed.

Held: (HL) The inquest, as the means of implementing the Article 2 requirement for investigation of deaths in custody, ought to result in an expression of the jury's conclusion on the central factual issues in the case. In some cases the traditional verdict in short form was not adequate to meet the Article 2 requirement. The scheme as enacted should be interpreted so that the question how the deceased met his death should mean by what means and under what circumstances. It was not appropriate for the coroner to ask the jury to hand up a private note since this detracted from the public nature of the proceedings. [2004] UKHL 10; [2004] 2 A.C. 182

Commentary
In this important procedural decision the House of Lords significantly extended the duties of juries in coroners' inquests as set out in r.36(l)(b) of the Coroner's Rules. (See also *R. (Sacker) v West Yorkshire Coroner* [2004] UKHL 11.)

Key Principle: **The state's duty under Article 2 included a requirement to hold a public inquiry into the circumstances of a racist killing in prison.**

R. (Amin) Secretary of State for the Home Department
A prisoner in a young offender institution was murdered by his cellmate, who was known to be a violent racist and was subsequently convicted of his murder. The prisoner's family challenged by way of judicial review the Secretary of State's refusal to hold a public inquiry. The judge declared that an independent public investigation was needed to satisfy the state's procedural duty, under Article 2 of the European Convention, to investigate the killing. The decision was overturned in the Court of Appeal and the family appealed.

Held: (HL) The appeal would be allowed. The state's duty under Article 2 required it to protect its prisoners from criminal attack. Where death occurred, there should be sufficient public scrutiny to secure accountability and an appropriate level of participation by the next-of-kin. [2003] UKHL 51; [2004] 1 A.C. 653

Commentary
Lord Bingham stated that the minimum standards which should apply in such investigations had been set out in the main in

Edwards v UK (2002) 35 E.H.R.R. 35. In that case it was held that for an investigation into alleged unlawful killing by state agents to be effective, it may generally be regarded as necessary for the persons responsible for and carrying out the investigation to be independent from those implicated in the events. The investigation must also be effective in the sense that it is capable of leading to a determination of whether the force used in such cases was or was not justified in the circumstances and to the identification and punishment of those responsible. The authorities must have taken the reasonable steps available to them to secure the evidence concerning the incident, including, *inter alia*, eyewitness testimony, forensic evidence and, where appropriate, an autopsy which provides a complete and accurate record of injury and an objective analysis of clinical findings, including the cause of death. Any deficiency in the investigation which undermined its ability to establish the cause of death or the person or persons responsible would risk falling foul of this standard. A requirement of promptness and reasonable expedition was also implicit. Finally there must be a sufficient element of public scrutiny of the investigation or its results to secure accountability in practice as well as in theory. The degree of public scrutiny required may well vary from case to case. In all cases, however, the next-of-kin of the victim must be involved in the procedure to the extent necessary to safeguard his or her legitimate interests.

Key Principle: **The obligation to investigate killings by state agents is not retrospective.**

Re McKerr
The Royal Ulster Constabulary shot a man in 1982. The officers involved were acquitted and a coroner's inquest was abandoned when police refused to disclose their investigation report. The dead man's family took the case to Strasbourg, where the court held that their Article 2 rights had been violated by the failure to hold an effective official investigation. The Government nonetheless refused to reconsider. The family brought judicial review proceedings, which succeeded in the Northern Ireland Appeal Court. The Secretary of State appealed.

Held: (HL) The appeal would be allowed. The Human Rights Act was not retrospective and did not require an investigation of a death occurring before it came into force. The Government might have been in breach of its treaty obligations in not holding an investigation, but it was not in breach of any domestic law obligations, since there was no common law right to effective investigation of the death. [2004] UKHL 12; [2004] 2 All E.R. 409

Commentary

This decision has been much criticised. Clayton, Keane and Dunlop ("Key Human Rights Cases in the Last 12 Months". EHRLR 2004, 6. 614–630 p.9) argue it was wrongly decided and cannot be reconciled with the European Court of Human decision in *Cyprus v Turkey* (2002) 35 E.H.R.R. 30. They suggest that the correct approach was that taken by Jackson J. in *R (on the application of Wright) v Home Secretary* [2001] 1 Lloyd's Rep Med 478 at 488 in holding that a failure to investigate a pre-HRA death was a breach of a continuing procedural obligation.

Abortion

Key Principle: **Article 2 could restrict the availability of an abortion but national authorities enjoy a wide margin of appreciation and recognising the absolute right to life of a foetus would be contrary to the object and purpose of the Convention.**

Paton v UK

A husband living separately from his wife, tried to stop her having an abortion. The operation was carried out under legislation which permitted abortions after 10 weeks to avert the risk of injury to the physical or mental health of the pregnant woman.

Held: (Commission) Case inadmissible. Article 2 does not require states to put a complete ban on abortions since a foetus has no "absolute right to life". "The life of the foetus is intimately connected with and cannot be regarded in isolation of the pregnant woman. If Article 2 were held to cover the foetus and its protection under the Article were, in the absence of any express limitation, seen as absolute, as abortion would have to be considered as prohibited even where the continuance of the pregnancy would involve a serious risk to the life of the pregnant woman". The Commission held this outcome as unacceptable since it would mean that the "unborn life" of the foetus would be taken to have a higher value than the life of the pregnant woman. The Commission observed that there were two other possible interpretations of Article 2 namely that the foetus had no right to life or that any right it did have was subject to limitations. Since in this case even if the second interpretation was accepted there was no breach of Article 2, the Commission did not see the need to pronounce which of the two interpretations was correct. (1980) 19 D.R. 244

Commentary
This case concerned the abortion of a foetus of under 10 weeks. At that stage viable life outside the mother is impossible. Although not excluding the possibility that under certain circumstances Article 2 does protect the foetus, the Commission was silent on what those circumstances were. In *Open Door Counselling and Dublin Well Woman v Ireland* (1993) 15 E.H.R.R. 244 the court held that injunctions preventing women from leafleting in favour of abortion were disproportionate and therefore there were violations of Article 10. This case thus concerned the applicants' rights to disseminate information about abortion rather than the right to abortion. However, the court did state that Article 2 could in principle restrict the availability of abortion while acknowledging that "National authorities enjoy a wide margin of appreciation in matters of morals, particularly in an area such as the present which touches on matters of belief concerning the nature of human life." It also stated that Article 10 should not be interpreted in such a way as to limit the right to life. Note that Article 2 does not declare that life starts at conception in contrast with Article 4 of the American Convention on Human Rights. Abortion may also raise rights of the parents under Article 8 (see below).

No Right to Assisted Suicide

Key Principle: **Section 21(1) of the Suicide Act 1961 was not incompatible with the European Convention on Human Rights.**

Pretty v DPP
P was terminally ill with motor neurone disease. She wished to take her own life but her physical incapacity meant she required assistance to commit suicide. Section 21(1) of the Suicide Act 1961 made it a criminal offence for a person to assist the suicide

of another. Section 2(4) of the Act provided that no proceedings for that offence could be instituted except by or with the consent of the Director of Public Prosecutions (DPP). P appealed from a decision of the Divisional Court that the DPP had correctly refused to undertake not to prosecute P's husband if he were to assist his wife to commit suicide. She submitted that Article 2 of the European Convention on Human Rights when read in conjunction with Protocol 6 Article 1 and Protocol 6 Article 2 of the Convention guaranteed that an individual could choose whether or not to live. She also submitted that the DPP's refusal subjected her to inhuman or degrading treatment in breach of Article 3 of the ECHR.

Held: (HL) (1) Article 2 did not confer a negative right to end life; (2) there was no common law right to take a life; (3) P had the burden of proof to establish the DPP's decision breached the ECHR; (4) Articles 2 and 3 were complementary and there was nothing in Article 3 that affected an individual's right to choose not to live; (5) Rights under Article 8, 9 or 14 were not infringed; the 1961 Act did not confer a right to commit suicide, it merely abrogated the rule of law that it was a crime. [2001] UKHL 61

Commentary
The House drew on Convention and common law principles in making its judgment. At common law someone else cannot take a person's life (see *Airedale NHS Trust v Bland* [1993] A.C. 789) nor could fatality be a primary aim of treatment (see *Re J (a minor) (wardship: medical treatment)* [1991] Fam. 33. The House considered that the most detailed and erudite discussion of the issues raised by the appeal was to be found in the Canadian case *Rodriguez v Attorney-General of Canada* (1994) 2 L.R.C. 136. The applicant also alleged breaches of Articles 8, 9 and 14 and that the United Kingdom's blanket refusal to allow assistance with suicides was disproportionate in view of P being in full command of her mental faculties, the absence of harm to anyone else, the imminence of her death and her willingness to commit suicide herself were she able to. The House found no breaches of those Articles.

Key Principle: **Article 2 does not encompass a right to die.**

Pretty v UK
Having exhausted the English process without success, the applicant complained to the European Court of Human Rights

that s.2(l) of the Suicide Act 1961 violated Articles 2, 3, 8, 9 and 14.

Held: (ECtHR) Application dismissed. The "right to life" guaranteed in Article 2 could not be interpreted as conferring a right to die; nor could it create a right to self-determination in the sense of conferring on an individual the entitlement to choose death rather than life. The UK authorities' refusal to give Mr Pretty immunity from prosecution did not constitute cruel or inhuman treatment. Nor did the fact that she would face an undignified and distressing death amount to interference with her right, to respect for private life under Article 8(1). Section 2 of the Suicide Act, was designed to safeguard life by protecting the weak and vulnerable, and a blanket ban on helping suicide was not disproportionate. Nor were the applicants' claims a manifestation of religion or belief protected by Article 9(1). There was no discrimination, since there was objective and reasonable justification for not distinguishing those who kill themselves from those who needed help to do so. (2002) 25 E.H.R.R. 1

Commentary
In *Widmer v Switzerland* (1993) unreported, the Commission held that Article 2 does not require states to make passive euthanasia a crime.

Key Principle: **Article 3 of the ECHR—Prohibition of torture: "No one shall be subjected to torture or to inhuman or degrading treatment or punishment."**

Key Principle: **Article 3 covers three levels of conduct defined as:**

"a Torture: deliberate inhuman treatment causing very serious and cruel suffering.

b Inhuman treatment or punishment: the infliction of intense physical and mental suffering.

c Degrading treatment: Ill treatment designed to arouse in victims feelings of fear, anguish and inferiority capable of humiliating and debasing them and possibly breaking their physical and moral resistance."

Ireland v UK

Detainees in Northern Ireland were obliged to stand against a wall for hours in extremely uncomfortable positions. They were interrogated wearing dark hoods and deprived of sleep and adequate food and drink. They were also subjected to noise.

Held: (ECtHR) The court disagreed with the Commission's findings that these techniques amounted to torture. They did however constitute inhuman and degrading treatment. The court listed the factors to take into account. These included sex, age and the state of health of the victim. It stated that the authority's activities should reach a minimum level of severity to bring them within the Article. "Degrading" did not mean simply disagreeable or uncomfortable. Actions in private as well as in front of others could fall within the Article. (1979) 2 E.H.R.R. 25

Key Principle: **Torture can consist of the imposition of mental suffering.**

Denmark v Greece (The Greek Case)

Prisoners in Athen's jails were subjected to severe overcrowding in cells and corridors with little natural light, were given no beds or mattresses. They were refused or had access delayed to medical treatment. They were also physically ill-treated.

Held: (Commission) The treatment amounted to torture in that it included "the infliction of mental suffering by creating a state of anguish and stress by means other than bodily assault. The Commission's finding of torture was confirmed by the Council of Ministers. The Commission stated that "mental suffering leading to acute psychiatric disturbances falls into the category of treatment prohibited by Article 3 of the Convention". (1969) 12 YB Spec. Vol.

Commentary

This is one of the few cases where a state has taken action against another state. The Commission found that slaps or blows to the head might not breach Article 3 but this position has been changed somewhat in subsequent case law see for example *Tomasi v France* (1993) 15 E.H.R.R. 1. The Commission's finding was upheld by the Committee of Ministers. For another acknowledgement that mental anguish can constitute torture see also *Ireland v UK* (1978) 2 E.H.R.R. 25.

Key Principle: **States have a positive obligation to prevent torture.**

Chahal v UK

The applicant was faced with deportation to India because his presence in the United Kingdom was considered not conducive to the public good on the grounds of national security. He had been denied asylum. He claimed that there was a violation of Article 3 since his deportation would expose him to a real risk he would be tortured in India.

Held: (ECtHR) Despite the difficulties faced by states in protecting their citizens from terrorist violence "the Convention prohibits in absolute terms torture or inhuman or degrading treatment or punishment, irrespective of the victim's conduct." There was therefore a violation of Article 3. (1997) 23 E.H.R.R. 413

Commentary

This case emphasises the absolute nature of the prohibitions in Article 3. However undesirable or dangerous the activities of the individual in question they cannot be a material consideration. There was also a violation in *D v UK* (1997) 24 E.H.R.R. 423 where the person threatened with deportation had AIDS. He would have neither emotional nor financial support in the receiving country where there was a poor quality of medical care. The absolute prohibition contained in Article 3 should be respected whether or not the applicant had been given leave to enter the United Kingdom.

Key Principle: **Torture may arise where the threatened treatment is lawful.**

Soering v UK
A German national faced extradition from Britain to face capital charges in the United States. He was in a prison hospital due to his dread of violence and homosexual abuse from other inmates. He claimed violations of Article 3 in that both the death penalty itself and waiting on "death row" for execution in the United States amounted to inhuman and degrading treatment.

Held: (ECtHR) The death penalty in itself was not an inhuman and degrading punishment within the meaning of Article 3. Article 3 did not in itself prohibit the death penalty since that would have nullified one of the exceptions to the right to life under Article 2(1). The court acknowledged that many Contracting States had abolished the death penalty which might be taken to abrogate the exception under Article 2(1). However the specific provision in the Sixth Protocol for the abolition of the death penalty was an indication that Article 3 could not have the meaning the application argued. There was nonetheless a violation of Article 3. Although the death penalty in the United States was not in itself illegal, the fact that the applicant might well be held for years on death row pending execution was a violation for which the United Kingdom would be responsible if the extradition went ahead. Extradition to non-contracting states may give rise to a positive obligation under Article 3 if there is a real risk of torture or inhuman or degrading treatment or punishment in the requesting country. (1989) 11 E.H.R.R. 439

Commentary
The court stated that despite its decision in this case the circumstances of the death penalty could in principle give rise to an application under Article 3. A relevant factor would be changing attitudes in the contracting states to executions. The court referred to the United Nations Convention for the Prevention of Torture and Other Cruel, Inhuman or Degrading Treatment or Punishment and in particular Article 3 which states that "No State Party shall . . . extradite a person . . . where there are substantial grounds for believing that he would be in danger of being subjected to torture" and that it would be compatible with the values of the Convention that such an obligation existed. Protocol 6 Article 1 of the ECHR provides: "The death penalty shall be abolished. No one shall be condemned to such penalty or executed." It is a matter of some controversy whether the judicial Committee of the Privy Council which sits as the final court of appeal for certain former colonial countries will be bound by Protocol 6 in their decisions in death

penalty cases. In ratifying Protocol 6 the United Kingdom only extended it expressly to Jersey, Guernsey and the Channel Islands. Article 56 of the European Convention on Human Rights, which was not included in the HRA, allows the state to extend the provisions of the Convention to "all or any territory for whose international relations it is responsible". This has not included the Caribbean. However the Privy Council in considering appeals involving the death penalty has drawn on case law from international and European Convention organs. (See *Pratt v Attorney-General for Jamaica* [1993] 3 W.L.R. 995).

Responsibility for Torture

Key Principle: **Former heads of state do not have immunity in respect of acts of torture committed while head of state contrary to the 1984 International Convention Against Torture.**

R. v Bow Street Metropolitan Stipendiary Magistrate Ex p. Pinochet Ugarte (No. 3)

The former Chilean dictator was arrested in London on a Spanish warrant. The warrant alleged that he had ordered torture and hostage-taking while he was in power. The Divisional Court held that the applicant as a former head of state was entitled to immunity from civil and criminal process in the English courts in respect of acts committed in the exercise of sovereign power. The House of Lords allowed an appeal by the prosecutor, but this decision was set aside because one of the judges, Lord Hoffman, was an office-holder in a charity controlled by Amnesty International. The case was reheard before a differently constituted court.

Held: (HL) Though a former head of state had immunity from the criminal jurisdiction of the United Kingdom for acts done in his official capacity as head of state, torture was an international crime against humanity and there was a universal jurisdiction to extradite or punish a public official for torture. That principle extended to heads of state because the state parties who had created the international jurisdiction by the International Convention Against Torture could not have intended to create an immunity for a head of state who was a torturer. [1999] 2 W.L.R. 827

Commentary
Two of their Lordships, Lords Millett and Phillips, stated that the systematic use of torture was an international crime for which there could be no immunity even before the United Nations Convention Against Torture came into effect and consequently there was no immunity under customary international law for the offences relating to torture alleged against the applicant. This decision shows that English courts are prepared to apply customary international human rights law. Pinochet subsequently avoided extradition by pleading ill-health.

Key Principle: **The state may be responsible for the acts of its agents even when they are acting in breach of orders.**

Cyprus v Turkey
The Cypriot Government claimed that the Turkish Government held responsibility for outrages on detainees including rapes.

Held: (Commission) The Commission accepted the allegations that a number of detainees had suffered rapes by Turkish soldiers and in two cases by Turkish officers and that the Turkish authorities had not taken sufficient measures to prevent this. (1982) 4 E.H.R.R. 482

Commentary
This case illustrates that the principle of strict liability applies to Article 3 since "It has not been shown that the Turkish authorities took adequate measures to prevent this happening or that they generally took any disciplinary measures following such incidents. The Commission therefore considers that the non prevention of the said acts is imputable to Turkey under the Convention." This approach was also evident in *Ireland v UK* (see above) where the court held that the higher authorities of the state "are strictly liable for the conduct of their subordinates; they are under a duty to impose their will on subordinates and cannot shelter behind their inability to ensure that it is respected".

Investigations into state's use of force

Key Principle: **Investigation into the use of force by state agents does not necessarily require a fully public process.**

R. (Green) v Police Complaints Authority
The claimant was knocked down and seriously injured by an unmarked police car, and complained that the driver had hit him deliberately. The Police Complaints Authority investigated and reported. The driver was then convicted of driving without due care. The Authority announced that there would be no further disciplinary action in relation to the incident because there was no "irrefutable evidence" that he had acted deliberately. When it was pointed out that this was not the appropriate test, the Authority undertook to look again at the driver's conduct. The claimant sought disclosure of the statements and documents in the authority's hands. The Authority refused and the claimant brought proceedings for judicial review, which succeeded at first instance but were overturned on appeal. The claimant appealed.

Held: (HL) The appeal would be dismissed. The Police Act 1996 permitted the authority to disclose material to the claimant only so far as this was necessary for the discharge of the Authority's functions. Disclosure was not necessary to the decision whether disciplinary proceedings should be brought. The degree of involvement of the claimant was sufficient to safeguard his legitimate interests and thus did not breach Article 3 of the European Convention. [2004] UKHL 6; [2004] U.K.H.R.R. 939

Commentary
This decision should be contrasted with *R. (on the application of Amin) v Secretary of State for Home Department*, see p.53.

Prison conditions

Key Principle: **In the context or the treatment of prisoners the treatment must go beyond the usual element of humiliation associated with imprisonment after a criminal conviction in order to be a violation of Article 3.**

Tyrer v UK
For facts and holding see p.9.

Commentary
The court made it clear that in order to cross the minimum threshold regard will be taken of all the circumstances of the case

which include "the nature and context of the punishment itself and the manner and method of its execution". The personal characteristics of the victim are relevant including age, gender and state of health.

Key Principle: **The fact that the person concerned has brought the treatment on himself may be a relevant consideration in assessing whether a violation of the Article has occurred.**

McFeeley v UK
IRA prisoners had as a protest against their prison status smeared their cells with food and excrement. They claimed that their continued detention in the cells was inhuman and degrading treatment.

Held: (Commission) The self imposed condition of the cells could relieve the state from its responsibilities for the welfare of prisoners. The state had an obligation to keep the situation under constant review. There was no violation of Article 3. (1984) 38 D. & R. 11

Commentary
The Commission also found that there was nothing inherently degrading or objectionable about the requirement to wear prison uniform or to be subjected to intimate body searches. The Commission also considered that the object of achieving political prisoner status was not supported by international law. In other cases the Commission stated that the fact that a person has brought the treatment on himself cannot in itself absolve the state of its obligations under Article 3. Although such cases show the Commission has not absolved the state of all responsibility for self-inflicted harm under Article 3, it has in fact not found any violations. In *Hilton v UK* (1981) 3 E.H.R.R. 104 the self-inflicted conditions were a result of an innate characteristic of the prisoner, namely his stressful personality which meant that he was incapable of accepting imprisonment. His distrust of fellow prisoners and warders led to his total isolation and his reduction to an animal like state. The majority view of the Commission was that although it was critical of many of the measures taken by the authorities some of them were positive and there was no violation of Article

3. However the strong dissenting view of four commissioners was that the state's responsibility was engaged.

Key Principle: **A degrading punishment does not lose its degrading character just because it is believed to be or actually is an effective deterrent to or aid to maintain discipline.**

Tyrer v UK
See p.9.

Commentary
The Government sought to rely on what was then Article 63(3) of the Convention, now Article 56(3). This allows a state to extend the Convention to territories for whose international relations it is responsible. However the provisions should be applied with due regard to "local requirements". The Government argued that public opinion in the Isle of Man supported birching, making it a "local requirement". However the court considered that there would have to be positive and conclusive proof of a requirement and beliefs and local opinion on their own were not sufficient.

Key Principle: **Lack of adequate specialist medical supervision of a known suicide risk prisoner violated Article 3.**

Keenan v UK
The son of the applicant had died in Exeter Prison from asphyxia caused by self suspension. His medical history included symptoms of paranoia, aggression, violence and deliberate self harm.

Held: (ECtHR) The lack of effective monitoring of Mark Keenan's condition and the lack of informed psychiatric input into his assessment and treatment disclosed defects in the medical care provided to a mentally ill person known to be a suicide risk. In these circumstances the imposition of additional disciplinary punishment was not compatible with the standard of treatment required in respect of a mentally ill person. There was therefore a breach of Article 3. (App. No. 27229/95), April 3, 2001.

Commentary
The court rejected the application to find a violation of Article 2. It was not apparent that the authorities omitted any step which should have reasonably been taken. Other cases have underlined that conditions of incarceration have to be very poor to engage Article 3. In *Delazarus v UK* (1993) (App. No. 17525/90) February 16, a prisoner was segregated for over four months as a disciplinary measure. He was not allowed to communicate or associate with other prisoners and was locked in a cockroach infested cell for 23 hours a day with two half hour breaks in a pen the size of a tennis court. The application was held inadmissible.

Immigration and Racial Discrimination

Key Principle: **Racial discrimination may amount to degrading treatment.**

East African Asians v UK
The applicants were citizens of the United Kingdom and colonies and husbands of Commonwealth citizens who were already resident in the United Kingdom. The authorities refused them admission into the United Kingdom. The legislation however would have permitted wives to come into the United Kingdom to join their husbands. The Commission was asked to decide whether the discriminatory effect of the legislation applicable at the time could be regarded as degrading treatment under Article 3 on the grounds that "to single out a group of persons for different treatment on the basis of race may constitute a special form of affront to human dignity and might therefore be capable of constituting degrading treatment".

Held: (Commission) In relation to one group the Commission considered that "the racial discrimination to which the applicants have been publicly subjected by the . . . immigration legislation, constitutes an interference with their human dignity which amounted to . . . degrading treatment in the sense of Article 3 of the Convention". This group had been promised free entry to the United Kingdom and their continued residence in East Africa was illegal and they were stateless. With regard to the group of "protected persons" who were not British subjects since here the legislation did not distinguish between categories of persons on any racial basis there was no violation of Article 3. (1981) 3 E.H.R.R. 76

Commentary

The use of immigration controls is not in itself a violation of the ECHR. but controls based on racial discrimination could as here amount to degrading treatment.

Key Principle: **Asylum claimants must be dealt with by a fair procedure which respects their human rights.**

R. (Q) v Secretary of State for the Home Department

People who sought asylum after leaving the port of entry were refused asylum support under s.55 of the Nationality, Immigration and Asylum Act 2002 because they had not claimed it as soon as practicable after arrival. All had been interviewed using a standard form questionnaire. The decision whether or not to grant them support was made entirely on the basis of their answers by a more senior officer who did not meet them. The claimants had no opportunity to rebut the conclusions drawn from their answers. On judicial review the judge held the decision-making process to be unfair. The Secretary of State appealed.

Held: (CA) It was for the claimant to satisfy the Secretary of State that he could not reasonably be expected to have claimed asylum earlier than he did. In determining that question the Secretary of State should take account of the asylum seeker's state of mind at the time, including what he had been told by the agent who facilitated his entry. Refusal of asylum support could amount to treatment for the purposes of Article 3, but would become inhuman or degrading only if it involved actual bodily disease or intense physical or mental suffering. The Secretary of State was under an obligation to provide support to an asylum seeker whose actual condition verged on the degree of severity capable of breaching Article 3. A number of features of the existing decision process were unfair, and the Secretary of State had to establish a fair system, including interview by the decision-taker and an opportunity to rebut suggestions of incredibility. [2003] EWCA Civ 364: [2004] Q.B. 36

Commentary

The effect of this judgment is that although the court held that the s.55 process was unfair it was in principle permissible to deny support to asylum seekers. The court approved the approach taken in *Pretty v UK* to Article 3. It would be necessary to provide the claimant with benefit where he or she is so patently vulnerable that to refuse support carries a high risk of an almost immediate breach of Article 3 or 8. That was a high threshold. The court did not agree with the decisions below of Collins J. who considered that there would be a breach of Article 3 if the Secretary of State refused permission to an asylum seeker where there was a real risk that, because he would receive no support from any alternative source, he would decline into the kind of state described in *Pretty v UK*. The "real risk" test was one that the Strasbourg court had applied in the case of removal to a country in circumstances where the removing state will no longer be in a position to influence events. The court did not believe that it was an appropriate test in the present context. The court observed that some who claim asylum may already be in a condition which verges on the degree of severity capable of engaging Article 3 described in *Pretty v UK*. For those s.55(5) of the 2002 Act would permit and s.6 of the Human Rights Act 1998 would oblige the Secretary of State to provide or arrange for the provision of support. The fate of others was uncertain. Those who had been in-country long enough to demonstrate that they have found other means of subsistence may be able to fend for themselves. But it was manifest that some recent arrivals who had no recourse to work, to funds or to help may also be caught by s.55(l). It was a possibility that, the Attorney-General submitted, charitable bodies or individuals would come to their assistance. But equally there must be a possibility that some will be brought so low that they would be driven to resort to crime or to prostitution in order to survive. Unlike Collins J. the court did not consider that the fact that there was a real risk that an individual asylum seeker would be reduced to this state of degradation of itself engaged Article 3. It was not unlawful for the Secretary of State to decline to provide support unless and until it was clear that charitable support had not been provided and the individual is incapable of fending for himself. That was what s.55(l) required him to do. He must, however, be prepared to entertain further applications from those to whom he had refused support who have not been able to find any charitable support or other lawful means of fending for themselves.

Key Principle: **For there to be a violation of Article 3 it is not** necessarily required required that the state should positively intend to degrade someone.

Price v UK
The applicant, a victim of the drug Thalidomide, was four limbed deficient. She was sentenced to seven days jail for refusing, in a judgment debt hearing, to answer questions on her financial position. She alleged that her committal and her treatment in prison violated Article 3. She had particular difficulty over reaching the bed and toilet, hygiene and fluid intake and mobility.

Held: (ECtHR) There was no evidence of any positive intention to humiliate or debase the applicant. However it constituted degrading treatment under Article 3 to imprison a severely disabled person in conditions where she was dangerously cold, risked developing bed sores and was unable to go to the toilet or keep clean without difficulty. (App. No. 33394/96) July 10, 2001

Commentary
It was considered significant that the documentary evidence submitted indicated that the police and prison authorities were not able to cope adequately with the applicant's special needs.

Key Principle: **Denial of state benefits could engage Article 3.**

R. (Limbuela) v Secretary of State for the Home Department
Destitute asylum seekers successfully challenged by way of judicial review a decision to refuse them benefit on the ground that they had failed to apply for asylum as soon as reasonably practicable after their arrival. Their challenge was that the refusal caused them such suffering as to amount to a breach of their Article 3 right not to be subject to inhuman or degrading treatment. The Government appealed.

Held: (CA) The Government's appeal would be dismissed. Destitution resulting from denial of assistance could involve a breach of Convention rights if it caused either intense physical or mental suffering or humiliation of a degree sufficient to break moral or physical resistance. No single test at a single point in time could determine whether that threshold had been crossed, and the government's obligation was to ensure that asylum-seekers did not cross it, by providing appropriate support. There was a presumption that such suffering would imminently follow if a person had no means offending for himself and could not obtain charity. Lord Justice Carnwath stated that "shelter of some form from the elements at night" was a "basic amenity". The court should set a legal standard and ensure that systems were in place to meet it. [2004] EWCA Civ 540. [2004] Q.B. 1440

Commentary
The decision in *Limbuela* has been held as a landmark one in its condemnation of Home Office policy which was described as "abhorrent, illogical and very expensive". In a powerful dissenting judgment Lord Justice Laws stated that the relevant principles in this area were "more than usually elusive". He observed (para.58) ". . . we are left with a state of affairs in which our public courts are driven to make decisions whose dependence on legal principles is at best fragile, leaving uncomfortable scope for the social and moral preconceptions of the individual judge". The Home Office has revised its guidance several times on the benefits for asylum-seekers in the light of this and a number of court decisions. The *Limbuela* decision effectively meant that state benefits could not be denied unless the authorities were sure that asylum seekers had alternative means of support.

Children

Key Principle: **Corporal punishment of juveniles may amount to a breach of Article 3.**

Tyrer v UK
The applicant, who was convicted of assault by a juvenile court in the Isle of Man, was sentenced to three strokes of the birch when he was 15. He complained to the Commission that the United Kingdom being responsible for the Isle of Man's international relations was in breach of Article 3.

Held: (ECtHR) The facts of the case did not amount to torture or inhuman punishment. It was, however, degrading treatment, and "although the applicant did not suffer any severe or long-lasting physical effects, his punishment—whereby he was treated as an object in the power of the authorities—constituted an assault on precisely that which is one of the main purposes of Article 3 to protect, namely a person's dignity and physical integrity. Neither can it be excluded that the punishment may have had adverse psychological effects. (1978) 2 E.H.R.R. 1

Commentary

Judicial corporal punishment on the mainland had been abolished in 1948 and in Northern Ireland in 1968. Corporal punishment in schools came under challenge in *Campbell and Cosans v UK* (1982) 4 E.H.R.R. 293, an application brought by the mothers of two Scottish school boys threatened by the tawse. Here the court found it had not been established that the pupils had been humiliated or degraded in the eyes of others. However the failure to respect the parents' wishes that their sons should not be beaten was a violation of Protocol 1, Article 2 (see p.9). A series of cases led to the Government banning corporal punishment in state schools (see *Warwick v UK* (1986) 60 D.R. 5). See *Costello-Roberts v UK* (1995) for the use of corporal punishment in independent schools. In that case the court found no breach of Articles 2 or 8. This case was distinguished from *Tyrer* in that the punishment was given in private, and consisted of three strokes with a rubber-soled slipper on the buttocks through shorts. There the minimal level of severity required by Article 3 had not been reached. See also pp.42, 64 and 66.

Key Principle: **States have a positive responsibility to safeguard children from physical punishment.**

A v UK

The applicant was a boy whose stepfather regularly beat him with a garden cane causing considerable bruising. The father was acquitted of assault on the basis that the beatings amounted to reasonable chastisement. The boy complained that the state had failed to safeguard his rights under Article 3.

Held: (ECtHR) The boy's treatment did reach the level of severity prohibited by the Article and the law allowing "reasonable chastisement" did not provide adequate protection to children's Convention rights. (1999) 27 E.H.R.R. 611

Commentary

At the trial the stepfather had successfully raised the defence of lawful punishment. The prosecution had the burden of proving beyond reasonable doubt that the assault was not lawful. The Government has accepted that the defence of lawful chastisement is too wide.

Z v UK

Four children were neglected and beaten by their parents, despite monitoring by the social services. Proceedings brought by the Official Solicitor on behalf of the children were struck out in the House of Lords on the grounds of public policy. The House of Lords held that local authorities should not be liable in negligence for having failed to safeguard the welfare of children in their area. [2002] 34 E.H.R.R. 3

Held: (ECtHR) The system had failed to protect the applicant from serious, long-term neglect and abuse. This was a violation of Article 3. The courts had failed to provide them with an adequate remedy.

Commentary

These cases make it clear that there is a positive obligation under Article 2 to prevent, investigate and punish private domestic violence. This case was the sequel to the House of Lords decision in *X (Minors) v Bedfordshire CC* [1995] 2 A.C. 633.

Prohibition of Slavery and Forced Labour

Key Principle: **Article 4 of the ECHR—Prohibition of Slavery and forced labour:**

"1 No one shall be held in slavery or servitude.

2 No one shall be required to perform forced or compulsory labour.

3 For the purpose of this article the term 'forced or compulsory labour' shall not include:

a any work required to be done in the ordinary course of detention imposed according to the provisions of Article 5 of this Convention or during conditional release from such detention;

b any service of a military character or, in the case of conscientious objectors in countries where they are recognised, service exacted instead of compulsory military service;

c any service exacted in case of an emergency or calamity threatening the life or well-being of the community;

d any work or service which forms part of normal civic obligations."

Key Principle: **Military service, even for those who enlist below the age of majority does not generally amount to "slavery or servitude".**

W, X, Y and Z v UK

The applicants had joined the army or navy at the age of 15 or 16 with the consent of their parents. Their contracts were for nine years, which was calculated from the date at which they reached the age of 18 and they could not leave the services before this time other than in "exceptional circumstances". The applicants alleged violations of Articles 6, 8, and 13 as well as 4, the latter on the grounds of relief from "oppressive compulsory service tantamount to the status of servitude".

Held: (Commission) The clause excluding military service expressly from the scope of the terms "forced or compulsory labour" does not forcibly exclude such service in all circumstances from an examination in the light of the prohibition directed at "slavery or servitude". Generally the duty of a soldier whether enlisting before or after the age of majority doesn't amount to an impairment of rights which could come under the terms "slavery or servitude". (1968) 11 Y.B. 562 (App. No. 3435–38/67)

Commentary

In an interesting example of its jurisprudential approach the Commission drew on the history of the provision including Convention Number 29 of the International Labour Organisation on Forced or Compulsory Labour.

Key Principle: **For labour to be forced or compulsory it must be performed involuntarily and the requirement to do the work must be unjust or oppressive or the work itself involve avoidable hardship.**

Van der Mussele v Belgium
Belgian law required pupil advocates to represent clients without payment. The applicant had provided some 750 hours of unpaid work as a pupil barrister. He alleged violation of Articles 4, 6, 14 and Article 1 of the first Protocol.

Held: (ECtHR) The barrister had entered the profession of his own free will, knowing that *pro bono* work was expected of him. The labour imposed on him was not a "burden which was so excessive or disproportionate to the advantages attached to the future exercise of the profession that the service could not be treated as having been voluntarily accepted". There were no violations. (1984) 6 E.H.R.R. 163

Commentary
The work performed could be considered as a "normal civil obligation". The majority of claims under Article 4 have been brought by serving prisoners.

4. DUE PROCESS AND A FAIR TRIAL IN CRIMINAL COURTS

Detention

Key Principle: **Article 5 of the ECHR—Right to liberty and security:**

"1   Everyone has the right to liberty and security of person. No one shall be deprived of his liberty save in the following cases and in accordance with a procedure prescribed by law:

   a   the lawful detention of a person after conviction by a competent court;
   b   the lawful arrest or detention of a person for non-compliance with the lawful order of a court or in order to secure the fulfilment of any obligation prescribed by law;
   c   the lawful arrest or detention of a person effected for the purpose of bringing him before the competent legal authority on reasonable suspicion of having

committed an offence or when it is reasonably considered necessary to prevent his committing an offence or fleeing after having done so;

d the detention of a minor by lawful order for the purpose of educational supervision or his lawful detention for the purpose of bringing him before the competent legal authority;

e the lawful detention of persons for the prevention of the spreading of infectious diseases, of persons of unsound mind, alcoholics or drug addicts or vagrants;

f the lawful arrest or detention of a person to prevent his effecting an unauthorised entry into the country or of a person against whom action is being taken with a view to deportation or extradition.

2 Everyone who is arrested shall be informed promptly, in a language which he understands, of the reasons for his arrest and of any charge against him.

3 Everyone arrested or detained in accordance with the provisions of paragraph 1.c of this article shall be brought promptly before a judge or other officer authorised by law to exercise judicial power and shall be entitled to trial within a reasonable time or to release pending trial. Release may be conditioned by guarantees to appear for trial.

4 Everyone who is deprived of his liberty by arrest or detention shall be entitled to take proceedings by which the lawfulness of his detention shall be decided speedily by a court and his release ordered if the detention is not lawful.

5 Everyone who has been the victim of arrest or detention in contravention of the provisions of this article shall have an enforceable right to compensation."

Key Principle: **No one shall be deprived of his liberty save under the exceptions listed in Article 5 and in accordance with a procedure prescribed by law.**

de Wilde v Belgium

The applicants were arrested as vagrants and held without trial for up to 21 months. All had unsuccessfully petitioned for release but had not appealed since Belgian case-law appeared to rule out an appeal from a magistrate's administrative decision. They complained of a violation of their rights under Article 5(4), on the basis that there was no judicial remedy for their imprisonment.

Held: Article 5(4) had been breached because the applicants had no remedy before a court against the detention orders. The Convention required that where a person was deprived of his liberty by an administrative decision he was entitled to have the lawfulness of his detention supervised by a court. (1979–1980) 1 E.H.R.R. 373 ECHR

Commentary
The cases illustrates that even if an individual waives his rights under the Article and agrees to his detention that detention can still be unlawful. The court stated "the right to liberty is too important in a 'democratic society' within the meaning of the Convention for a person to lose the benefit of the protection of the Convention for the single reason that he gives himself up to be taken into detention."

Key Principle: **An authority should furnish acceptable evidence of the grounds for "reasonable suspicion" of an individual having committed an offence for which he is being detained.**

Fox, Campbell and Hartley v UK
The applicants were detained in Northern Ireland for periods between 30 and 44 hours under a power to arrest without warrant "any person suspected of being a terrorist". They were informed in general terms of the reason for their arrest when they were held, and learned the details during interrogation.

Held: The legislation allowed for arrest on "reasonable" (which in domestic law meant "honestly held") suspicion. Reasonableness depended on the circumstances. Past terrorist convictions were not in themselves enough to justify arrest. The applicants' rights under Article 5(1) had been violated. (1990) 13 E.H.R.R. 157

Commentary
The court accepted that "reasonable suspicion" was not necessarily "a genuine and bona fide suspicion". In terrorist crimes in

particular the police may have to act on the basis of information which cannot be revealed to the suspect. In *Brogan v UK* (1989) also the court was prepared to accept that reasonable suspicion of being a terrorist satisfied the requirements of the article. Although the power was expressed in subjective terms the question is whether, as a matter of fact, the suspicion was based on reasonable grounds.

Key Principle: **Anyone arrested should be brought promptly before a judge or other judicial officer and should be tried within a reasonable time or released pending trial.**

Brogan v UK

Four applicants were detained under s.12 of the Prevention of Terrorism Act 1978 and held for periods of between four and 16 days without being charged or brought before a magistrate.

Held: The Convention required that suspects be produced "promptly". The court accepted that subject to the existence of adequate safeguards, the context of terrorism in Northern Ireland had the effect of prolonging the allowable detention period. But four days and six hours was too long. (1989) 11 E.H.R.R. 117

Commentary

As a result of this case the United Kingdom issued a notice of derogation (see p.10).

Key Principle: **A detained person has a right to have the lawfulness of his detention reviewed by a body independent of the executive and the parties.**

T v UK; V v UK

The applicants had been convicted of the abduction and murder of a two-year-old boy. They had been 10 at the time of the murder and 11 at the time of the Crown Court trial. They were sentenced to be detained indefinitely during her Majesty's pleasure and according to English law had first to serve a tariff period to satisfy the requirements of retribution and deterrence.

Detainees would be released on expiry of the tariff unless, in the view of the parole board, they were a danger to the public. The Home Secretary's tariff of 15 years for each of the applicants had been quashed by the House of Lords and no new tariff had been set. The applicants claimed first that their trial and sentence was a violation of Article 3 of the ECHR; secondly that they had been denied a fair trial under Article 6, and the fact that it was a government minister who was responsible for setting the tariff was a violation of Article 6; thirdly that the sentence imposed was a breach of Article 5 and that there was a further breach of that article in that they had been denied the opportunity to have the lawfulness of their detention examined by a judicial body.

Held: (ECtHR) There was no breach of Article 3 since the age of 10 could not be said to be so young as to differ disproportionately to the age limit set for trial by other European states. There had been a breach of the right to a fair trial and that the setting of the tariff and the absence of judicial scrutiny of it were also violations of Articles 6 and 5. (1999) 30 E.H.R.R. 121

Commentary
Successful challenges under Article 5(4) have also been made in relation to continuing detention in discretionary period life sentences (see *Weeks v UK* (1988) 10 E.H.R.R. 293, *Thynne v UK* (1990) 3 E.H.R.R. 666). The court has stressed that it is crucial to recognise that circumstances could change over time. As a result of *Thynne* the United Kingdom introduced oral hearings to consider discretionary life paroles. These have the power to direct a prisoner's release when he is no longer dangerous. (See also *Wynne v UK* (1994) 19 E.H.R.R. 333).

Bail

Key Principle: **Facts relevant to a decision on whether a defendant had broken a condition of bail did not have to be proved to the criminal standard to comply with Article 5.**

R. v Havering Magistrates' Court, Ex p. DPP
There were two joined cases concerning the effect of the HRA on the Bail Act 1976. The defendants in the two cases were arrested for breach of bail conditions and brought before the magistrates. In the first case the justices held that Articles 5 and 6 ECHR applied and that the prosecution was obliged to call

oral evidence to prove the breach of bail conditions. In the second case the justices held that Article 5 but not Article 6 applied and oral evidence was not required. The applications were for judicial review by the prosecution in the first case and by the defendant in the second as to whether the ECHR required formal proof to be given of a breach of bail conditions.

Held: (DC) The rights under Article 6 had no relevance to proceedings under s.7 of the 1976 Act. While Article 5 was relevant to proceedings under s.7, Articles 5 and 6 related to two separate sets of proceedings which had different objects and the procedural requirements of Article 6 were not to be assimilated to the considerations relevant to Article 5. Article 5 did not require the underlying facts relevant to detention under s.7 to be proved to the criminal standard of proof or that only evidence which would be admissible at trial could be relied on. To comply with Article 5 it was necessary for the magistrates to evaluate the material and its nature in the light of the serious potential consequences to the defendant and form an honest and rational opinion. [2001] 1 W.L.R. 805

Commentary
The court here applied the existing law in *R. v Liverpool City Justices Ex p. DPP* [1993] Q.B. 233. In *Caballero v UK, The Times* February 29, 2000, the then existing bail conditions were found to be a violation of Article 5(3) and as a result s.25 of the Criminal Justice and Public Order Act was amended. In one of the earliest cases under the HRA, *Burgess v Home Office* [2001] 1 W.L.R. 93 the Court of Appeal found that Article 5 "added nothing to the claimant's case". It was held that the detention of the claimant, who was required to surrender to custody from one hour before each day's hearing until half an hour after the court rose for five days during his criminal trial did not entitle him to have that period taken into account on sentence.

Key Principle: **A new offence charged on the same facts could give rise to fresh custody time limit and was not incompatible with Articles 5(1) or 5(3).**

R. v Leeds Crown Court Ex p. Wardle
In July 1998 a man died during a burglary or robbery at his home. The defendants were originally charged with murder and

a new charge of manslaughter was substituted on the last day of the custody time limit for the murder charge. The magistrates' court found that a new custody time limit had thereby been created. The decision was upheld by the judge, although he held that if the old custody time limits had applied it would not have been appropriate to have extended them, as the prosecution had not acted with due expedition. The applicants sought judicial review of the decision submitting that it was an abuse of process that new custody time limits should be created in these circumstances. The Divisional Court had found that it was not an abuse of process for the prosecution to change the charge on the last day of the custody time limit thereby creating a new custody limit, even when the old custody time limit would not have been extended because the prosecution had not acted with expedition. The applicants also applied for writs of habeas corpus.

Held: (HL) When a new charge had been laid in the magistrates' court on the last day of the custody time limit of the original charge, the true question was whether the new charge had been brought solely for the purpose of avoiding a custody time limit and the prosecutor was required to demonstrate why the bringing of the new charge was necessary. Murder and manslaughter were distinct in law and were separate offences attracting separate custody time limits. It was plain that Parliament had intended there to be limits on the period during which a person could be detained. It was recognised that where there was an abuse of process by adding additional or substituted charges, a new period of custody time limits did not operate. A mere change in the details of the charge did not of itself mean that time would begin to run again. However, where the new charge was plainly distinct from any original charges, the new charge attracted its own separate time limit. It would clearly be an abuse of process to bring a new charge simply to keep an accused in custody for a longer period. However, if the purpose was genuinely to introduce a new charge on a revised assessment of the case, the fact that the accused began a new custody period did not in itself constitute an abuse of process. There was no breach of Article 5 ECHR as D had been deprived of his liberty in accordance with a procedure prescribed by law and the domestic law complied with the general requirements of the Convention. Appeal dismissed. [2001] 2 W.L.R. 865

Commentary
This was a controversial decision and some commentators expected a challenge in Strasbourg.

Presence of Defendants

Key Principle: **Fair procedure will generally, but not always, require the presence in person of the party concerned.**

Monnell and Morris v UK
The applicants had persisted in hopeless appeals against conviction and sentence and the Appeal Court ordered in their absence that part of the time they had already served since conviction should not count towards their sentences. They claimed this was a violation of Article 5(1).

Held: (ECtHR) Under English law a sentence of imprisonment was to be served subject to any order for loss of time the Court of Appeal might make. The power to order loss of time served a legitimate purpose of discouraging futile appeals. Article 5(1) had not been violated. The applicants had been warned that they might lose time if they persisted with their appeals and had not been denied the benefit of fair procedure. (1988) 10 E.H.R.R. 205

Commentary
In this case the principle of "equality of arms" was protected since neither the applicants nor the prosecution were represented by a barrister or by a solicitor before the court.

Right to a Fair Trial

Key Principle: **Article 6 of the ECHR—Right to a fair trial:**

"1 In the determination of his civil rights and obligations or of any criminal charge against him, everyone is entitled to a fair and public hearing within a reasonable time by an independent and impartial tribunal established by law. Judgment shall be pronounced publicly but the press and public may be excluded from all or part of the trial in the interests of morals, public order or national security in a democratic society, where the interests of juveniles or the protection of the private life of the parties so require, or to the extent strictly necessary in the opinion of the court in special circumstances where publicity would prejudice the interests of justice.

2 Everyone charged with a criminal offence shall be presumed innocent until proved guilty according to law.

3 Everyone charged with a criminal offence has the following minimum rights:

    a to be informed promptly, in a language which he understands and in detail, of the nature and cause of the accusation against him;

    b to have adequate time and facilities for the preparation of his defence;

    c to defend himself in person or through legal assistance of his own choosing or, if he has not sufficient means to pay for legal assistance, to be given it free when the interests of justice so require;

    d to examine or have examined witnesses against him and to obtain the attendance and examination of witnesses on his behalf under the same conditions as witnesses against him;

    e to have the free assistance of an interpreter if he cannot understand or speak the language used in court."

Key Principle: **The accused's right to a fair trial is not to be subordinated to the public interest in the detection and suppression of crime.**

Montgomery v HM Advocate; Coulter v HM Advocate

Three white men, the defendants and C, were charged with murdering an Asian youth. Only C was indicted and at trial he raised a special defence of incrimination, naming the defendants as the perpetrators. C was convicted of assaulting, but acquitted of murdering, the victim. After the verdict the trial judge criticised the prosecution for not having had all three tried together. The judge's remarks were publicly criticised by the Lord Advocate, the head of the Scottish prosecution system. After a public campaign the defendants were indicted for the Asian's murder. They complained that the pre-trial publicity had made it impossible for them to have a fair trial as required by Article 6 ECHR. Further publicity about the case was banned some seven weeks after the defendants were indicted. The trial judge rejected the contention that the defendants would not be able to have a fair trial. The defendants appealed.

Held: (PC) Dismissing the appeal, that the only issue to be considered under Article 6 was the defendants' right to a fair trial, and considerations of the public interest did not arise. The decisive question was whether the doubts raised about the tribunal's impartiality were objectively justified. It had to be borne in mind that the trial judge could warn the jury to ignore prejudicial pre-trial publicity, and that listening to witnesses and thinking about the evidence would be likely to have a greater impact on the jury than their recollections of matters they had read in the past. [2001] 2 W.L.R. 779

The content of a criminal charge

Key Principle: **A criminal charge is an official notification to an individual by the competent authority of an allegation that he has committed a criminal offence and covers measures which substantially affect the situation of a suspect.**

Campbell and Fell v UK
The applicants, in prison for terrorist offences, faced disciplinary proceedings as a result of disturbances, were convicted and lost privileges and remission. They alleged that the proceedings were the determination of a "criminal charge" and so should have complied with Article 6.

Held: (ECtHR) The classification by the national state of the nature of proceedings was not decisive although there was a necessary distinction between disciplinary and criminal matters. The court was entitled to consider the nature of the proceedings and, taking account of the gravity of the offences charged, and the severity of the penalty the applicants risked, Article 6 was applicable. (1985) 7 E.H.R.R. 165

Commentary
The question of what is or is not a criminal charge is not defined in the ECHR and therefore must be derived from the jurisprudence. The court was faced here with deciding whether the disciplinary adjudications of the prison governor attracted the protection of Article 6. In other cases the Strasbourg Court had afforded Article 6 protection to searches of premises but not to the questioning of witnesses. The determination of the proceedings is crucial since the complete protection of Article 6 is only afforded to criminal hearings not civil, see *Benham v UK* (pp.101, 219).

In *Eckle v Germany* (1983) 5 E.H.R.R. 1 being charged was defined as "the official notification given to an individual by the competent authority of an allegation that he has committed a criminal offence". It was made clear in *Neumeister v Austria (No. 1)* (1979–1980) 1 E.H.R.R. 91 that the period covers the whole of the time for the proceedings to be completed, including appeal proceedings.

Key Principle: **An award of additional days' imprisonment as a result of prison disciplinary hearings did not mean that the proceedings should be regarded as "criminal" for the purposes of Article 6.**

R. (Carroll) v Secretary of State for Home Department
The appeals arose from dismissals of applications for judicial review by serving prisoners. They argued that internal prison disciplinary hearings which resulted in further days in prison should be subject to Article 6. It was also argued that the requirement of legality meant that prison officers should give reasons for squat searches which otherwise violated Article 8.

Held: (CA) The proceedings were disciplinary under domestic law; the additional days imprisonment did not add to the sentence they merely postponed release on licence and the punishment powers were not disproportionate. Article 6 did not apply. Individual prison officers should decide if it was necessary to give reasons for the searches. *The Times,* August 16, 2001

Commentary
This is a narrowly based decision which does not appear to follow the reasoning of *Campbell and Fell.* It has been criticised as leaving the interpretation of the provisions of the Convention to prison officers rather than the courts (see Commentary in the journal *Human Rights* (December 2001) p.243).

Key Principle: **The imposition of a civil evasion penalty in respect of value added tax or excise duty gave rise to a "criminal charge" within Article 6(1) of the European Convention on Human Rights.**

Han & Yau v Customs & Excise Commissioners

This was a trial of a preliminary issue in relation to three appeals concerning whether the imposition of a civil evasion penalty on the three appellants under s.60 of the Value Added Tax Act 1994 (VATA) or s.8 of the Finance Act 1994 (FA) gave rise to a "criminal charge" within Article 6(1) of the European Convention on Human Rights. In each case no point was taken that the penalty in question was imposed before the HRA 1998 came into force. In each appeal the appellant taxpayer was appealing from a civil penalty assessment which had been imposed upon him for alleged dishonest evasion of tax. Each appellant contended by way of preliminary issue that the imposition of such a penalty gave rise to "criminal charges" within the meaning of Article 6 of the Convention. The tribunal had determined the issue in favour of the taxpayers by reference to the three criteria laid down in *Engel v The Netherlands* (1976) 1 E.H.R.R. 706, namely: (i) the classification of the proceedings in United Kingdom law; (ii) the nature of the offence; and (iii) the severity of the penalty that might be imposed.

Held: (CA) The court accepted that the imposition of a civil penalty gave rise to a criminal charge within the meaning of Article 6 of the Convention. In particular, the court accepted that (a) the civil penalty regime replaced the earlier criminal regime; (b) the offence to which the penalty related involved fraud/dishonesty; and (c) the amount of the penalty that could be imposed was substantial and its purpose was punitive and deterrent. [2001] 1 W.L.R. 2253

Commentary

The labelling of the charge here as civil as also in cases under the regime of the Inland Revenue suits the administrative convenience of government departments and has some advantages to defendants in that for example they do not give rise to a criminal record. The court referred to Strasbourg cases in its judgment including *AP, MP and TP v Switzerland* (1998) 26 E.H.R.R. 541 and *Georgiou v UK* [2001] S.T.C. 80 as being at the heart of the case law. It did not consider it was now appropriate to place the jurisprudence of the United Kingdom out on a limb in an area where the Strasbourg cases had sought to develop an autonomous integrated test. The previous case law indicated that there are three criteria to be taken into account when it is being decided whether a person was "charged with a criminal offence" for the purposes of Article 6. They were the classification of the offence under national law, the nature of the offence, and the nature and degree of severity of the penalty the person concerned risked. These requirements were not a formula for a three stage test. They were factors which should be taken into account in examining whether on the facts as a whole the measure should be treated as criminal. The categorisation of proceedings as "civil" and "criminal" for the purposes of Article 6 ECHR has led to a great deal of litigation. The approach is decided on a case-by-case basis and it is difficult to derive a clear principle. In *McCann v Manchester Crown Court* [2002] UKHL 39 the House of Lords held that Anti-Social Behaviour Orders were civil in nature, although the applicant for the order should prove the case to the criminal standard.

Key Principle: **Confiscation proceedings arising from drug trafficking offences do not concern a criminal charge.**

McIntosh v HM Advocate

The defendant had been convicted of being concerned in the supply of heroin. The prosecutor applied for a confiscation order against him under the Proceeds of Crime (Scotland) Act 1995. This allowed the court to make assumptions about of the source of property of the convicted drug dealer. The Scottish High Court of Justiciary held that the presumption of innocence was violated. HM Advocate appealed.

Held: (PC) The confiscation order was not a criminal charge. Even if the respondent appellant had been entitled to take advantage of Article 6(2) his right to a fair trial would not have been violated in this case. [2001] 3 W.L.R. 107

Commentary

The Privy Council referred to the reasoning in *R. v Benjafield* [2001] 2 Cr.App.R. 87 where it was held that confiscation orders were criminal charges but that Article 6 was not violated by the imposition of a reverse burden of proof since the legislation was a proportionate response to a grave social evil. Perhaps surprisingly in *McIntosh* it also stated that in concluding that Article 6(2) had no application to the prosecutor's application for a confiscation order the result did not leave the respondent unprotected since "he was entitled to all the protection afforded him by Article 6(1) which applied at all stages, the common law of Scotland and the language of the statute" (*per* Lord Bingham).

Key Principle: **Confiscation orders do not amount to criminal charges but the defendant is entitled to a fair proceeding under Article 6(1).**

Phillips v UK

The applicant who had been convicted of importation of cannabis was subject to a drug confiscation order under the Drug Trafficking Act 1994. This empowers a court to assume that all property held by a person convicted of a drug trafficking offence in the previous three years represented the proceeds of drug trafficking. He complained that the application of the statutory presumption violated his right to the presumption of innocence under Article 6(2).

Held: (ECtHR) (1) A person against whom a confiscation order was made was not a person charged with a criminal offence. (2) A person's right in a criminal case to be presumed innocent forms part of the general notion of a fair hearing under Article 6(1). (2001) Crim.L.R. 817

Commentary

The court endorsed the approach of the Privy Council in *HM Advocate v McIntosh*. The judgment raises quite difficult problems of interpretation. Although confiscation proceedings do not concern a criminal charge it appears the ECtHR still applies the procedural safeguards of Article 6(1) since "In addition to being specifically mentioned in Article 6(2) a person's right in a criminal case to be presumed innocent and to require the prosecution to bear the onus of proving the allegations against him or her forms part of the general notion of a fair hearing under Article 6(1)". The court considered that an issue relating to fair procedure might arise in drug confiscation orders but on the facts of this case the operation of the statutory assumption did not violate the notion of a fair hearing under Article 6(1).

Reasonable Time

Key Principle: **In the determination of any criminal charge against him everyone is entitled to a fair and public hearing within a reasonable time.**

Attorney-General's Reference (No. 2 of 2001)

A judge had stayed an indictment against seven defendants facing charges of violent disorder on the grounds that to proceed would be a breach of Article 6(1) due to delay between the interview and the summons. The Attorney-General asked two questions of law: (1) whether criminal proceedings could be stayed on the grounds that there had been a violation of the reasonable time requirement in Article 6(1) in circumstances where the accused could not demonstrate any prejudice from the delay; and (2) when in the determination of whether a criminal charge had been heard within a reasonable time the relevant period began. The relevant time period would usually commence when the defendant was charged or served with a summons.

Held: (HL) Time does not run from an interview in terms of Article 6(1). Stay of proceedings should only be granted in situations where to continue with the trial would be an abuse of the process of the court. Other remedies were available such as a reduction in sentence or compensation. Absent prejudice, there would normally be no justification for a stay. [2004] 2 A.L 72

Commentary

Most cases on delay in the Strasbourg Court involve Italy. In *Howarth v UK* (2001) 31 E.H.R.R. 37 the court held that a delay of two years between the the original sentence and the imposition of a greater sentence following an Attorney-General's reference was excessive. It is interesting to note that the Crown Court does not have power to award compensation for breach of the Convention. See also *McLean v HM Advocate* [2000] U.K.H.R.R. 73 where it was held that delay without prejudice can result in proceedings being staged.

In *Mellors v UK* (2003) the UK was responsible for a breach of Article 6(1) where appeal proceedings had lasted more than three years and eight months.

Access to the criminal courts

Key Principle: **There is no power to extend the time allowed for the prosecution to apply for leave to appeal from the Court of Appeal to the House of Lords.**

R. v Weir

The Court of Appeal had quashed the defendant's conviction for murder, burglary and assault on the grounds that the DNA evidence used to convict him had been inadmissible under s.64(3B) of the Police and Criminal Evidence Act 1984 (PACE) as amended by s.57 of the Criminal Justice and Public Order Act 1994. The Court of Appeal certified the point of law of general public importance but the DPP lodged his application for leave to appeal to the House of Lords one day after expiry of the 14-day time limit laid down in s.34 of the Criminal Appeal Act 1968 and the application was rejected by the Judicial Office. Subsequently in another case (*Attorney-General's Reference No. 3 of 1999* [2001] 2 W.L.R. 56) the House ruled that pursuant to s.78 of PACE trial judges had a discretionary power to admit evidence of the type used to convict the defendant. The DPP lodged a petition seeking leave to apply to the House for leave to appeal on the grounds that the House had a discretion to extend the statutory time limit and that it would be contrary to the HRA for the time limit not to be extended.

Held: (HL) The appellate jurisdiction of the House in criminal matters was statutory and by s.34 of the 1968 Act Parliament had provided for time to be extended on application for leave to appeal by a defendant but not by that of the prosecutor. The situation did not engage the human rights of the DPP in any way. [2001] 1 W.L.R. 421

Commentary

In this case the House of Lords considered Articles 2, 3 and 8 as well as 6 and held that if the Court of Appeal made an erroneous decision in law in favour of a defendant it could be corrected by the House of Lords. The House of Lords underlined here the main purpose of the Convention as being to protect the individual against oppressive state action. It stated: "the Convention was concerned to protect the rights of private citizens against abuse of power by the state and could not be interpreted as strengthening the rights of prosecutors against private individuals".

Impartiality

Key Principle: **The accused is entitled to an independent and impartial tribunal established by law.**

Sander v UK
After a trial where the Asian applicant was the defendant a juror had transmitted a note to the judge indicating that another juror had made racist comments during deliberations. The judge had given the jury a redirection. The applicant was convicted. He alleged a violation of Article 6.

Held: (ECtHR) The judge's decision to deal with the allegation of racial bias in the jury by means of a redirection rather than a discharge did constitute an infringement of the right to a fair trial as guaranteed by Article 6(1). *The Times*, May 12, 2000

Commentary
The court considered that the judge should have reacted in a more robust manner than merely seeking vague assurances that the jurors could set aside their prejudices and try the case solely on the evidence. The judge had not therefore provided sufficient guarantees to exclude any objectively justified or legitimate doubts as to the impartiality of the court. In *Mills v UK* (App. No. 35686/97) June 5, 2001 the court found there had been a violation of Article 6(1). The applicant who served in the army was tried by a court martial. The court held that this did not meet the requirement of independence and impartiality under Article 6(1) in view particularly of the central part played by the commanding officer.

Guidance as to steps which may be taken by a juror who feels he has taken part in a miscarriage of justice was given by the House of Lords in *Attorney-General v Scotcher* [2005] UKHL 36. The juror would not be in contempt if he wrote to the judge or to the Court of Appeal to draw attention to the supposed miscarriage. However, it was contempt for a juror to tell the defendant's mother what had happened in the jury room.

Key Principle: **Magistrates should not exercise powers to bind over defendants to be of good behaviour in respect of their conduct in court.**

Practice Direction (Magistrates' Courts: Contempt)
Guidance was sought as to the way to deal with contempt in the face of the court where the same bench was deciding the contempt and the substantive trial.

Held: (DC) Detailed guidance was set out. In particular where contempt was not admitted the justices' power was limited to making arrangement for a trial to take place. They should not at this stage make findings against the defendant. The trial should take place at the earliest opportunity and should be before a bench of justices other than those justices before whom the alleged contempt took place. The accused's rights under Article 6 should be respected. [2001] 1 W.L.R. 1254

Commentary
The Direction gave very specific advice for situations where the courts had previously adopted a different position but where now the Convention rights must be observed.

Key Principle: **It was not necessarily a breach of Article 6 for the same bench to decide the public interest immunity (PII) hearing and the substantive trial.**

R. (Acton Youth Court) v DPP

The District Judge at Acton youth court had heard an *ex parte* application for a PII certificate and had ruled in favour of the prosecution that the evidence should not be disclosed to the defence. He had disqualified himself from hearing the trial. The DPP applied for judicial review.

Held: (DC) Review allowed. The general rule was that justices who had ruled on PII should use their discretion as to whether or not to remit the trial to another bench on the basis of whether or not any reasonable and fair-minded person could reasonably have suspected the defendant could not have a fair trial before the same bench. The procedure in the Crown Court could be followed and the case should not be remitted as a matter of practice. *The Times*, June 21, 2001

Commentary
The court referred to *R. v Stipendiary Magistrates for Norfolk Ex p. Taylor* (1997) 161 J.P. 773 as setting out the proceedings for the Crown Court. It noted that the European Court had endorsed this approach in *Fitt v UK* (2000) 30 E.H.R.R. 480 and there was no reason why such an approach should not be followed in the magistrates' courts.

Right to Silence

Key Principle: **The right to remain silent under police questioning and the privilege against self-incrimination are generally recognised international standards which lie at the heart of the notion of a fair procedure under Article 6.**

Funke v France
Customs officers searched the applicant's home to obtain details of his overseas assets and seized documents. The operation did not result in criminal proceedings under the relevant financial dealing regulations, but there were parallel proceedings for disclosure of documents and interim orders. The applicant was convicted and fined for failing to provide statements of his overseas bank accounts.

Held: The applicant's conviction was an attempt to compel him to provide evidence of other offences he had allegedly committed. His right to remain silent and not to incriminate himself had been infringed. (1993) 16 E.H.R.R. 297 ECHR

Key Principle: **Where answers are given on the course of compulsory proceedings their use by the prosecution at a subsequent criminal trial may violate Article 6.**

Saunders v UK
A company chief executive was questioned by Department of Trade inspectors investigating a takeover battle. He was obliged by law to answer their questions on pain of up to two years' imprisonment. The inspectors recommended prosecution and transcripts of his interrogation by the inspectors were used against him at trial.

Held: (ECtHR) The use of the transcripts at trial violated the applicant's right not to be forced to incriminate himself. The right was primarily concerned with respecting the will of the accused to remain silent. (1997) 23 E.H.R.R. 313

Commentary
The court saw no inherent objection to legislation which compels parties to answer questions in the course of non-judicial inquiries

but "the public interest cannot be invoked to justify the use of answers compulsorily obtained in a non-judicial investigation to incriminate the accused during trial proceedings." It did not extend to evidence which might be obtained by compulsion but was independent of the suspect's will, such as breath samples. In the wake of this decision the Attorney-General issued guidelines designed to prevent the Crown from using what were known as items of "derivative evidence" obtained in extra-judicial investigations. The Youth Justice and Criminal Evidence Act 1999 Sch.3 has amended those provisions such as s.434 of the Companies Act 1985 which formerly purported to render admissible in subsequent criminal proceedings evidence procured by compulsion during investigations. Subsequently the applications of the three co-defendants of Saunders succeeded on identical grounds at Strasbourg, see *ILJ, GMR and AKP v UK, The Times* October 13, 2000. In *R. v Hertfordshire County Council Ex p. Green Environmental Industries Ltd* [2000] A.C. 412 Lord Hoffman acknowledged that although the relevant statute, namely the Environmental Protection Act 1990, did not expressly provide that answers obtained in non-judicial inquiries would be admissible in any subsequent prosecution, the trial judge if faced with such a request from the prosecution will be required under the HRA to consider whether such derivative evidence conforms with Article 6. If it does not it should be excluded under s.78 of the PACE.

In *Kansal v UK* (2004) E.C.H.R. 179 the applicant ran a chain of chemists' shops which went into liquidation and he was made bankrupt. He was publicly examined by the official receiver, who had the power to compel the applicant to answer his questions. Failure to comply could have resulted in a fine or imprisonment for contempt of court. A few days after being made bankrupt, the applicant had borrowed some £265,000 from building societies. His wife had taken some of the money to India in a bin liner. He was prosecuted and convicted on the basis of the evidence he had given before the official receiver. His conviction was overturned on appeal on the grounds that the admission of the evidence breached Article 6 of the European Convention. But the decision was reversed in the House of Lords, which held that the Article did not protect a defendant tried before the Human Rights Act came into force. The applicant took the case to the Strasbourg Court which held that the proceedings infringed the applicant's right not to incriminate himself, and he had been deprived of a fair trial in violation of Article 6(1). No compensation was awarded. The court held that the case was indistinguishable from that of *Saunders*. For discussion on retrospectivity see p.33

Key Principle: **The right to remain silent is not an absolute.**

Murray v UK

The applicant had been found guilty of aiding and abetting unlawful imprisonment after being arrested in an IRA safe house. He was interviewed without a solicitor and remained silent. The trial judge informed the applicant that because of his failure to account for his presence at the house and because he had not given evidence at trial, he had drawn adverse inferences under the Criminal Evidence (Northern Ireland) Order 1988. The applicant claimed violations of Article 6.

Held: (ECtHR) The right to remain silent under police questioning and the privilege against self incrimination are generally recognised international standards which lie at the heart of the notion of fair procedure under Article 6. But these immunities were not absolutes. There was no breach of Article 6 in the drawing of inferences from silence but there was a breach in that the suspect's access to a solicitor had been delayed. (1996) 22 E.H.R.R. 29

Commentary

The provisions in the Order were applied to the mainland in ss.34 to 38 of the Criminal Justice and Public Order Act (CJPOA) 1994. While refusing to uphold the right to remain silent in the face of police questioning as an absolute the decision makes it clear that the drawing of adverse inferences when the suspect had not had access to legal advice prior to the failure to reply to questions will breach Article 6. The court made it clear that its findings were confined to the particular facts of the case in particular that the trier of fact was a judge in a Diplock Court who had expertise to appraise the evidence. The court stated that it would be incompatible with Articles 6(1) and (2) "to base a conviction solely or mainly on the accused's silence or refusal to answer questions".

Key Principle: **The fact that an accused has been advised to**

**remain silent by his solicitor is one of the relevant factors to
be weighed in the balance when assessing the fairness of the
trial but does not in itself render the trial unfair.**

Condron v UK

A solicitor refused to allow his clients to be interviewed about a
suspected offence of supplying heroin because he believed that
they were suffering from withdrawal symptoms and therefore
unfit to be interviewed. The doctors called to examine them
thought otherwise. At the trial the two accused relied on facts
they could have told the police at interview. The trial judge had
failed to direct the jury along the lines recommended by the
Judicial Studies Board to the effect that if they concluded,
having regard to any explanation advanced to explain the
accused's silence or the absence of explanation, that the
accused's silence can only sensibly be attributed to the accused's
having no answer to the case against him or no answer likely to
stand up to cross examination they may draw an adverse
inference against him. The Court of Appeal refused despite this
to overturn the conviction because it found that the evidence
against the defendant was overwhelming. The applicants
alleged violations of Article 6.

Held: (ECtHR) The applicants had not had a fair trial since the
Court of Appeal should not have found that the conviction was
safe despite the erroneous direction of the judge to the jury.
Since the court could not know what part the silence played in
allowing the jury to come to its decision it should have allowed
the appeal. [2000] 8 B.H.R.C. 290

Commentary

The ruling makes it unclear under what circumstances the drawing
of adverse inferences will be a violation of Article 6. The principle
from *Murray* clearly underlines the importance of legal advice
which the domestic decision in *Condron* undermined but the
Strasbourg ruling in *Condron* does not give guidance on when a no
comment interview based on legal advice should be excluded or as
to the reasons which might be regarded as sound for advising a
suspect to remain silent. Even if the accused's solicitor advises him
to remain silent, the drawing of adverse inferences is not necessarily a violation. The crucial question is that the judge should give
specific directions to the jury on what adverse inferences, if any,
might be drawn. The absence of such a direction will constitute a
violation of Article 6(1). The Strasbourg Court has followed this

approach in *Beckles v UK* (2002) B.H.R.C. 522. See also *R. v Beckles* [2004] EWCA Crim 2766.

Key Principle: **Although the overall fairness of a criminal trial could not be compromised the rights enshrined in Article 6 were not absolute.**

Stott (Procurator Fiscal, Dunfermline) v Brown

The defendant was arrested at a supermarket on suspicion of stealing a bottle of gin. Police were called and noticed that the defendant appeared to have been drinking. They asked how she had come to the store and she told them she had come by car. She was arrested and taken to a police station where she was required under s.172 of the Road Traffic Act 1988 to say who had been driving the car when she came to the supermarket. She admitted she had been the driver, was breathalysed and charged with driving with excess alcohol. She maintained it was contrary to Article 6(1) of the ECHR for the prosecution to rely at her trial on her admission that she had been driving, since it had been compulsorily obtained. The High Court of Justiciary allowed her appeal against conviction on that ground. On appeal by the prosecutor.

Held: (PC) Allowing the appeal, that the right to a fair trial under Article 6 was absolute and could not be compromised, but the privilege against self-incrimination was not absolute, since it was a right implied from Article 6, and could be limited, provided the limitation was proportionate to achieving its aim. There was a clear public interest in enforcing drink-driving legislation. Section 172 of the Road Traffic Act allowed for the putting of one simple question subject to a moderate and non-custodial penalty for failure to answer, and improper coercion could not be used to obtain an answer. It was not incompatible with the Convention for the defendant's answer to be used against her at trial. [2001] 2 W.L.R. 817

Commentary

In this instance some balancing of rights seemed to be necessary. Lord Bingham stated that the ECHR had recognised the need for a fair balance between the general interest of the community and the personal rights of the individual. It was permissible to qualify the right in Article 6 if any qualification was reasonably directed by the national authorities. Commentators have contrasted the decision here and that in *Montgomery* (see example in Marshall, "Things We Can Say About Rights" (2001) *Public Law* at 207). By contrast to the approach in *Stott*, *Montgomery* seemed to suggest that the right to a fair trial is compromised if any balancing of the public interest is allowed. It is arguable that although the overall unqualified right cannot be balanced any or all of its constituent elements can be balanced as long as the response is proportionate.

Presumption of Innocence

Key Principle: **Everyone charged with a criminal offence shall be presumed innocent until proved guilty according to law but that does not preclude the imposition of presumptions of fact and law.**

Salabiaku v France
The applicant was convicted of smuggling prohibited goods. The prosecution had proved that he was in possession of the goods, but relied on a presumption in the criminal code that a person in possession of prohibited goods was criminally liable.

Held: (ECtHR) Presumptions of fact or law were not in principle contrary to the Convention, though states were obliged to remain within reasonable limits in making such presumptions. It had been open to the applicant to prove *force majeure* and obtain acquittal or to plead mitigating circumstances. Article 6(2) had not been violated. (1991) 13 E.H.R.R. 379

Commentary
The implications of this controversial decision are that the existing common law position (see *Woolmington v DPP*) meets up with the requirement of Article 6 in accepting that the burden of proof could shift by implication on occasion. In *R. v DPP Ex p. Kebilene* (1999) the House of Lords was asked to consider whether the reverse burden provisions in the Prevention of Terrorism Act violated Article 6(2). In the Divisional Court Lord Bingham had declared that these sections "in a blatant and obvious way" undermined the presumption of innocence. The House of Lords did not pronounce on this point since it was decided that the matter was not reviewable. However their Lordships took a pragmatic approach to the shifting of the burden of proof. Lord

Hope stated: "As a matter of general principle . . . a fair balance must be struck between the demands of the general interest of the community and the protection of the fundamental rights of the individual." A relevant factor to consider was whether the defendant was being required to prove an essential element of the offence or establish a special defence or exception, which would be less objectionable.

Key Principle: **It may be contrary to the ECtHR to interpret legislation so as to impose the legal burden of proof on the defendant in criminal trials.**

R. v Lambert
For facts see p.5.

Held: (HL, *obiter*) It was not justifiable to use s.28 of the Misuse of Drugs Act 1971 so as to transfer the legal burden on the accused and require him to prove he did not know the bag contained a controlled drug. It was possible to construe s.28 as imposing an evidential rather than a legal burden and such a requirement was not a violation of the Convention. On the facts if the trial judge had given the direction to the jury that the burden on the accused was only an evidential burden the jury would have reached the same result. The conviction should not be quashed. [2001] 3 W.L.R. 206

Commentary
This was a majority decision and the judges gave differing reasons for their decision. Lord Hutton dissented on this point stating that "it is not unprincipled to have regard to practical realities where the issue relates to knowledge in a drugs case". Lord Steyn argued for outlawing reverse burdens where the defence bears directly on the moral blameworthiness of the defendant. An important factor in this case was the seriousness of the offence charged. See the discussion above on the nature of a criminal charge for the preliminary conditions for the application of the presumption of innocence. *McIntosh, Benjafield* and *Phillips* all lead to the conclusion that the presumption of innocence guaranteed in Article 6(2) is a specific example of the more general obligation of fair trial rights enshrined in Article 6(1).

Key Principle: **Reversals of the burdens of proof may be**

permitted so long as they were confined within reasonable limits that took account of the importance of what was at stake and maintained the rights of the defence.

R. v Johnstone

Police officers found 500 bootleg records at the defendant's home and charged him with trade mark violations. He was convicted and contended successfully on appeal that to establish an offence under s.92 Trade Marks Act 1994 the prosecution had to prove a civil infringement of the trade mark. The prosecution appealed to the House of Lords.

Held: (HL) Appeal dismissed. It was for the prosecution to prove as a fact that the trade mark concerned was being used as an indication of trade origin and not merely as an indication of the artiste on the disc. [2003] UKHL 28

Commentary

In *Attorney-General's Reference (No. 1 of 2004)* [2004] EWCA 1025 the Court of Appeal addressed what it stated was a significant difference in emphasis between the approaches of Lord Steyn in *Lambert* and Lord Nicholls in *Johnstone*. In practice a legal burden was much more likely to have to be reduced to an evidential burden on Lord Steyn's approach. Until there was a House of Lords decision clarifying the position the lower courts should follow the approach of Lord Nicholls rather than Lord Steyn. Courts should strongly discourage the citation of authority to them other than *Johnstone*. Reverse legal burdens were probably justified if the overall burden remained on the prosecution but Parliament had for significant reasons concluded that it was fair and reasonable to make an exception in respect of a particular aspect of the offence. See also *Attorney-General's Reference (No. 4 of 2003)* [2004] UKHL 43 where the House stated that Parliament's intentions may be disregarded if the fairness of the trial is threatened. The case concerned the burden of proof of membership of a proscribed organization. In effect s.11 of the 2000 Act requires a suspect to prove either that the organization was not proscribed or that he has not participated in its activities while it was proscribed. The court held that this placed a legal, not an evidential burden on the defendant which might be contrary to the presumption of innocence under Article 6(2) of the Convention, but was in any event justified and proportionate.

Legal Aid and Equality of Arms

Key Principle: **Everyone charged with a criminal offence has the right to defend himself in person or through legal assistance of his own choosing, or if he had not sufficient means to pay for legal assistance to be given it free when the interests of justice so require.**

Benham v UK

The applicant was imprisoned for non-payment of the community charge after a hearing in the magistrates' court under its civil jurisdiction. The proceedings were classified as civil and he was denied legal aid. He alleged violations of Articles 5 and 6.

Held: (ECtHR) Since the defendant's liberty was at stake the interests of justice required that the matter be treated as a criminal charge. Legal representation should have been allowed. [1996] 22 E.H.R.R. 293

Murray v UK

For facts see above.

Held: (ECtHR) In view of the fact that remaining silent had serious consequences at the trial the pressure on the defendant to speak to the police was sufficiently great to warrant the presence of a lawyer. The failure to secure the solicitor's presence therefore was a breach of Article 6(3). (1996) 22 E.H.R.R. 29

Commentary

The importance of legal professional privilege has been acknowledged. In *S v Switzerland* the ECtHR (1992) 14 E.H.R.R. 670 held that "free communication between a lawyer and his detained client is a fundamental right which is essential in a democratic society above all in the most serious cases." In *Campbell and Fell v UK* (1984) 7 E.H.R.R. 165 the court accepted however that although in principle those consultations should be conducted in private there were exceptional circumstances where this need not be so, for example if there were reasonable grounds to suspect counsel of abusing his professional position, perhaps by colluding with his client to destroy evidence. As a result of *Murray v UK* the law was amended so that inferences from silence when questioned can be drawn only if the accused has been offered an opportunity to consult a solicitor (see CJPOA 1994, ss.34–37 as amended by the Youth Justice and Criminal Evidence Act 1999). As a result of this decision the Youth Justice and Criminal Evidence Act 1999 has amended the CJPOA to impose an additional condition that if the defendant was at an authorised place of detention at the time of his failure or refusal, no inference may be drawn unless he was afforded an opportunity to consult a solicitor before the request was made. The cases illustrate that the requirement of the availability of legal aid will vary according to the complexity of issues for the particular defendant and the severity of the penalty. Legal aid is not available for some criminal charges under English law and it may be that this will lead to successful claims under Article 6.

Key Principle: **A system of fixed fees for defendants' solicitors in legal aid cases does not breach the principle of equality of arms.**

McLean and McLean v Procurator Fiscal Fort William
Under the Criminal Legal Aid (Fixed Payments) (Scotland) Regulations 1999 (S.I. 1999/491) solicitors were paid fixed sums for cases no matter what the complexity. In the instant case the expenditure incurred exceeded the fee payable. It was argued that breached the principle of equality of arms since the prosecution had no such limits.

Held: (PC) There was no breach of Article 6. Article 6 guaranteed the right to effective representation and the question was whether the system was institutionally incapable of providing adequate representation rather than what people were paid. While the regulations were not likely to cause a breach in this case, there was a real likelihood that they could do so in another serious case. However fixed fees were not wrong in principle. [2001] U.K.H.R.R. 793

Commentary
The Privy Council left open the possibility of a claim being brought if the regulations were not changed. The principle of equality of arms runs throughout Article 6 and particularly impact on the rights of legal representation and the right to examine witnesses.

Right to Question Witnesses

Key Principle: Since everyone charged with a criminal offence has the right to examine or have examined witnesses against him and to obtain the attendance and examination of witnesses on his behalf under the same conditions as witnesses against him the testimony of anonymous witnesses may generally not be admitted.

Saidi v France

The applicant was sentenced to 10 years' imprisonment for drug offences. The case was based on identification evidence of three persons but the applicant was denied any opportunity to confront the witnesses.

Held: (ECtHR) As a rule the defendant should be given an adequate and proper opportunity to challenge and question a witness against him whether the witness was making his statement out of court or at a later stage of the proceedings. The court was aware of the difficulties of the fight against drug trafficking, in particular with regard to obtaining and producing evidence, and of the ravages caused to society by the drug problem but such considerations could not justify restricting the rights of the defence to such an extent. (1994) 17 E.H.R.R. 251

Doorson v Netherlands

The applicant was convicted of drug trafficking on the evidence of witnesses who had not been heard in his presence and whom he had not been given an opportunity to question. He complained of violation of Articles 6(1) and (3)(d).

Held: (ECtHR) Use of anonymous witnesses was not in all circumstances compatible with the Convention. While Article 6 does not refer explicitly to the protection of the interests of witnesses and victims, these are protected by other Articles of the Convention. The Court of Appeal was entitled to consider that the applicant's interests were outweighed by the need to insure the safety of witnesses. The court had not based its finding solely on the anonymous evidence. (1996) 22 E.H.R.R. 330

Commentary

If witnesses are potentially vulnerable to attack from defendants then written submissions may be acceptable. In *Doorson* the court observed that "principles of a fair trial also require that in appropriate cases the interests of a defendant are balanced against those of witnesses or victims, called upon to testify". The potential clash between these interests has arisen on a number of issues, particularly those relating to rape trials. Under s.41 of the Youth Justice and Criminal Evidence Act 1999 defendants are not allowed to cross-examine an alleged victim in person. English criminal procedure does not normally allow pre-trial hearings without the defendant being present so that the safeguard present in *Doorson* is not available. As regards hearsay evidence admitted for the prosecution the Court of Appeal considered in *R. v Gokal* (1997) 2 Cr.App.R. 266 that there had been no breach of Article 6 in admitting documentary hearsay because the whole basis of s.26 of the Criminal Justice Act 1988 (now repealed) is to assess the interests of justice by referring to the risk of unfairness to the accused (See also *Trivedi v UK* [1997] E.H.R.L.R. 521). The Criminal Justice Act 2003 has made major changes to the law relating to hearsay evidence.

Fairness of Whole Proceedings

Key Principle: **The taking of evidence is governed primarily by the rules of domestic law and compliance with the European Convention on Human Rights is judged by whether the proceedings in their entirety, including the way in which evidence was taken, were fair.**

Blastland v UK
The applicant had been convicted of murder and buggery of a boy. He denied murder but stated that he had attempted buggery and run when he had seen another man M near the scene. He sought to adduce evidence of witnesses that M had told them a boy had been murdered before the body had been discovered. The trial judge refused to allow this evidence and the House of Lords had decided that the evidence had been rightly excluded. It was untested hearsay and would be treated as having probative force it did not possess. He claimed a violation of Article 6.

Held: (Commission) Application failed. The accused's right to a fair trial was protected procedurally since he was entitled in theory to call M as a witness. [1987] 10 E.H.R.R. 528

Commentary
This is a disturbing case since the defendant had been denied the right to adduce evidence of an implied admission by a third party

of guilt. The Commission however felt that as a whole the rule against the admissibility of hearsay evidence did not violate Article 6. Since the defendant in this case had the right to challenge the ruling it could not be said that there was no "equality of arms". If this had not been so the Strasbourg Court might have come to a different decision. In *Vidal v Belgium* (1992, unpublished) the court upheld the defendant's complaint that he had not had a fair trial where the Brussels Court of Appeal had refused to allow the defendant to call possibly relevant defence evidence because they had given no reason for their refusal. It is possible that the rule against hearsay evidence may be subject to challenge under the HRA. Article 6(3)(d) does not apply to the defence in the same way as to the prosecution so it is possible to argue that hearsay evidence which the prosecution could not adduce should be excluded if tendered by the defence. English law does not differentiate between defence and prosecution evidence in relation to hearsay. Thus the exclusion of cogent exculpatory evidence could constitute a violation of the right to a fair trial. However where there are a number of defendants the exercise by one defendant of a right to put in hearsay evidence might be fair under the Convention from that defendant's point of view and yet be unfair as against another defendant.

Key Principle: A breach of the fair trial guarantees under the ECHR will almost always lead to the trial being unfair and any conviction overturned on appeal.

R. v Togher, Doran, Parsons
The applicants pleaded guilty to offences of drug dealing arising from seizures by the authorities of cocaine in Madrid. They were convicted. Prior to this they had been convicted of drug offences at Frugal. This latter conviction was appealed and a retrial ordered. At the retrial the judge ordered a stay of proceedings because the prosecution had, by means which were arguably unlawful, deprived the defence of its strategic ability to challenge the integrity of the prosecution case. It was not disputed that the separation of the Madrid and Frugal indictments had been because of case management considerations and the defendants argued that the trial judge's ruling in the retrial should have applied to the Madrid indictment and they should not have been required to plead.

Held: (CA) An appeal against conviction where there had been a guilty plea could be allowed if the proceedings had been an abuse of process such that it would be inconsistent with the due administration of justice to allow the plea to stand. On the facts the failures on the part of the prosecution did not amount to the category of misconduct which had to exist before it was right to stay a prosecution. The defendants were only unaware of material which could but for their pleas have been used in order to attack the credibility of the prosecution witnesses. *The Times*, November 21, 2000

Commentary

Togher has been endorsed by the House of Lords in *R. v Forbes* [2001] 2 W.L.R. 1. It is one of a number of cases where the court has considered the effect of a breach of the ECHR on the safety of convictions. The problem is acute when there is factual evidence of the truth of the conviction but that the integrity of the process is flawed. An earlier Court of Appeal decision, *R. v Chalkley*, had adopted a narrow approach to this, holding that in cases of guilty pleas the Court of Appeal should concentrate on the reliability of the verdict. This Court of Appeal considered in *Togher* that now the ECHR was part of domestic law it should follow the broader approach of the ECtHR in *Condron v UK* "The question whether the rights of the defence guaranteed to an accused under Article 6 of the Convention were secured in any given case cannot be assimilated to a finding that his conviction was safe in the absence of any inquiry into the issue of fairness." As a matter of first principles the Court of Appeal did not consider that either the use of the word "unsafe" in the legislation or the previous cases compelled an approach which did not correspond with that of the ECtHR. It follows that a finding of unfairness should lead to a conviction being unsafe. An illustration of the effect of this new approach is seen in *Rowe* where eventually the Court of Appeal decided it had no choice but to overturn the convictions. See also *R. v Williams*, *The Times* March 30, 2001 where the Court of Appeal considered that a breach of Article 6(2) would not automatically mean that a conviction was unsafe.

Unlawfully or Improperly Obtained Evidence

Key Principle: **There is no rule that requires that illegally or improperly obtained evidence should be excluded from a trial.**

Exclusion is a matter of discretion for the trial judge based on the effect on fairness to the proceedings.

Khan v UK

The applicant had been convicted of involvement in importing heroin. The evidence against him came from an electronic listening device installed by police in a private house he visited. He claimed violations of Articles 6 and 8.

Held: (ECtHR) The evidence had been obtained in violation of Article 8 but it had not been unlawful in the sense of being contrary to domestic criminal law. The authenticity of the recordings was not in question only their admissibility. Since the domestic courts could exercise discretion whether or not to admit such evidence and had concluded its admission would not affect the fairness of the trial there was no breach of Article 6. (2000) 8 B.H.R.C. 310

Commentary

The court found a breach of Articles 8 and 12 since there was no legal basis and thus no redress for the invasion of privacy (see p.135 *et seq*). Subsequently such covert operations have been placed on a statutory footing in the Regulation of Investigatory Powers Act 2000. If the communication falls outside the statute intercept evidence is generally admissible. In *R. v P* [2001] 2 W.L.R. 463 the House of Lords upheld a judge's ruling that telephone intercept evidence lawfully acquired by the authorities in a foreign jurisdiction could be used at trial. Deriving support from *Khan v UK*, the House rejected a claim that Article 8 inevitably demanded the exclusion of intercept evidence not covered by the 2000 Act. In *Edwards v UK* (1993) 15 E.H.R.R. 417 the court had stated that the right to a fair trial extends not merely to the trial but also to pre-trial procedures. Clearly however the mere fact that the evidence had been obtained illegally does not render the trial unfair. The Strasbourg Court has expressed itself willing to leave questions of the admissibility of evidence to national rules and discretion. For an example of a case where the House of Lords has stated that unlawfully obtained intercept evidence was wrongly admitted at trial see *R. v Sargent* [2001] 3 W.L.R. 992. Its admission in this instance had rendered a conviction unsafe. See also *Perry v UK* (2003).

Attorney-General's Reference (No. 3 of 1999)

Under s.64(1) of the PACE 1984 a sample taken from a suspect during the investigation of an offence must be destroyed if that person is "cleared" of that offence and according to s.64(3B) such sample "shall not be used in evidence against that person . . . or for the purposes of any investigation of an offence". In two cases, one involving murder and one rape, the Crown had put forward as part of its case DNA evidence collected during other investigations which had both led to the defendants being acquitted. The Court of Appeal had declared that s.64 was mandatory and such evidence was inadmissible. The Court of Appeal at the request of the Attorney-General referred a question for the opinion of the House of Lords as to whether in such circumstances a judge had a discretion to the relevant evidence notwithstanding the terms of s.64(3B).

Held: (HL) Decision of Court of Appeal reversed. Whereas s.64(3B) of the 1984 Act made express prohibition against the use of a DNA sample which should have been destroyed, s.64(3B) in prohibiting the use of an unlawfully retained sample for the purposes of any investigation did not amount to a mandatory exclusion of evidence obtained as a result of a failure to comply with the prohibition. It should be read along with s.78 which left the question of its admissibility to the discretion of the trial judge. A decision by a judge in the exercise of his discretion to admit such evidence would not breach Articles 8 or 6 of the Convention. The information obtained as a result of the failure to destroy the DNA sample ought not to have been rendered inadmissible. [2001] 2 A.C. 91

Commentary
Lord Steyn referred specifically to the principle of fairness for all sides and reasoned that a consideration of the public interest reinforced his interpretation of the application of s.78. With regard to the argument that Article 8 of the ECHR required the interpretation which the Court of Appeal had come to, he said that "the interpretation was in accordance with law" as judicial discretion under s.78 governed admissibility. The interference was plainly necessary in a democratic society to ensure the investigation and prosecution of serious crime. Lord Steyn pointed out: "respect for the privacy of defendants is not the only value at stake. . . . There must be fairness to all sides. In a criminal case this requires the court to consider a triangulation of interests. It involves taking into account the position of the accused, the victim and his or her family and the public. In my view the austere interpretation which the Court of Appeal adopted. . . produces results which are contrary to good sense." It has been observed

that this was indeed a sensible decision. It is of interest that in *R. v Z* [2000] 2 A.C. 483 the House of Lords held that acquittals are not to be treated as findings of innocence.

Entrapment

Key Principle: **In entrapment cases the ultimate question was whether the fairness of the proceedings would be adversely affected by admitting the evidence of the agent provocateur or evidence which was available as the result of his action or activities.**

Teixeira de Castro v Portugal
Two plain clothes police officers had asked a known petty drug trafficker to obtain heroin. He mentioned the name of the applicant who eventually obtained packets of the drug for the undercover officers. The applicant was arrested, charged and convicted. He claimed breaches of Articles 3, 6 and 8. He claimed that the officers had engaged in immoral conduct since he had supplied the drug solely at the officers' request. They had not been carrying out drug trafficking searches pursuant to a court order.

Held: (ECtHR) There was a violation of Article 6 and it was not necessary to consider violations of Articles 3 and 8. The officers had instigated and incited the offence and there was nothing to suggest that but for their intervention it would have been committed. The applicant had been denied the right to a fair trial. [1999] 28 E.H.R.R. 101

R. v Shannon
The defendant was convicted of supplying drugs to a journalist posing as an Arab sheikh, part of a stratagem to obtain evidence of drug offences against him. The judge refused an application to exclude the evidence as unfairly obtained.

Held: (CA) Appeal against conviction dismissed. There was no general rule requiring a court on grounds of fundamental fairness not to entertain a prosecution in all cases of incitement or instigation by an agent provocateur regardless of whether the trial as a whole could be fair in the procedural sense. The judge found correctly in that the evidence fell short of establishing actual incitement or instigation of the offences and in any event

the admission of the evidence would not have an adverse effect
on the procedural fairness of the trial. [2001] 1 W.L.R. 51

Commentary
The Court of Appeal referred to *Teixeira de Castro v Portugal* and
considered that the end result of that case, couched as it was in
terms of incitement and causation, was not necessarily at odds
with English law. It considered that the approach of the Strasbourg
Court was not inconsistent with the approach in *R. v Smurthwaite*
[1994] 1 All E.R. 898 namely that the evidence would be open to
exclusion if the incitement had caused the offence.

Key Principle: **In assessing whether to exclude evidence or
stay criminal proceedings in cases of entrapment the requirements of Article 6 of the ECHR are compatible with s.78 of the
PACE and the common law.**

R. v Looseley; Attorney-General's Reference (No. 3 of 2000)
An undercover police officer who had been given the defendant's name as a potential source of drugs, arranged with him
to exchange heroin for money. The defendant was charged with
supplying or being concerned in supplying to another a class A
controlled drug, contrary to s.4 of the Misuse of Drugs Act 1971.
The trial judge refused a preliminary request to exclude
evidence or stay proceedings. The defendant pleaded guilty. In
a separate case two undercover police officers who offered
contraband cigarettes for sale at a housing estate were introduced to the accused as a potential buyer. They sold him
cigarettes and asked if he could get them heroin, a request to
which he agreed and complied after initial hesitation. He was
charged with supplying heroin. The trial judge stayed the
proceedings on the ground that the police had incited the
commission of the offence and that otherwise the accused would
be denied his right to a fair hearing under Article 6(1) of the
ECHR. The stay was lifted, the prosecution offered no evidence
and the accused was acquitted. The Attorney-General referred
for the opinion of the Court of Appeal the question whether in
cases of entrapment the judicial discretion conferred by s.78 of
PACE and the power to stay proceedings as an abuse of process
had been modified by Article 6(1) of the ECHR. The Court of
Appeal held it had not and that the trial judge had been wrong

to stay the proceedings. The defendant in the first case appealed and the reference was made from the Court of Appeal in the second.

Held: (HL) The court must in such cases balance the need to uphold the rule of law by convicting and punishing those who committed crimes with the need to prevent law enforcement agencies acting in a way which offended ordinary notions of fairness. The House distinguished between entrapment which might lead to exclusion of evidence and entrapment which will lead to a stay of prosecution. There is not one simple test. The court must ask the central question which was whether the actions of the police were so seriously improper as to bring the administration of justice into disrepute. If there has been an abuse of state power, then the appropriate remedy is a stay of the indictment, rather than exclusion of the evidence under s.78 of the PACE. The appeal of the defendant in the first case was dismissed since the undercover officer did no more than present himself as an ordinary customer to an active drug dealer and there was nothing in the officer's conduct which constituted incitement. In the second case on the facts the trial judge had been entitled to stay the proceedings on the ground that the officers had instigated the offence by offering inducements which would not ordinarily be associated with the commission of that offence. The decision of the Court of Appeal was reversed in part. [2001] 1 W.L.R. 2060

Commentary

The House stated that the principle to be applied was that it would be unfair and an abuse of process if a person had been lured, incited or pressurised into committing a crime which he would not otherwise have committed but that it would not be objectionable if a law enforcement officer, behaving as an ordinary member of the public, gave a person an unexceptional opportunity to commit a crime and that person freely took advantage of the opportunity. The judgment demonstrated strong judicial recognition of the dangers of excessive police behaviour in cases of entrapment and the need for the courts to protect citizens. Following this judgment the focus of the court's approach must be on an objective assessment of the conduct of the police rather than the predisposition of the defendant. Thus, for example, the defendant's criminal record is unlikely to be relevant. Lord Nicholls specifically recognised that *R. v Sang* [1980] A.C. 402 had been "overtaken" by statute and case law. Lord Hoffman stressed the importance of the "protection of the integrity of the criminal justice system". Their Lordships considered that their judgment was compatible with *Teixeira de Castro v Portugal.* It it did not follow from *Teixeira* that taking any active steps, such as offering to buy drugs, necessarily amounts to "incitement". The law was and is that entrapment is not a defence *per se.* Lord Nicholls stated that if there has been entrapment, then even where there is other evidence, the abuse of state power is such that the case should be stopped entirely by means of a stay. Among the factors to be considered will be the following: the nature of the offence; the factual basis for the police carrying out the operation; the degree and extent of the police inducement. The former test of whether the offender was predisposed to commit such an offence was not appropriate.

Disclosure of Evidence

Key Principle: **Failure by the prosecution to disclose documents to the defence may impair the fairness of the proceedings.**

Rowe and Davis v UK
The appellants had been convicted of murder. They contended that their convictions were obtained in violation of Article 6 since they were based on unreliable evidence from witnesses who had vindictive motives for giving evidence, were police informers or had obtained rewards. The trial judge had accepted a prosecution request to not disclose documents to the defence and had not reviewed the documents; the Court of Appeal had reviewed them and refused disclosure.

Held: (ECtHR) The applicants had been denied a fair trial and the Court of Appeal had not been able to remedy the defect of the non inspection of the documents by the trial judge. The trial judge was best placed to decide whether non disclosure of public interest immunity evidence would be unfairly prejudicial to the defence. A fundamental principle of a fair trial in the adversarial system was that there was equality of arms. There may be occasions when documents were not made available to the defence but this had to be "strictly necessary".

Commentary
The court referred approvingly to *R. v Ward* [1993] 1 W.L.R. 619 in its judgment. The convictions of the appellants were overturned

by the Court of Appeal which held that a conviction may be unsafe even where there was no doubt about guilt but the trial process had been "vitiated by serious unfairness or significant legal misdirection" (see *R. v Rowe and Davis, The Times*, July 25, 2000). By contrast to the ruling in *Rowe v UK*; *Jasper v UK*; *Fitt v UK* (2000) there was no violation of Article 6(1) since the defence were notified of the *ex parte* hearing and were allowed to present their case to the judge. The court observed in the latter cases that disclosure of relevant evidence is not an absolute right and that competing interests of national security, protecting witnesses and preserving the secrecy of police investigative methods have to be balanced against those of the accused. These considerations affect the operation of the doctrine of public interest immunity. However a more general issue is the disclosure of prosecution evidence to the defence. It is arguable that the regime under the Criminal Procedure and Investigations Act 1996, whereby secondary disclosure is postponed until after a defence statement, may not be compatible with the Convention. This case is commonly known as the M25 Case. (For another example of the same principle see *Atlan v UK* (App. No. 36533/97) June 19, 2001). *Edwards and Lewis v UK* (2003) 15 B.H.C.R. 189 concerned the request by the defence to disclosure of the identity of an informer. The court held that the prosecution should not be permitted to refuse to disclose information to the defence without adequate safeguards.

No punishment without law

Key Principle: **Article 7 of the ECHR—No punishment without law:**

> "1 No one shall be held guilty of any criminal offence on account of any act or omission which did not constitute a criminal offence under national or international law at the time when it was committed. Nor shall a heavier penalty be imposed than the one that was applicable at the time the criminal offence was committed.
>
> 2 This article shall not prejudice the trial and punishment of any person for any act or omission which, at the time when it was committed, was criminal according to the general principles of law recognised by civilised nations."

Key Principle: **An order which was designed to protect the public rather than inflict punishment did not infringe Article 7.**

Gough v Chief Constable of Derbyshire

The appellant argued that a football banning order was a violation of Article 7 in that when he committed the relevant act the maximum penalty was 3 years which was later increased to 6. He had been given 6 years.

Held: (CA) The order was not a penalty for the purposes of Article 7 since it was to protect the public at home and abroad from the threat of football violence. Such measures to counter this sickening menace were proportionate. [2001] 3 W.L.R. 1392

Commentary

It was also submitted that the orders were contrary to the free movement of people under EU law. The court held that it was possible to derogate from these laws on public policy grounds.

Key Principle: **A strong indication of a regime of punishment will engage Article 7.**

Welch v UK

The applicant was convicted of drug offences. The trial judge imposed a confiscation order under the Drug Trafficking Act 1986 which came into force after the applicant's arrest but before conviction. He claimed this was a violation of Article 7.

Held: (ECtHR) Factors to be taken into account in deciding whether an order was a penalty were: whether the order was imposed after a criminal conviction; its nature and purpose; its characterisation under national law; its severity; and the procedures involved in its making and implementation. In view of the combination of punitive elements there was a violation of Article 7. (1995) 20 E.H.R.R. 247

Commentary

Drug confiscation orders have also been subject to scrutiny under Article 6 (see p.116 *et seq*). In 1994 the Drug Trafficking Act replaced the earlier legislation. Confiscation orders are no longer mandatory. Either the prosecution may seek an order or the court of its own motion may do so.

5. DUE PROCESS AND A FAIR TRIAL IN CIVIL PROCEEDINGS

Key Principle: Article 5 of the ECHR—Right to liberty and security:

> "1 Everyone has the right to liberty and security of person. No one shall be deprived of his liberty save in the following cases and in accordance with a procedure prescribed by law:
>
> . . .
>
> (f) the lawful arrest or detention of a person to prevent his effecting an unauthorised entry into the country or of a person against whom action is being taken with a view to deportation or extradition."

Detention of Asylum Seekers

Key Principle: **The detention of asylum seekers awaiting determination of their applications is both lawful under domestic law and does not violate the right to liberty under Article 5.**

R. (Saadi) v Secretary of State for the Home Department
Four asylum seekers had claimed judicial review of the lawfulness of their temporary detention at Oakington reception centre after their arrival in the United Kingdom. Oakington had been established as a reception centre for asylum seekers whose claims could be decided usually within 10 days of arrival. It was accepted that none of the claimants presented any risk of absconding or of otherwise failing to comply with the terms of temporary admission while their claims for asylum were being processed and the sole reason for their detention was to facilitate the "fast track" disposal of their claims. Collins J. in the administrative court had held that the detention was unlawful under Article 5. The Secretary of State appealed.

Held: (CA) The claimants' detention fell within the express statutory powers of immigration officers. Article 5 allowed detention to prevent an "unauthorised entry into the country". "Unauthorised entry" was an entry which had not be authorised. No disproportionality was demonstrated. Appeal allowed. [2002] 1 W.L.R. 356

Commentary

The court stated that the Convention was a living instrument and when interpreting it and considering the Strasbourg jurisprudence it was necessary to bear in mind that its effect might change in step with changes in the standards applied by member states. But as a starting point it was sensible to consider the position in 1951 when the Convention was agreed. In accepting Article 5 member states were not binding themselves to grant aliens unlimited license to enter their territories and enjoy liberty within them. The right of the state to determine whether aliens should enter was a firmly entrenched principle of international law. The exception to the right to liberty in Article 5(1)(f) was intended to preserve the right of member states to decide whether to allow aliens to enter.

Fair Trial Rights

Key Principle: **Article 6 of the ECHR—Right to a fair trial:**

"1 In the determination of his civil rights and obligations or of any criminal charge against him, everyone is entitled to a fair and public hearing within a reasonable time by an independent and impartial tribunal established by law. Judgment shall be pronounced publicly but the press and public may be excluded from all or part of the trial in the interests of morals, public order or national security in a democratic society, where the interests of juveniles or the protection of the private life of the parties so require, or to the extent strictly necessary in the opinion of the court in special circumstances where publicity would prejudice the interests of justice."

Access to the courts

Key Principle: **The state cannot preclude access to a judicial procedure.**

Golder v UK

A prisoner in Parkhurst was accused by a prison officer of having taken part in a disturbance. The officer later withdrew the allegation and the prisoner petitioned for the right to consult a solicitor with a view to bringing a libel action against the officer. The Home Secretary refused. The applicant claimed his right of access to justice under Article 6 had been denied.

Held: (ECtHR) Article 6(1) contains the right of access to a court and in civil matters "one can scarcely conceive of the rule of law without there being the possibility of having access to a court". The right to institute civil proceedings is one aspect of the right of access to a court. This right was not an absolute and could be subject to limitations. On the facts in this case there was an infringement of Article 6(1). (1979–80) 1 E.H.R.R. 524

Commentary

In its judgment the court demonstrated how it dealt with a new issue coming before it. It looked both at the content of Article 6(1) and its relationship to other Articles, particularly Articles 5(4) and 13, pointing out that "the three provisions do not operate in the same field. The concept of 'civil rights and obligations' is not co-extensive with that of 'rights and freedoms as set forth in this Convention', even if there may be some overlapping". It also referred to theoretical and abstract issues particularly the "rule of law". As a result of this important case the Prison Rules in force then were amended to allow a prisoner to institute proceedings or to consult a solicitor.

Key Principle: **Article 6 offers protection against procedural restrictions to access to the courts for those civil rights which are recognised in domestic law.**

Matthews v Ministry of Defence

The claimant had become ill as a result of exposure to asbestos while serving in the Royal Navy. He issued personal injury proceedings against the Ministry of Defence alleging negligence of breach of statutory duty. The judge rejected the Ministry's submission that the claim was barred by s.10 of the Crown Proceedings Act 1947. which exempts the Crown from liability in tort for injuries suffered by servicemen as a consequence of events before 1987. The Court of Appeal allowed an appeal by the Ministry. The claimant appealed.

Held: (HL) Appeal dismissed. Article 6(1) protected only those civil rights which could be recognised under domestic law and where the restriction on the right of access was procedural in nature. Here, the bar imposed by s.10 and by the common law was a matter of substantive law under which the claimant had no civil rights to which Article 6 could apply. [2003] UKHL 4; [2003] I.C.R. 247.

Commentary

The difference between procedural rights, protected by Article 6, and substantive law rights has been a matter of controversy. In *Osman v UK* (1999) the Strasbourg Court had held that the immunity of the police from suits in negligence had violated Article 6 but it subsequently retracted from that approach.

In *Osman* the Strasbourg Court had stretched Article 6(1) to include not only procedural guarantees but the availability of a cause of action. The blanket ban on actions against the police derived from *Hill v Chief Constable of West Yorkshire Police* was a violation of an individual's right. This was potentially a far reaching decision and its effect was seen for example in *Hall v Simons* [2000] 3 W.L.R. 543 where the House of Lords removed the immunity in civil suit of advocates. However the Strasbourg Court subsequently appeared to retreat from the robust ruling in *Osman*. In *Z v UK* [2001] ECHR 29392/95 the court stated (at para.100) that it

> "considers that its reasoning in the *Osman* judgment was based on an understanding of the law of negligence . . . which has to be reviewed in the light of the clarifications subsequently made by the domestic courts and notably the House of Lords. . . . In the present case, the Court is led to the conclusion that the inability of the applicants to sue the local authority flowed not from an immunity but from the applicable principles governing the substantive right of action in domestic law. There was no restriction on access to court of the kind contemplated in the *Ashingdane v United Kingdom* (1985) judgment."

In *Barrett v Enfield LBC* [1999] 3 All E.R. 193 the House of Lords had implemented reforms to the tort of negligence. In *Z v UK* the court had found no violation of Article 6 arising from the fact that children who had suffered neglect in local authority care could not sue the authority in negligence. This rule was the application of substantive law principles by the domestic courts and it was not for the ECtHR to rule on the appropriate content of domestic law.

Key Principle: **Access to the courts must not be made practically impossible by high court fees.**

R. v Lord Chancellor Ex p. Witham

The Lord Chancellor increased the fees for issuing a writ and abolished exemption from paying fees for litigants in person in receipt of income support. The applicant was an unemployed man in receipt of income support who wished to issue proceedings in person for defamation for which legal aid was not available. He was not able to afford the fees and sought judicial review of the Lord Chancellor's decision.

Held: (DC) Access to the courts was a constitutional right at common law and could be abrogated only by a specific statutory provision in primary legislation. The Lord Chancellor had no power to prescribe fees so as to deny the poor access to the courts and his decision to do so was *ultra vires* and unlawful. [1998] Q.B. 575

Commentary

The judgment of Laws J. contains a full survey of English cases on the common law and rights of access to justice. Laws J. made reference to Article 6 but stated that "the common law provides no lesser protection to the right of access to the Queen's courts than might be vindicated in Strasbourg". See also *R. v Home Secretary Ex p. Leech* [1994] Q.B. 198

Key Principle: **The right of access to the courts is not an absolute one.**

Ashingdane v UK

The applicant who had been convicted of a criminal offence, was sent to a secure special hospital. The Home Secretary ordered he be transferred to a local psychiatric hospital but this was delayed because of industrial action. Legislation protected the authorities from civil suit for failure to comply with an order as long as there was no allegation of negligence or bad faith. The applicant complained there was a breach of Article 6(2) since he was thus prevented from challenging at law his prolonged detention in a secure hospital.

Held: (ECtHR) Any restrictions on the right of access to the courts must be proportionate and must not restrict or reduce access in such a way that the right itself was impaired. The court accepted that the objective of the legislation was to reduce the risk of unfair harassment of those responsible for these mental patients. This was a legitimate aim and did not "transgress the principle of proportionality". There was thus no violation of Article 6(1). (1985) 7 E.H.R.R. 528

Commentary
There are a number of groups of litigants or would be litigants who are disadvantaged in getting to court at all. These include prisoners, mental patients, bankrupts. *Ashingdane* makes it clear that although the essential right of access to the courts to pursue civil claims must be upheld some procedural limitations are acceptable in cases of this type.

Key Principle: **Limitation periods must be proportionate and pursue a legitimate aim.**

Stubbings v UK
The applicant claimed that she had been abused for a number of years by her adoptive father and his son and that as a result she had suffered severe psychological damage. She only realised the cause when undergoing psychiatric treatment years later. Her claim against the alleged perpetrators was time barred under the Limitation Act 1980. She claimed a breach of Article 6.

Held: (ECtHR) Limitation periods served the legitimate aim of ensuring legal certainty and finality and a six-year limitation period was not unduly short. There had been no violation. (1997) 23 E.H.R.R. 213

Commentary
The court recognised that society's attitude to the offence of child sex abuse and its effects on victims might change. It stated: "It is

possible that the rules on limitations of actions applying in Member States of the Council of Europe may have to be amended to make special provision for this group of claimants in the near future."

Key Principle: **The right of access to a court extends only to disputes over civil rights and obligations which are recognised under domestic law.**

Al-Fayed v UK
The applicants had acquired ownership of the House of Fraser. The Government appointed two inspectors to investigate the take over and they published a report which was critical of the applicants. The applicants complained that they had no redress in law and there was a violation of Article 6.

Held: (ECtHR) The state had not exceeded its margin of appreciation in limiting the access to a court; there were safeguards in the procedure of investigative inquiry which was not determinative of a civil right or criminal liability. There was no violation of Article 6(1). (1994) 18 E.H.R.R. 393

Commentary
In *Al-Fayed* the court recognised that the protection of public interests was an important factor in the activities of the investigators operating under the Companies Act 1985 and therefore it was important that inspectors were allowed freedom to report with "courage and frankness". The case illustrates also that Article 6(1) does not necessarily apply to official inquiries. The court concluded that there was an important difference between adjudication which was covered by Article 6(1) and investigation which was not. The finding that the applicant was dishonest as a result of the investigation was not a "determination" since it was not "dispositive of anything" in the way of legal rights and duties.

Legal Aid

Key Principle: **Legal aid in civil proceedings may be necessary in order to secure the right of access to a court.**

Airey v Ireland
For facts see p.136.

Held: (ECtHR) The Convention was intended to guarantee rights that are not theoretical or illusory but rights that are practical and effective. Legal aid was required to allow the applicant to pursue her case in view of the complexity of the issues. (1979) 2 E.H.R.R. 305

Commentary
After referring to criminal legal aid in Article 6(3)(c) the court stated "despite the absence of a similar clause for civil litigation, Article 6(1) may sometimes compel the State to provide for the assistance of a lawyer. . .". The court stressed that it did not hold that legal aid must be provided in all civil proceedings. Legal aid was needed only where it was "indispensable for effective access to court either because legal representation was compulsory" or because of the "complexity of the procedure or of the case". It noted in *Winer v UK* (1986) 48 D.R. 154 there was no breach where legal aid was not available for defamation cases. In *Airey* the court commented that simplifying procedures might be one way of ensuring an effective right of access. The case does suggest that the complete absence of legal aid to enable a litigant to press a claim may be an infringement of Article 6. Some commentators have questioned whether the conditional fee system might be regarded as an adequate substitute.

Key Principle: **Equality of arms may require that the blanket ban on legal aid in defamation cases be set aside where the case is particularly complex.**

Steel & Morris v UK
The applicants had been found liable for libelling the McDonald's fast food chain in leaflets distributed outside one of its branches in London. The trial was the longest civil case in English legal history, but the defendants were denied legal aid.

Held: (ECtHR) The denial of legal aid to the applicants deprived them of the opportunity to present their case effectively before the courts and contributed to an unacceptable inequality of arms with McDonald's. Their rights under Article 6.1 had been violated. *The Times*, February 15, 2005

Commentary
There is no statutory provision for legal aid in defamation proceedings. The government will be obliged in future to consider

granting legal aid to an impecunious defendant facing too heavy a burden, because of the likely length or complexity of the case.

Impartiality and Equality of Arms

Key Principle: **Civil rights and obligations should be determined by an independent and impartial tribunal.**

Starrs and Chalmers v Procurator Fiscal
The Lord Advocate appointed temporary sheriffs to hear a large proportion of criminal cases in Scotland. It was argued that such an appointment system including lack of security of office and the discretion of the Lord Advocate, was incompatible with the right to a fair trial.

Held: (Court of Session) The appointment of temporary sheriffs under s.11(4) of the Sheriff Courts (Scotland) Act 1971 was incompatible with Article 6(1) as they did not constitute an independent and impartial tribunal. (2000) U.K.H.R.R. 78

Commentary
While the HRA was in force in England from October 2000 it was in effect in Scotland on the devolution of power to the Scottish Parliament in 1998 and cases in Scotland gave an early indication of the impact of the Act. With regard to impartiality a key requirement is that the tribunal should be independent of the executive. The Lord Advocate controlled appointments and he was also head of the prosecution service. In *Langborger v Sweden* (1990) 12 E.H.R.R. 416 the court set out the factors which should be considered in determining whether the tribunal was independent. These included the manner of appointment of the members, their term of office, the existence of guarantees against outside pressure, whether the body in question presents an appearance of independence. There should be both lack of actual bias and of the appearance of bias. *Starrs* has implications for the system of judicial appointments throughout the United Kingdom. The court recognised that the fact that the executive appoints judges does not in itself threaten judicial independence but that where a judge is appointed on a temporary basis and his appointment lies at the discretion of the Executive judicial independence may be at risk.

Key Principle: **Justice must be seen to be done and the** composition of tribunals should avoid the possibility of subconscious bias.

Lawal v Northern Spirit Ltd
Counsel in an appeal to the Employment Appeal Tribunal had previously sat as a part time judge in the E.A.T. with one of the lay members hearing the appeal. The claimant argued that this gave rise to a real risk of bias since it might dispose the lay member to accept counsel's submissions more readily than he would otherwise have done. The case made its way to the House of Lords.

Held: (HL) Appeal allowed. Public confidence in the administration of justice might be undermined by the practice whereby leading counsel sat as part-time judges in the E.A.T. so that counsel might have sat as a judge with one or more of the lay members of the panel before which he was appearing. The practice should be discontinued. The principle to be applied was whether a fair-minded and informed observer would conclude there was a real possibility of bias. [2003] UKHL 35; [2003] I.C.R. 856

Commentary
Lord Steyn put the test for apparent bias as: "The principle to be applied is that stated in *Porter v Magill*, whether a fair-minded and informed observer, having considered the given facts, would conclude that there was a real possibility that the Tribunal was biased. Concretely, would such an observer consider that it was reasonably possible that the wing member may be subconsciously biased?"

Key Principle: **Decisions by the Secretary of State were not incompatible with Article 6(1) provided they were subject to review by an independent and impartial tribunal.**

R. (Alconbury Developments Ltd) v Secretary of State for Environment, Transport and the Regions
In three separate planning cases the Secretary of State played a part in deciding whether or not planning permission should be granted. It was argued that the Secretary of State's role was contrary to the right to have their civil rights and obligations

determined by an independent and impartial tribunal guaranteed by Article 6(1) of the Convention. The Divisional Court held that the Secretary of State's powers were incompatible with Article 6(1) but that his exercise of those powers was not unlawful because s.6(2) of the HRA applied. The Secretary of State appealed to the House of Lords.

Held: (HL) Although the Secretary of State was not himself an independent and impartial tribunal, decisions taken by him were not incompatible with Article 6(1) if they were subject to review and by an independent and impartial tribunal. The reviewing body did not need full power to redetermine the merits of the decision. It would be undemocratic for the courts to review ministerial policy decisions on their merits. Compatibility with Article 6(1) was ensured by the power of the High Court in judicial review proceedings to review the legality of the decision and the procedures followed. [2001] 2 W.L.R. 1389

Reasonable Time

Key Principle: **The state has responsibility to ensure civil proceedings between private parties take place within a reasonable time.**

Obasa v UK
The applicant had brought discrimination proceedings in the employment tribunal against her employer, a local authority, in December 1991. The case was delayed while an internal hearing took place and there were interlocutory issues, so that the tribunal decision was not handed down until December 1994. The council appealed to the Employment Appeal Tribunal, which quashed the discrimination finding in October 1996. The applicant's appeal to the Court of Appeal was dismissed in February 1998 and the House of Lords refused her leave to appeal in April 1999.

Held: (ECtHR) The reasonableness of the length of proceedings fell to be assessed in the light of the complexity of the case, the conduct of the applicant and the authorities and the importance of the issues at stake. While the delay in the first instance hearing might be reasonable in the circumstances, and a delay of a year between appeal hearings might be acceptable, it was not acceptable that there was a delay of at least a year between each of the stages of appeal. The overall duration was simply too long. [2003] January 16

Commentary
The Government is responsible for the overall duration of proceedings. It might need to show some mechanism for ensuring that a case completes all its stages within a reasonable time. In *Price and Lowe v UK* [2003] Application No 00043185/98 and 00043186/98 the European Court of Human Rights stated that states had responsibility to ensuring that civil proceedings took place within a reasonable time even though the initiative in taking proceedings was with the parties. Possible ways of avoiding delay included increasing the number of judges or imposing automatic time-limits and directions. Although there are no absolute limits beyond which proceedings are held to have taken an unreasonable time relevant considerations are the complexity of the case, the conduct of the applicant and the importance of the issues at stake. Time was of particular importance in cases involving children or the very ill.

Key Principle: **Civil hearings should usually be public ones.**

Campbell and Fell v UK
For facts see p.84.

Held: There was a no breach of Article 6 in failing to hold the hearing in public since there were sufficient reasons of public order and security justifying the exclusion of the press and public. But there was no justifiable reason why the decision of the board should not have been made public and to this extent there was a violation of Article 6(1). (1984) 7 E.H.R.R. 165

Commentary
Article 6(1) lists grounds under which the press and public may be excluded from all or part of a trial. These are: the interests of morals, public order, national security, where the interests of juveniles or respect for the private life of the parties so require or to the extent strict publicity would prejudice the interests of justice. In *B v UK* and *P v UK* (2001), *The Times*, May 15, 2001 the court made it clear that the right to a public hearing is not

absolute and in this case a private hearing was in the interests of the children involved. In *Pelling v Bruce-Williams* [2004] the Court of Appeal overturned restrictions on the naming of the parties in a case involving children and said that such cases should not be automatically anonymised. Anonymity should be decided on a case-by-case basis.

Key principle: **Where there was a determination of rights under schemes of regulation and social welfare it was "inappropriate" to regard Article 6 as requiring in all cases that the primary facts and inferences from primary facts were to be fully within the remit of the independent and impartial judicial body.**

Runa Begum v Tower Hamlets London Borough Council (First Secretary of State intervening)

The claimant was offered accommodation by her local authority as a homeless person in priority need. She rejected the accommodation but the council's offer was upheld on review by a reviewing officer, who decided it was reasonable for her to accept the offer. The county court judge allowed her appeal under s.204 of the Housing Act 1996, but his decision was reversed by the Court of Appeal. She appealed and the Secretary of State intervened as an interested party.

Held: (HL) Assuming that the decision of the reviewing officer was a determination of the claimant's civil rights under Article 6(1) of the Convention, the extension of the fair trial principle to the administrative decision-making required substantial modification of the full judicial model. The reviewing officer as part of the council's administration was clearly not an independent tribunal, but the independence of the process could nonetheless be guaranteed by ensuring that the appellate court had jurisdiction to deal with the case as the nature of the decision required. The decision here involved a classic exercise of administrative discretion and convention judicial review provided sufficient safeguard for the claimant's rights. [2003] 2 A.C. 430

Commentary

This is another in a number of cases drawing a distinction between the requirements for administrative and judicial decision making.

It is not a breach of Article 6(1) for a decision to be taken by a tribunal which did not itself possess the necessary independence provided measures were in place to safeguard the fairness of the proceedings and the decision was subject to ultimate judicial control by an independent court.

Key Principle: Each party in civil proceedings must be afforded a reasonable opportunity to present his case, including his evidence, under conditions that do not place him at a substantial disadvantage with regard to his opponent.

McGinley and Egan v UK
The applicants had been refused a war pension. They claimed they suffered medical problems arising from their exposure to high levels of radiation. They complained that the Government had withheld documents which would have helped their claim.

Held: (ECtHR) There was an effective procedure for the determination of claims under the Pension Appeals Tribunal Rules 1981 which the applicants had failed to use. There was no breach of Article 6. (1999) 27 E.H.R.R. 1

Commentary
Although the court rejected the applicants' claim on the facts it emphasised that denial of access to documents which would assist a party's case was a breach of the right to a fair hearing. The court has insisted that the principle of the equality of arms means that proceedings which determine civil rights and obligations should be adversarial (see *Ruiz–Mateos v Spain* (1993) 16 E.H.R.R. 505). In *McMichael v UK* (1995) 20 E.H.R.R. 205 Article 6(1) was breached where parents in care proceedings were not given full disclosure of documents including social reports.

Reasons

Key Principle: Domestic courts should give reasons for their judgments.

Van de Hurk v Netherlands
The applicant, who owned a cowshed, claimed the procedure under which his claim to extend his milk quota was rejected

violated Article 6(1) on three counts. First his case had not been dealt with by an "independent and impartial" tribunal since the Crown and thus the minister could decide that a judgment of the industrial appeals tribunal should not be implemented; secondly he had not been afforded a "fair hearing" and thirdly the tribunal had not sufficiently dealt with the arguments he had advanced in a reasoned judgment.

Held: (ECtHR) Article 6(1) obliges courts to give reasons for their decisions but cannot be understood as requiring a detailed answer to every argument. The court did not find that the judgment of the industrial appeals tribunal was insufficiently reasoned. (1994) 18 E.H.R.R. 481

Commentary
The court did find a violation in the first of the applicant's claims but not in the second. One reason why it is important that reasons be given is so that parties can exercise their rights of appeal. Some civil trials are held in front of a jury who are not required to give reasons.

Costs

Key Principle: **There must be fair rules for allocating costs.**

Robins v UK
The applications arose out of a dispute between the applicants and their neighbours over sewerage. The applicants contended that the costs proceedings after the conclusion of the civil litigation were not concluded in a reasonable time, in violation of Article 6(1).

Held: (ECtHR) The legal costs were incurred during the resolution of the dispute which involved the termination of civil rights and obligations. Article 6(1) was violated in view of the unreasonable delay in dealing with the case. (1997) 26 E.H.R.R. 527

Commentary
The cost proceedings involved the Legal Aid Board and had taken four years to complete. The courts recognised that the state authorities could not be held responsible for the totality of the delays. However the Department of Social Security had been at fault and for a period of 16 months the court authorities had been

totally inactive. The Commission had held that costs proceedings after the civil litigation was over were not covered by Article 6(1) but the court disagreed stating that Article 6(1) "requires that all stages of legal proceedings for the determination of . . . Civil rights and obligations, not excluding stages subsequent to judgment on the merits, be resolved within a reasonable time. The ECHR is silent on whether the successful party should be awarded costs. It is implicit in *Robins* that all matters relating to costs should be settled fairly. The court stated in *Grepne v UK* [1990] 66 D.R. 268 that "it is not an unreasonable requirement of civil litigation that the unsuccessful party may have to pay the adversary's costs."

Key Principle: **High security for costs orders do not necessarily infringe Article 6(1).**

Tolstoy Miloslavsky v UK

The applicant had been successfully sued for libel by Lord Aldington whom he had accused in a pamphlet of arranging the perpetration of a major crime. Record damages were awarded by the jury in the High Court. The applicant wanted to appeal but was prevented from doing so by an order of the Court of Appeal that he pay into court nearly £125,000 within 14 days as security for his opponent's costs. He failed to do so and his appeal was dismissed. He complained that the damages award infringed his freedom of expression and that the security for costs order infringed his right to access to the Court of Appeal.

Held: (EctHR) Although the exceptionally high damages award infringed Article 10 there was no breach of Article 6. (1995) 20 E.H.R.R. 442

Commentary

The court stated that its task was not to "substitute itself for the competent British authorities in determining the most appropriate policy for regulating access to the Court of Appeal in libel cases nor to assess the facts which led the court to adopt one decision rather than another. The court's role is to review under the Convention the decision that those authorities have taken in the exercise of their powers of appreciation." The court stressed that it was here concerned with the appeal stage so its reasoning may not necessarily apply to orders for costs at the trial stage before evidence has been submitted.

Delay

Key Principle: **Delay in concluding civil proceedings may breach Article 6.**

Darnell v UK
The applicant, a consultant microbiologist with the Thames Regional Health Authority, had faced disciplinary hearings and been dismissed in 1984. His dismissal was confirmed two years later by the Secretary of State. The applicant successfully challenged the fairness of the procedure leading to his dismissal in a judicial review. The Secretary of State, having been asked to reconsider, confirmed the dismissal in 1988. Another application for judicial review was refused. In 1990 the industrial tribunal, whose proceedings had been stayed pending the outcome of the appeals, held the dismissal was not unfair. In 1993 the Employment Appeal Tribunal (E.A.T.) dismissed the appeal. The applicant contended that the period of nine years from his dismissal to the final E.A.T. ruling breached Article 6.

Held: (ECtHR) The long delay between the initial application to the Industrial Tribunal and the E.A.T. ruling was not reasonable. (1991) 69 D.R. 306

Commentary
The court has not applied a strict set of criteria for assessing whether the delay in civil cases is reasonable. A number of factors will be taken into account including the complexity of the case, the importance of the issue for the applicant, and the conduct of the courts and the applicant. Employment disputes are one example where fairness would require a prompt outcome (see *Obermeier v Germany*).

Employees

Key Principle: **Internal workplace disciplinary hearings do not attract the protection of Article 6.**

Darnell v UK
See above.

Held: (ECtHR) The period which engaged Article 6 did not include the time it took to hear the internal disciplinary hearings. (1991) 69 D.R. 306

Commentary

A number of commentators are sceptical about the potential impact of Article 6 on employment law matters. Professor Hepple has argued that Article 6 adds nothing to the procedural safeguards which exit under the Employment Tribunals Act 1996 for both private and public employees. See also *C v UK* where the Commission noted "whilst internal professional disciplinary proceedings against persons employed in public service may not attract the guarantees of Article 6(1) of the Convention, when a contract of employment, albeit in the public service, permits access to the civil courts to determine the respective civil liabilities of the parties, the proceedings before the normal courts may usually be said to determine civil rights and obligation within the meaning of Article 6(1) of the Convention." (1987) 54 D.R. 162

Key Principle: **The right to a reputation is a civil right but school exclusion proceedings do not embrace the determination of that right.**

R. (B, T and C) v Secretary of State for Education and Employment

The applicants had been excluded, expelled from or declined admission to various schools. Their appeals to the schools' independent appeal tribunals were rejected. They sought review of the decisions on the basis that they had a right to a good reputation, that this right was affected by the decisions of the tribunal and that they should be able to protect that civil right in a tribunal which observed the fair trial guarantees of Article 6(1).

Held: (DC) Article 6 did not apply. The issue in the case went to the content of the right to a reputation rather than its definition and so an authoritative definition of such a civil right was not needed. The content of a right to a reputation was "the right to enjoy a fair reputation". The appeal proceedings did not directly decide the reputations of the pupils and Article 6 did not apply to them. *The Times,* June 8, 2001

Commentary

In *Le Compte, Van Leuven and de Meyere v Belgium* (1982) E.H.R.R. 47 it was held that to gain the protection of Article 6 the hearing must be "directly decisive of the right in question". In deciding the nature of a civil right the court has looked at the character of the right and its classification in domestic law (*Konig v Germany* (1979–80) 2 E.H.R.R. 170) and also whether there is a uniform European practice (*Feldbrugge v Netherlands* (1986) 8 E.H.R.R. 425).

Key Principle: **Public law rights are not embraced within the definition of civil rights and so are not protected by Article 6.**

Balfour v UK
A former diplomat challenged his employers' use of PII in proceedings he had taken over his dismissal.

Held: (Commission) Application inadmissible since the applicant was a public official and Article 6(1) did not apply. (1997) E.H.R.L.R. 665

Commentary
One way that Article 6(1) may cover public sector employees is that some public employees may not be categorised as civil servants. In *C v UK* (1987) 54 D.R. 162 a school caretaker was entitled to claim Article 6 protection. The Commission noted: "whilst internal professional disciplinary proceedings against persons employed in public service may not attract the guarantees of Article 6(1) of the Convention, when a contract of employment, albeit in the public service, permits access to the civil courts to determine the respective civil liabilities of the parties, the proceedings before the normal courts may usually be said to determine civil rights and obligation within the meaning of Article 6(1) of the Convention." Proceedings over purely economic issues such as payment of a salary may be covered by Article 6. See also *Vogt v Germany* (1995) 21 E.H.R.R. 205 where it was held that German schoolteachers were not "members of the administration of the State" and there could be an issue of a civil right relating to freedom of expression in a dismissal case.

Key Principle: **The right not to be discriminated against on grounds of religious belief or political opinion in employment is a civil right within the meaning of Article 6(1).**

Devlin v UK

The applicant, a Catholic and a member of the Irish National Foresters, was unsuccessful in his application for a post of administrative assistant with Northern Ireland Civil Service. Following several appeals the Secretary of State for Northern Ireland issued a certificate stating that the reason for refusal of employment was an act "done for the purpose of safeguarding national security and protecting the public". He was refused permission to challenge this by judicial review. He complained that his rights under Article 6(1) were infringed.

Held: (ECtHR) Article 6 was applicable since the discrimination engaged a civil right. The applicant was not outside the protection of Article 6(1) by virtue of the fact that the post he was applying for was a civil service one. The test now laid down (following *Pelligrin v France*) only excluded from Article 6(1) disputes raised by public servants whose "duties typify the specific activities of the public service in so far as the latter is acting as the depository of public authority responsible for protecting the general interests of the State or other public authorities." (2002) 34 E.H.R.R. 43

Commentary

In this significant decision which revisits the decision in *Balfour* the court noted that the post of "administrative assistant" was not a post where it can be said the incumbent is "wielding a portion of the State's sovereign power" so as to exclude Article 6(1) rights. The right to a court was not absolute but any limitation must pursue a legitimate aim and there must be a reasonable relationship of proportionality between the means employed and the aim sought to be achieved. Here there was no independent scrutiny of the facts, and no evidence as to why the applicant was a security risk. Article 6(1) was breached.

Appeals

Key Principle: **A refusal of leave to appeal does not constitute a determination of civil rights and obligations.**

Porter v UK

The applicant claimed that a refusal of leave to appeal by the House of Lords violated Article 6(1).

Held: (Commission) The application was inadmissible since a refusal of leave did not constitute a determination of civil rights and obligations. [1987] 54 D.R. 207

Commentary
This position was reaffirmed by the Commission in *Comninos & National Justice Compania Naviera SA v UK* (1996) 23 E.H.R.R. CD.

6. PRIVACY AND FAMILY LIFE

Key Principle: **Article 8 of the ECHR—Right to respect for private and family life:**

"1 Everyone has the right to respect for his private and family life, his home and his correspondence.

2 There shall be no interference by a public authority with the exercise of this right except such as is in accordance with the law and is necessary in a democratic society in the interests of national security, public safety or the economic well-being of the country, for the prevention of disorder or crime, for the protection of health or morals, or for the protection of the rights and freedoms of others."

General

Key Principle: **There is a positive obligation on public authorities to protect the rights in Article 8.**

Johnston v Ireland
The first applicant's marriage broke down and he went to live with the second applicant. They had a daughter who was the third applicant. Because the Irish constitution did not allow divorce, the first two applicants were unable to marry, so their daughter was illegitimate. They claimed violations of Articles 8, 9, 12 and 14 of the Convention, concerning their inability to marry, the legal status of unmarried couples and the status of illegitimate children.

Held: (ECtHR) Articles 8, 9 and 12 were not violated by the absence of any provision for divorce. The public authorities had not interfered with the applicants' ability to live together. States were not obliged to establish for unmarried couples a status analogous to that of married couples, or a special regime for couples who would marry if there were divorce. Article 8 did however require that the daughter should be placed legally and socially in a position akin to that of a legitimate child. The absence of an appropriate legal regime reflecting the daughter's natural family ties was a breach of Article 8. (1987) 9 E.H.R.R. 203

Airey v Ireland

The applicant claimed that the absence of a provision for legal aid in civil proceedings for a judicial separation violated her right under Article 6 to a fair hearing for the determination of her civil rights, since it effectively denied her access to the courts. She also said Article 8 had been violated by the state's failure to provide an accessible legal procedure for the deter-mination of rights and obligations in family law.

Held: (ECtHR) Articles 6 and 8 had both been violated. Convention rights were intended to be practical and effective. It was not realistic to expect the applicant to conduct her own case in the High Court. (1979) 2 E.H.R.R. 305

Commentary

It is clear from this case that the state has a duty to protect the quality of a person's private life. In *Costello-Roberts* (see p.145) the court stated that although in some circumstances there might be a breach of Article 8 arising from physical punishment in a school,

> "having regard to the purpose and aim of the Convention taken as a whole and bearing in mind that the sending of a child to school necessarily involves some degree of interference with his or her private life, the court considers that the treatment complained of by the applicant did not entail adverse effects for his physical or moral integrity sufficient to bring it within the scope of the prohibition contained in Article 8."

Both these cases illustrate that although the ban on divorce was not in itself a breach of the Article, the state had a duty to protect children born out of wedlock. In *Airey* the court declared:

> "Although the object of Article 8 is essentially that of protecting the individual against arbitrary interference by public authorities, it does not merely compel the state to abstain from such interference. In addition to this primarily negative undertaking, there may be positive obligations inherent in an effective respect from private and family life."

Protecting family life also implies the right of divorced parents to have contact with their children. In *Hendricks v Netherlands* the Commission stated "The right to respect for family life within the meaning of Article 8 of the Convention includes the right of a divorced parent, who is deprived of custody following the break up of marriage, to have access to or contact with his child." The Convention recognises however that the child's interest will be overriding and on occasion this may require curtailing the access of a parent (see *Whitear v UK* (1997) E.H.R.L.R. 291).

Key Principle: **Even events which take place in public may raise questions of the right to privacy.**

Peck v UK

The applicant, who was suffering from depression, had slashed his wrists with a kitchen knife while walking down Brentwood High Street. The operator of a closed circuit television camera operated by the local authority saw the knife and called the police, who gave him medical assistance and arrested him under the Mental Health Act 1983. The council used the footage to publicise the effectiveness of its surveillance of the high street, and the video, on which the applicant was recognisable, appeared on local and national television. Recognisable pictures taken from the closed circuit TV clip were published in local newspapers. He complained to the Broadcasting Standards Authority that his privacy had been infringed. He also complained unsuccessfully to the Press Complaints Commission. Having been refused judicial review and denied permission to appeal, he took the case to Strasbourg.

Held: (ECtHR) The applicant's actions had been seen to an extent which far exceeded any exposure to a passer-by or to security observation and to a degree surpassing what he could possibly have foreseen. It was a serious interference with his right to respect for his private life. There was no justification for the local authority releasing still pictures of the applicant without his consent or for its failure to protect his identity. The fact that the applicant had subsequently appeared on television to complain about the treatment he had suffered did not diminish its seriousness. The law had failed to provide the applicant with an effective remedy for the violation of respect for his private life. [2003] 36 E.H.R.R. 719

Commentary
In previous decisions the Strasbourg Court had held that the right
to privacy was not violated by taking photographs in public places.
In *Peck* the court stated: " The present applicant was in a public
street but he was not there for the purposes of participating in any
public event and he was not a public figure". The case has
significance for local authorities and other public bodies who are
increasingly using CCTV. The seriousness with which the court
viewed the issues raised by the case is seen in the relatively high
award of damages.

Developing Right to Privacy

Key Principle: **The common law does not recognise a tort of
privacy.**

Kaye v Robertson
A newspaper reporter and photographer invaded the hospital
room of a television actor when he was recovering from serious
head injuries, violating hospital instructions. The actor obtained
an injunction requiring the newspaper to refrain from publishing the interview and photographs the journalists had obtained.
The newspaper editor and the publisher appealed.

Held: (CA) There was no right of action for breach of a
person's privacy. [1991] F.S.R. 62

Commentary
Glidewell L.J. stated: "the fact of the present case are a graphic
illustration of the desirability of Parliament considering whether
and in what circumstances statutory provision can be made to
protect the privacy of individuals." Bingham L.J. stated: "this case
none the less highlights, yet again, the failure of both the common
law of England and statute to protect in an effective way the
personal privacy of individual citizens." But although there was an
invasion of privacy the court decided it could do nothing. This
case has now to be considered in the light of *Douglas v Hello!* (see
below). The court reviewed the existing law on privacy. Referring
to *Kaye v Robertson* Brooke L.J. stated that in contrast to the
uncompromising position of the Court of Appeal in that case
"both academic commentary and extra-judicial commentary by
judges over the last 10 years have suggested from time to time that

a development of the present frontiers of the breach of confidence action could fill the gap in English law which is filled by privacy law in other countries". This commentary was given a boost recently by the decision of the European Commission of Human Rights in *Earl Spencer v UK* (1998) 25 E.H.R.R. CD 105, and by the coming into force of the HRA 1998. Sedley L.J. concluded that the Q.C. for the actors "has a powerfully arguable case to advance at trial that his two first named clients have a right to privacy which English law will today recognise and where appropriate, protect". He saw privacy as "a qualified right recognised and protected by English law". Regard had also to be given to Article 10 although this did not have a presumptive priority over other rights. In *Secretary of State for the Home Department v Wainwright, The Times*, January 4, 2002 the Court of Appeal held that since at common law there was no tort of invasion of privacy and because the conduct complained of occurred before the coming into force of the HRA the Act did not apply to introduce a right of privacy retrospectively.

Key Principle: **The test where information was private was whether a reasonable person of ordinary sensibilities in the claimant's position would find its disclosure offensive.**

Campbell v MGN Ltd

The claimant, a well-known model gave media interviews in which she claimed untruthfully that she did not take drugs. The defendant newspaper exposed her lies, showing that she was indeed taking drugs, and was attending meetings of Narcotics Anonymous. She was covertly photographed leaving a meeting of the drug-takers' help group. The claimant sued the newspaper for breach of confidentiality. She succeeded at first instance, but the Court of Appeal held that in the context the newspaper's disclosure of the fact that she was attending a self-help group was peripheral and a reasonable person of ordinary sensibilities would not find its disclosure offensive. She appealed.

Held: (HL) Appeal allowed. The test where information was private was whether a reasonable person of ordinary sensibilities in the claimant's position, would find its disclosure offensive. The details of the self-help therapy for drug addiction were akin to medical records and their publication required specific justification. Disclosure might deter a person in the claimant's position from continuing to attend the self-help group and setback her recovery. The publication of those details went beyond what was necessary to add credibility to the story that she had deceived the public. Though taken in a public place the photographs in context also intruded into her private life. The protection of her right to a private life outweighed the newspaper's right to freedom of expression and she was entitled to damages under Article 8. [2004] UKHL 22; [2004] 2 A.C. 457

Commentary
This decision seems to be confined to its own facts and is difficult to justify in principle. It remains a controversial decision. A minority of the Law Lords took the view articulated by Lord Hoffman that since judges were not newspaper editors, it was harsh in a case where the main substance of the story was justified, to hold the newspaper liable whenever the judge thought it had revealed too much personal information. This was especially so where three Court of Appeal judges had held the story to be perfectly justified. Striking a balance between Article 8 and Article 10 is likely to continue to cause problems with the courts.

Key principle: **The right to privacy is not a free-standing right in English law.**

Wainwright v Home Office
The claimants, a mother and her mentally impaired son, were strip-searched for drugs on a prison visit. The staff who conducted the search failed to follow the prison rules and humiliated the claimants who both won damages at first instance for trespass to the person and in the son's case for battery.The Court of Appeal allowed an appeal by the Home Secretary against the finding of trespass and reduced the son's damages. The claimants appealed.

Held: (HL) Appeals dismissed. Invasion of privacy was not a tort at common law. Legislation would be required to bring such a tort into existence. The UK did not need to create a free-standing right of privacy in order to fulfil its obligations under Article 8 of the European Convention. [2003] UKHL 53; [2004] 2 A.C. 406

Commentary
The House held that although privacy was a value underlying the law of breach of confidence it was not in itself a principle of law and there was no tort of the invasion of privacy. Article 8 did not require English law to develop such a tort. Lord Hoffman highlighted the difficulties of bringing a tort of privacy into being. It was important to distinguish between privacy as value underlying the existence of a legal rule and privacy as a principle of law itself.

Key Principle: **There is no free-standing right to privacy in English law but such a right may exist if there is a pre-existing legal relationship including contract.**

Douglas v Hello!
Two Hollywood stars, Michael Douglas and Catherine Zeta-Jones, gave exclusive publication rights in their wedding pictures to *OK!*, a celebrity magazine, retaining a veto over publication of particular photographs. All photography other than by the magazine's own photographer was banned: guests were searched for cameras on arrival, and the couple's employees signed undertakings that they would not take pictures at the wedding. Despite these precautions, photographs were taken surreptitiously at the wedding, and it came to the couple's notice that *Hello!*, a rival celebrity magazine, planned to publish them. It was not clear whether the photographs had been taken by a guest, an employee or an intruder. The claimants obtained an injunction to prevent the publication of the photographs pending trial of an action against *Hello!*, who then appealed.

Held: (CA) If the photographs had been taken by a guest or an employee, *Hello!* might rely on the existing law of confidence on the basis that the photographer had either acted (if an employee) in breach of contract, or (if a guest) in breach of confidence. However if the photographs had been taken by an intruder who was not under an obligation of confidence towards the couple, there was no relationship of trust on which the existing law could bite. In those circumstances the law recognised that it had to protect not only those whose trust had been abused, but also those whose personal lives were subjected to unwarranted intrusion. Sedley L.J. said the law no longer required the construction of an artificial relationship of confidentiality between intruder and victim. Privacy itself could be acknowledged as a legal principle drawn from the fundamental value of personal autonomy. In this particular case the court discharged the injunction against *Hello!*, on the basis that the judge who had granted to the injunction had failed to give his reasons. The case is also important because it establishes that the provision in Article 10(2) permitting restriction of the right of freedom of expression "for the protection of the reputation or rights of others" is to be given as much weight as the substantive right itself in deciding whether to order an injunction limiting freedom of expression. [2001] 2 W.L.R. 992 (CA)

Commentary
The court also considered s.12 of the HRA (see p.185) which prohibits prior restraint unless the claimant establishes a strong case that the restraint is justified. The court treated it as a balancing mechanism between existing codes of practice on privacy and freedom of the press. Breach of the Press Complaints Commission code was likely, Brooke L.J. said, to result in the grant of an injunction since the claimant's rights under Article 10(2) would then "trump" the publication's right to freedom of expression. The court extended the existing law on confidentiality to situations where the party that was intruding had no relationship of trust or confidence with the claimant. The court took the view that "a development of the present frontiers of a breach of confidence action could fill the gap in English law which is filled by privacy law in other developed countries." But it stopped short of creating a new cause of action which would have meant interpreting the HRA to have horizontal effect. In *A v B and C Plc, The Times*, March 13, 2002 the Court of Appeal set aside an injunction granted by Jack J. restraining a Sunday newspaper from naming a footballer, married with a family, who had sex with two women in one session. The story had been sold to the newspaper by one of the women. Jack J. had held that the law of confidentiality could apply to sexual relationships regardless of the existence of an express agreement to treat the matters as confidential. There was no public interest in the publication of the articles and the information they contained. The appeal court, however, held that a public figure should recognise that his actions would be closely scrutinised by the media whether or not he had courted publicity. The courts should not act as censors and arbiters of taste. The judge had ignored the importance of a free press. He should not have assumed that it was in the interests of the footballer's wife to

be kept in ignorance and he had been wrong to say there was no element of public interest in the disclosure, since the public and the media would inevitably be interested in the doings of a well-known footballer. An injunction would be an unjustified infringement of press freedom. It has been noted that there is now an emergent "right of celebrity" (see *The Times Law*, February 5, 2002, p.7) with the courts affording greater protection to public figures than the voluntary Press Complaints Commission. Litigation resulting from the Douglas-Zeta Jones nuptials had not concluded as this book went to press. In the latest proceedings, the Court of Appeal [2005] EWCA Civ 595 applied the European Court decision in *Von Hannover v Germany* (2005) 40 E.H.R.R. 1, a case brought by Princess Caroline of Monaco which stressed the need to give a high degree of protection against invasions of privacy by the press. The Court of Appeal held that the courts should do this by developing the action for breach of confidence so as to uphold rights under Articles 8 and 10. The Court appeared to urge legislation to protect privacy, when it commented: "We cannot pretend that we find it satisfactory to be required to shoe-horn within the cause of action of breach of confidence claims for publication of unauthorised pictures of a private occasion." Recent House of Lords authority established that the knowledge, actual or imputed, that information is private would normally impose on anyone publishing that information the duty to justify what, in the absence of justification, will be a wrongful invasion of privacy. It also showed that, in cases where privacy and freedom of expression were both involved, the court did not start with the balance tilted in favour of freedom of expression. Special considerations attached to photographs. Even where some photographs of an event were published, others of the same event might be protected from publication, since photographs were particularly intrusive and revealing. The decision also establishes that privacy rights are personal and cannot be traded as if they were commercial rights. It followed that OK! Magazine, which had bought the exclusive right to publish pictures of the wedding, had no privacy claim against Hello! The level of damages awarded to the Douglases for the privacy breach was relatively low, £3,750 apiece. This strongly suggests that damages in future cases will be sensibly restricted.

Key Principle: **The law of confidence could, exceptionally, be extended to cover information as to the identity or where-**

abouts of individuals where its disclosure would put them at risk of serious injury or death.

Venables v News Group Newspapers Ltd

Jon Venables and Robert Thompson, the killers of two-year-old James Bulger, were sentenced to be detained at Her Majesty's pleasure. They were aged 11 when they committed the crime, and when they reached 18 became eligible for parole. The mother of their victim headed an influential campaign against the grant of parole, and several newspapers wished to publish up-to-date photographs of the boys and details of their present whereabouts. Thompson and Venables sought a continuing injunction against such publication on the basis that injunctions were necessary to protect their rights of confidentiality and their rights to life and freedom from persecution and harassment under the Convention.

Held: (Fam. Div.) The ECHR did not give rise in private law proceedings to a free-standing cause of action based on Convention rights but the court as a public authority was obliged to act compatibly with Convention rights in adjudicating on common law causes of action, and had by s.12(4) of the HRA to give direct effect to the right to freedom of expression under Article 10. Freedom of the media could be restricted only if the need for restrictions was such that they were in accordance with the law, necessary in a democratic society and proportionate to the legitimate aim pursued. The law of confidentiality could extend to cover information about the identity and whereabouts of people in circumstances where publication could put their lives at risk. The injunctions were necessary to protect the applicants against the "real and strong possibility" of physical harm or death. Injunction granted against the whole world to stop publication of the identity and whereabouts of the claimants. [2001] 2 W.L.R. 1038

Commentary

The court was here applying *Douglas v Hello! Ltd.* These cases illustrate that a new right is developing out of existing law. Butler-Sloss P. referred to the rights of the boys under Articles 2 and 3 as well as 8 and stated:

> "under the umbrella of confidentiality there will be information which may require a special quality of protection. In the present case the reason for advancing that special quality is that, if the information

was published, the publication would be likely to lead to grave and possibly fatal consequences. In my judgement, the court does have the jurisdiction, in exceptional cases, to extend the protection of confidentiality even to impose restrictions on the press, where not to do so would be likely to lead to serious physical injury, or to death, of the person seeking that confidentiality and there is no other way to protect the applicant other than by seeking relief from the court."

It must be emphasised that this case was a particularly extreme example because the invasion of privacy might lead to threats to the lives of the boys. This is another case in which legal concepts of confidentiality have been stretched to the limit to impose restraint on the media. It demonstrates the judiciary's considerable power and discretion within the new regime brought about by the HRA. See also *Re A (Children, Conjoined Twins: Surgical Separation)* [2001] 2 W.L.R. 480.

Physical Integrity

Key Principle: **Article 8 may offer protection for physical integrity beyond that of Article 3.**

Costello-Roberts v UK
The applicant had been beaten as a punishment at an independent boarding school. Violations of Articles 3, 8 and 13 were alleged.

Held: (ECtHR) The treatment did not entail adverse effects for physical or moral integrity sufficient to bring it within the scope of the prohibition in Articles, 3 or 8. (1993) 19 E.H.R.R. 112

Commentary
The court accepted that there might be circumstances where Article 8 offered protection beyond that of Article 3 in relation to physical assault. (See also pp.42, 136).

Privacy at Work

Key Principle: **Individuals have a right to "private life" at work.**

Niemietz v Germany
Police searched the premises of a lawyer seeking information which would reveal the identity and possible whereabouts of a

suspect. The lawyer complained that the search violated his right under Article 8 to respect for his home and correspondence and had impaired the goodwill of his law office and his professional reputation.

Held: (ECtHR) The right to respect for private life included the right to develop relationships with others. Article 8 could not be applied equally to all unless professional and business activities were included in the notions of "home" and "family life". The fact that correspondence examined by the police was of a professional nature did not render Article 8 inapplicable. Though the interference was prescribed by law and intended to prevent crime it was not necessary in democratic society. (1993) 16 E.H.R.R. 97

Halford v UK

A senior police officer complained that telephone calls made from her office and from her home had been intercepted without warning, in violation of her rights to respect for private life and freedom of expression.

Held: (ECtHR) Telephone calls made from business premises were covered by the notions of private life and correspondence in Article 8. Employees making calls on an internal telephone system operated by their employer should have a reasonable expectation of privacy. Since domestic law did not regulate the interception of calls on an internal system the interception was not "in accordance with the law", as Article 8 required. There was insufficient evidence to determine whether or not the claimant's home phone had been tapped. (1997) 24 E.H.R.R. 523

Commentary

As a result of the latter case the Government introduced a statutory procedure to regulate interception of internal telecommunications systems, the Regulation of Investigatory Powers Act 2000 which affects the privacy of employees. The Government may now argue that interference is in accordance with the law although it is still open to the courts to declare the statute incompatible with the Convention.

Key principle: **Article 8 could be engaged in unfair dismissal claims.**

X v Y

The claimant was employed by a charity catering for young offenders. He was cautioned for gross indecency with a man in a public lavatory, but did not tell his employer. The employer found out about the incident and sacked the claimant for gross misconduct. He claimed unfair dismissal, and maintained that the sacking involved a breach of his rights under Articles 8 and 14 of the European Convention since an act of gross indecency could not be committed by a heterosexual couple or by two women, making him a victim of discrimination. The Employment Tribunal and the Employment Appeal Tribunal both dismissed the claim. The claimant appealed.

Held: (CA) Appeal dismissed. Tribunals should hear claims that a claimant's human rights had been breached in an employment context, since s.3 of the Human Rights Act 1998 drew no distinction between legislation governing public authorities and legislation governing private individuals. But on the facts the claimant's conduct did not take place in his private life, so Articles 8 and 14 were not engaged and no issues of compatibility with the European Convention arose. The employer had been entitled to treat the caution as an acceptance of guilt in a criminal offence. [2004] EWCA Civ 662; [2004] I.C.R. 1634

Commentary

Mummery L.J. stated that if an employee in a public authority is dismissed in breach of Article 8 or 14 then the dismissal will be unfair but it will not normally be unfair for a private sector employee to be dismissed for a reason which is an unjustified breach of Article 8. Section 98 of Employment Rights Act should be construed so as to give effect to Convention rights as was required by s.3 HRA.

Family life

Key Principle: **Legislation which discriminates against children born outside marriage is a violation of the right to respect for family life.**

Marckx v Belgium

A woman and her young daughter complained that Belgian illegitimacy law violated Article 8 and other provisions of the

Convention because it required a formal act of recognition to establish maternal affiliation and limited the mother's capacity to give or bequeath and the child's capacity to take or inherit property.

Held: (ECtHR) The legislation failed to respect the applicants' family life contrary to Article 8 and amounted to discrimination under Article 14 because there was no objective and reasonable justification for the different treatment of legitimacy and illegitimacy. (1979) 2 E.H.R.R. 330

Commentary
In this case the court recognised that the concept of a family should be a broadly interpreted one and one which should reflect changing social views. It stated that family life encompasses "at least ties between near relatives, for instance those between grandparents and grandchildren", since such relatives play a considerable part in family life.

Key Principle: **The rights of parents whose children have been removed from the home by a public authority must be protected.**

W v UK
The applicant complained that his access to his child in care had been terminated without due process. He had no viable remedy against the decision to terminate access and some of the proceedings had been over-long.

Held: (ECtHR) The natural family relationship was not terminated when the child was taken into care, so decisions restricting access to the child were interferences with rights under Article 8 and required to be justified. Though the authorities must be allowed some discretion, the need for protection against arbitrary interference was even greater, so it was open to the court to review it. The parents had not been involved in the process to a degree sufficient to provide them with the means of protecting their interests. (1988) 10 E.H.R.R. 29

Responsibilities of public authorities

Key Principle: **State agencies concerned with the welfare of families must consider the rights of individuals in their charge and involve them in any decision-making process.**

TP v UK
A local authority suspected that a child to whom it owed duties under the Child Care Act 1980 was being abused. The child took part in a video interview stating that she had been sexually abused by a man with the same name as her mother's boyfriend but not the boyfriend. The authority placed the child in a place of safety. One year later the mother saw the video. The mother alleged that the delay in providing the video was a breach of Article 8 since as a result the mother had not been able to take part in a meaningful way in the decisions over the child.

Held: (ECtHR) There was a breach of Article 8 and a failure to respect family life. The question whether to disclose the video should have been determined promptly to allow the applicant an effective opportunity to deal with the allegations that her daughter could not be returned safely to her care. App. No. 28945/95

Commentary
For the case's application to Article 6, along with *Z v UK* and the law of negligence see p.118. The case establishes that it is important that family members are involved in cases concerning children.

Abortion

Key Principle: **Legislation which which restricts abortion may be justified.**

Brüggemann and Scheuten v Federal Republic of Germany
Two women claimed that German law restricting abortion breached their rights under Article 8. The restrictions forced them to use other methods of contraception including renouncing sexual intercourse.

Held: (Commission) Article 8 was engaged since it embraces the right to establish sexual relationships with others. There was no breach because Article 8(1) could not be interpreted to mean that pregnancy and abortion are solely within the choice of the mother. (1976) 5 D.R. 103

Commentary
The Commission noted that many of the contracting states had laws which set up regulations for the conduct of pregnancy and abortion. In this sensitive area the concept of the margin of appreciation is especially important. For other judgments relating to abortion see also p.55.

Homosexuality

Key Principle: **Article 8 is violated by a state's prohibition of homosexual acts between consenting adults.**

Dudgeon v UK
The applicant, a resident of Belfast, complained that Northern Ireland law forbidding buggery and gross indecency amounted to unjustified interference with his right to respect for his private life under Article 8. He also claimed to have been discriminated against on sexual grounds and on grounds of his residence since such offences did not exist in the rest of the United Kingdom.

Held: (ECtHR) The prohibition on private homosexual conduct in Northern Ireland was an interference with the right to respect for private life, being unnecessary in a democratic society. The applicant's rights were not breached by the fact that homosexual acts were prohibited between persons under 21 years old. (1982) 4 E.H.R.R. 149

Commentary
The prosecution of sado-masochistic practices was not however a violation in *Laskey, Jaggard and Brown v UK* (1996) 24 E.H.R.R. 1. A key issue is whether the interference with private life is "necessary in a democratic society". Thus in *ADT v UK* (2000) App. No. 35765/97 there was a violation of Article 8 in a prosecution for gross indecency of a man who engaged in oral sex and mutual masturbation with four other men. Since the activities were of a non-violent nature the interferences fell outside the

narrow margin of appreciation allowed to the state and could not be justified.

Key Principle: **Different ages of consent for heterosexuals and homosexuals is a violation of Article 8 in combination with Article 14.**

Sutherland v UK
The applicant argued that the fixing of the minimum age for lawful homosexual activities at 18 was a violation of his rights to respect for his private life and was a violation of Article 14 since the age of consent was 16 years for heterosexual activities.

Held: (Commission) There was a violation of Articles 8 and 14 despite the fact that the applicant had not been prosecuted or threatened with prosecution. There was no objective and reasonable justification for the maintenance of a higher minimum age of consent to male homosexual rather than to heterosexual acts. (1998) 24 E.H.R.R. CD 22

Commentary
The Commission referred to the words of the court's judgment in *Dudgeon* that decriminalisation does not imply approval. It was not a good ground for maintaining the different age that some of the sectors of the population might otherwise be drawn misguided conclusions.

Key Principle: **Sexuality is a private matter and rules which invade people's privacy as to their sexuality or which discriminate on the grounds of sexuality may be a violation of Article 8.**

Smith and Grady v UK
Investigation into the applicants' homosexuality resulted in their discharge from the navy in pursuit of a policy of excluding homosexuals from the forces. The applicants complained of degrading treatment and violation of their right to a private life. They also complained that they had no effective remedy.

Held: (ECtHR) Though the interference with the applicants' right to respect for private life was "in accordance with law" and could be said to pursue legitimate national security aims, the perceived problems of allowing homosexuals in the armed forces were not justified because they were founded solely on the negative attitudes of heterosexual personnel. Article 8 had been violated, but the applicants' treatment was not so severe as to constitute degrading treatment. (2000) 29 E.H.R.R. 493

Commentary
The British Government had not produced convincing or weighty reasons to justify the policy on homosexuals in the armed forces. The case also established that employees' rights to privacy were invaded contrary to Article 8 when they were questioned intensively about their sexuality and relationships in cases involving personnel discharged from the armed forces on grounds of homosexuality. See also *Lustig-Prean and Beckett v UK* (2000).

Key Principle: **Homosexual relationships do not fall within the scope of the right to respect for family life ensured by Article 8.**

X and Y v UK
The applicants who were in a stable homosexual relationship complained that there was a violation of Articles 8 and 14 in that the United Kingdom immigration authorities had refused to allow the first applicant who was a Malaysian citizen the right to remain with the second applicant who was a British citizen.

Held: (Commission) The complaints were ill-founded since such relationships did not fall within the scope of the right to respect for family life ensured by Article 8. The right to respect for family life does not necessarily include the right to choose the geographical location of that family. (1983) 5 E.H.R.R. 601

Transsexuals and Gender Reassignment

See p.8.

Surveillance and Data Collection

Key Principle: **Secret surveillance by state authorities is tolerable only insofar as it is strictly necessary for safeguarding democratic institutions.**

Klass v Federal Republic of Germany

The applicants claimed violation of Articles 6 and 8 arising from German legislation which permitted the authorities to open their letters and monitor telephone conversations. They had no right to be informed of the surveillance and no recourse to the courts when the surveillance was ended.

Held: (ECtHR) States did not enjoy unlimited power to subject persons to covert surveillance and must provide adequate safeguards against abuse. The surveillance was in accordance with law, was necessary in the interests of national security and contained procedural safeguards. Failure to inform a person that they had been under surveillance was not in principle incompatible with Article 8(2). There was no violation of Article 8. (1979–80) 2 E.H.R.R. 214

Commentary

With reference to Article 8 the court stated that there must be "a balance between the exercise by the individual of the right guaranteed to him under paragraph 1 and the necessity under paragraph 2 to impose secret surveillance for the protection of the democratic society as a whole". It is clear that the main aim of Article 8 is to prevent individuals from being subject to arbitrary interference in their private lives. It is accepted that some interference by the state is necessary. In *MS v Sweden* (1999) 28 E.H.R.R. 313 the handing over of the applicant's medical confidential records to the Social Insurance Office was an interference with the right to privacy but it was justified since it was with the legitimate aim of the economic well being of the country in protecting public funds in a claim for compensation.

Malone v UK

The applicant had brought a civil action claiming that interception of his telephone calls during a police investigation was unlawful. The Government denied that his telephone had been tapped but conceded that he did belong to a class of persons liable to telephone interception since he was suspected of dishonestly handling stolen goods. Under existing law the police should have obtained a warrant issued by the Home Secretary before intercepting calls. The applicant claimed a violation of Article 8.

Held: (ECtHR) The law did not make clear sufficiently the scope and manner of exercise of the discretion conferred on police authorities. There was a violation of Article 8 since the interference was not in accordance with law. (1984) 7 E.H.R.R. 14

Commentary
The case led to the passing of legislation which placed such interception on a statutory footing.

Key Principle: **Article 8 may be violated if surveillance by investigatory bodies is not in accordance with law.**

Khan v UK
The applicant had flown to England from Pakistan on the same plane as his cousin who was found on arrival to be carrying prohibited drugs. Later the applicant visited premises which had secretly been bugged by the police drugs squad. In the course of conversation he admitted that he too had brought drugs into the country. The recording of the conversation was the only evidence at the applicant's trial, where he was convicted. He complained that the use made of the recorded conversation breached Articles 6, 8 and 13 of the Convention.

Held: (ECtHR) The bugging could not be considered to be "in accordance with law", since there was no statutory regulation of police surveillance, and Article 8 had been violated. But the use made of the recording had not undermined the fairness of the applicant's trial, since the applicant had been given every opportunity to challenge the admission of the evidence. (2001) 31 E.H.R.R. 45

Commentary
The court also considered that there had been a violation of Article 13 of the European Convention on Human Rights since the United Kingdom had not provided any remedy for the breach of Article 8.

Thus, irrespective of whether using such evidence makes a trial unfair, it may now be necessary to provide a remedy for breach of Article 8 in such circumstances. Under the Regulation of Investigatory Powers Act 2000 statutory guidelines have been set for state surveillance. Police action in secretly filming defendants in the cell area of a magistrates' court was held to be unlawful and a breach of their right to privacy since it was not in accordance with the law and could not be justified. However a judge had been entitled to admit the film in evidence at the defendants' trial as it had not interfered with the fairness of the trial; see *R. v Loveridge, The Times*, May 3, 2001. Overall the Strasbourg jurisprudence does not give clear answer on whether video surveillance is a breach of Article 8. In *JS v UK* (1993) the Commission rejected a complaint that covert surveillance by an insurance company was a breach of Article 8. On the grounds that the company's activities did not engage the responsibility of the state. See also *Perry v UK* (2003).

Key Principle: A general policy of retention of fingerprints and DNA profiles and samples taken from suspects who subsequently were not convicted did not contravene Article 8 or 14.

R. (S) v Chief Constable of the South Yorkshire Police; R. (Marper) v Chief Constable of Yorkshire Police (HL)
In the two cases the police retained fingerprints and DNA samples taken from suspects who were subsequently acquitted or not proceeded against. The suspects were told that the police were acting in accordance with s.64(1A) of the Police and Criminal Evidence Act 1984. The claimants sought judicial review on the basis that the retention of their DNA and fingerprints when they had not been convicted was a violation of their Article 8 right to privacy and their right under Article 14 not to be discriminated against. Their appeals from the Divisional Court's refusal of judicial review were dismissed by the Court of Appeal and the claimants appealed.

Held: (HL) The appeals were dismissed. The retention of fingerprints and DNA samples did not engage Article 8(1), but even if it was engaged, there was an objective reason within the meaning of Article 8(2) for keeping the prints and samples. Nor was there any breach of Article 14, since it was not a case involving discrimination on a proscribed ground, there was sufficient objective justification for keeping the prints to combat serious crime and the measure was not disproportionate. [2004] 1 W.L.R. 2196

Commentary

Section 82 of the Criminal Justice and Police Act 2001 had amended s.64 of the Police and Criminal Evidence Act 1984 to permit the retention of this evidence. Lord Steyn said that this amended section could play a significant role in the elimination of the innocent, the correction of miscarriages of justice and the detection of the guilty. Such "real evidence" had inestimable value.

Immigrants

Key Principle: **Applicants for immigration must demonstrate obstacles to establishing family life in their mother country for refusal of admission by a state to be a violation of Article 8.**

Abdulaziz, Cabales and Balkandali v UK

The applicants were lawfully and permanently settled in the United Kingdom, but under the immigration rules their husbands were refused permission to remain. The applicants claimed violations of Article 8.

Held: (ECtHR) Articles 8 and 14 had been violated on the grounds of sex, since the rules were stricter for husbands who wanted to stay than for wives. Contracting states enjoyed a wide margin of appreciation in determining steps to be taken to comply with the Convention. Although states had a margin of appreciation in determining whether differences in otherwise similar situations required different treatment in law, it was in the last analysis a matter for the court to decide. (1985) 7 E.H.R.R. 471

Commentary

This case illustrates that Article 8 cannot invalidate immigration controls in themselves. The court commented that ". . . the duty imposed by Article 8 cannot be considered as extending to a general obligation on the part of the contracting state to respect the choice by married couples of the country of their matrimonial residence and to accept the non-national spouse for settlement in that country."

Key Principle: **Where a fundamental right, such as family life, was engaged a court would insist that the decision-maker must demonstrate either that his proposed action did not interfere with that right or if it did that considerations existed which might reasonably be accepted as amounting to a substantial objective justification for the interference.**

R. (Mahmood) v Secretary of State for Home Department

The applicant faced removal as an illegal entrant though by the time the decision was taken to remove him he had married a woman legally settled in Britain and had two children. He claimed that his right to family life had been unlawfully interfered with.

Held: (CA) The decision-maker had to demonstrate either that his proposed action did not in truth interfere with the right, or if it did, that considerations existed which might reasonably be accepted as amounting to a substantial objective justification for the interference. Here there was interference but it was justified in the interests of orderly and fair control of immigration. [2001] 1 W.L.R. 840

Key Principle: **In reviewing executive decisions, including those which concern the effect of Article 8 on a deportation order made against an immigrant with no right to remain in the United Kingdom, the courts will acknowledge the extent of a discretionary area of judgment.**

R. (Isiko) v Secretary of State for the Home Department

The applicant faced deportation as an illegal immigrant. While under threat of deportation he had married a United Kingdom citizen who had a British child by a previous marriage. Since the child could not lawfully be separated from her father, the effect of the deportation would be to separate the applicant and his wife.

Held: It was lawful under the Convention for a state to have an immigration policy and the mere fact that its implementation could interfere with family life did not render the policy unlawful. The elected government of a country was entitled to lay down and enforce a general policy which did not offend the principle of proportionality. A deportation could be a disproportionate application of the policy, but in the instant case the Home Secretary had been entitled to deport. (2001) 1 F.L.R. 930

Commentary

These two cases raise similar issues of the extent to which the courts would defer to Parliament and executive bodies. In *Mahmood* Laws L.J. stated: "The Human Rights Act does not authorise the judges to stand in the shoes of Parliament's delegates, who are decision-makers given their responsibilities by the democratic arm of the state. . ." In *Isiko* the court recognised that "there will be an area of judgment within which the judiciary will defer, on democratic grounds, to the considered opinion of the elected body or person whose decision is said to be incompatible." This area, however, is an evolving one, see *R. v Secretary of State for the Home Department Ex p. Daly* [2001] on proportionality as a new ground of review, below.

Prisoners

Key Principle: **A prisoner's right to uncensored correspondence with a lawyer or judicial body is a fundamental aspect of access to justice.**

Golder v UK

A prisoner in Parkhurst was accused by a prison officer of having taken part in a disturbance. The officer later withdrew the allegation and the prisoner petitioned for the right to consult a solicitor with a view to bringing a libel action against the officer. The Home Secretary refused. The applicant claimed his right of access to justice under Article 6 had been denied.

Held: (ECtHR) The rule of law was scarcely conceivable without the possibility of access to the courts. Though the right was not absolute, the refusal of access to a solicitor had deprived the prisoner of his rights under Article 6 and under Article 8, since it was not necessary in a democratic society that he be prevented from instructing a solicitor. (1979–1980) 1 E.H.R.R. 524

R. (Daly) v Secretary of State for the Home Department

A prisoner kept in his cell correspondence with his solicitor about his security categorisation reviews and parole. He complained that prison officers following standard procedure had searched his cell in his absence and had examined, though they had not read, the correspondence with the solicitor.

Held: (HL) A prisoner retained, along with the right of access to the courts and to legal advice, the right to communicate confidentially with a legal adviser under the seal of legal professional privilege, that such rights could be curtailed only by express words and then only to the extent reasonably necessary to meet the ends which justified infringement, in this case the need to maintain security, order and discipline and prevent crime. The provision that privileged correspondence should always be examined in the prisoner's absence was void. [2001] 2 W.L.R. 1622

Commentary

The House of Lords here drew the conclusion that proportionality is a matter of law which is a ground of review. The result is likely to be that in cases involving human rights the courts will be more rigorous and robust in reviewing decisions of the executive. (See also p.158.)

Key Principle: **Any interference with family life had to be justified under Article 8(2) of the Convention.**

R. (P and Q and QB) v Secretary of State for Home Department

Under a Prison Service Order issued in May 2000, babies with their mothers in prison would be separated from their mothers at the age of 18 months. The applicants appealed against the dismissal of their application for a judicial review of the policy stating that such a policy was a violation of Article 8.

Held: (CA) Article 8 confers not an absolute right to family life but a right to respect for family life. There were necessary limitations on women who were imprisoned. In the great majority of cases mother and child would be separated at 18 months but rare cases would exist where the interests of mother and child outweighed other interests. Appeal for P dismissed and that of Q allowed. [2001] U.K.H.R.R. 1035

Commentary

The case is of interest also because the court stated that it would have reached a different decision had the HRA not been in force.

See also *X v UK* (1983) 5 E.H.R.R. 260 and *R. (Lalley) v Secretary of State for Health* (2001) 1 F.L.R. 406 and *R. (Mellor) v Secretary of State for Home Department* (p.167). In the same case, in the Divisional Court, it was considered that the prison service was operating a reasonable balance between the various considerations which was not flawed. It was not for the courts to intervene and run prisons. In this and a number of other cases the courts have adopted a cautious approach to interfering with prison policy.

Key Principle: **In interpreting the Rehabilitation of Offenders Act 1974 the court should uphold its national and international obligations in the field of child protection.**

N v Governor of Dartmoor Prison

The claimant had been convicted of a child sex offence in 1992 and by 1999 this conviction was "spent" pursuant to the Rehabilitation of Offenders Act 1974. In January 2000 he was convicted of drugs offences and sentenced to prison. The governor told the local social services department of the sentence and his release date. He did this following Prison Service instructions which required the governor to minimise the risk that prisoners convicted of sexual offences may present to children under 18 years.

Held: (QBD) On a proper construction of the 1974 Act the governor was committed to disclose the information to social services. It would make it difficult to comply with obligations under the UN Convention on the Rights of the Child 1989 if another interpretation was adopted. Also the impact of Articles 2, 3, 8 compelled the same approach. Owing to their vulnerability, children are accorded a special place in terms of international conventions both UN and ECHR. It is their human rights which have a high need of domestic protection. Balancing this with the invasion of the privacy of the applicant the balance was in terms of necessity on the side of the governor's decision. *The Times*, March 20, 2001

Commentary

It is clear that the rights of children and the responsibilities of the authorities to protect them are overwhelming over those of a prisoner who had not offended against children for eight years.

Home and Environment

Key Principle: **Article 8 does not reasonably go so far as to allow individuals' preference as to their place of residence to override the general interest.**

Buckley v UK

A gypsy and her three children lived in caravans parked on land which she owned. The district council refused her retrospective planning permission for the caravans and served a notice requiring their removal from the site.

Held: (ECtHR) The case concerned respect for the applicant's home. There was no doubt that the council's decision was made in pursuit of legitimate aims of public safety and national economic well-being. The means to achieve these aims were not disproportionate and did not exceed the state's margin of appreciation. (1997) 23 E.H.R.R. 101

Commentary

The European Court of Human Rights has considered the question of gypsies in two subsequent cases. In *Connors v UK* (*The Times*, June 10, 2004) it set out some general principles. It stated that:

> "The procedural safeguards available to the individual will be especially material in determining whether the respondent state has, when fixing the regulatory framework, remained with its margin of appreciation. In particular the court must examine whether the decision making process leading to measures of interference was fair and such as to afford due respect to the interests safeguarded to the individual by Article 8. . . The vulnerable position of gypsies means that some special consideration should be given to their needs and their different lifestyles both in the relevant regulatory framework and in reaching decisions in particular cases."

The Court referred to *Chapman v UK* (2001) as indicating that "there is a positive obligation imposed on the contracting states by virtue of Article 8 to facilitate the gypsy way of life." In *Connors* the availability of judicial review was not a sufficient procedural safeguard and there was a violation of Article 8 (see below).

Key principle: **Article 8 gives rise to a right to respect for a person's home as an aspect of the right to privacy but it does not give a right to a home.**

Harrow LBC v Qazi

The defendant and his wife were joint tenants of a council flat. The wife left the man and terminated the tenancy. The defendant's application to the council for sole tenancy was refused, but he continued to live in the flat and when he remarried brought his new wife there. When the local authority sought possession he resisted on Article 8 grounds. The housing authority's appeal reached the House of Lords.

Held: (HL) Article 8 could not be relied on to defeat proprietary or contractual rights to possession. In domestic law the council had a right to immediate possession under the clear terms of the original tenancy. The possession proceedings were not a violation of the defendant's rights under Article 8. [2004] 1 A.C. 983

Commentary

In the Court of Appeal the case turned on the narrower issue of whether the concept of "home" for the purposes of Article 8 of the European Convention is confined to dwellings or land which is lawfully occupied. The House of Lords agreed with the Court of Appeal unanimously that it was not so confined. A powerful minority judgment stated that all proceedings for possession of a home engaged Article 8 but the majority view was that to allow Article 8 to vest property rights in the tenant, and consequently diminish the landlord's rights, would attribute to Article 8 an effect it was not intended to have. Clayton, Keen and Dunlop (sup.cit p.10) comment, "The decision in *Qazi* is somewhat surprising. The idea that legal form trumps substance is alien to the Strasbourg jurisprudence; and Strasbourg cases certainly do not dictate the result". In March 2004 however, the European Court of Human Rights decided that Mr Qazi's application did not disclose any appearance of a breach of the Convention and declared his application inadmissible.

The English courts are thus taking the position that once a landowner asserts lawful ownership of premises the occupier has no proprietary right to respect for a home under Article 8. Gypsies however might be considered a special case. In *Connors v UK* the

ECtHR held there was a breach of a number of Convention rights including Article 8 when the licence of a gypsy family to occupy land was terminated on the basis of nuisance allegations. The local authority had decided to evict the applicant and his family on the expiry of notices to quit. In another tenancy case which applied in *Qazi, Gavin Kay v (1) London Borough of Lambeth and (2) Quadrant Housing Trust* (2004) 3 W.L.R. 1396, the Court of Appeal observed that the general statement of principle in the Strasbourg's Court's judgment in *Connors* drew on *Buckley v UK* and *Chapman v UK* (see above). Both of these had been cited in the House of Lord's decision in *Qazi*. The Court of Appeal in *Gavin Kay* concluded that, "The *Connors* case is therefore only of assistance to the courts of this country in relation to cases involving gypsies". (See above p.161).

Key Principle: **Interference with the right to respect for an individual's home must be proportionate.**

Gillow v UK

The applicants had lived for some years in Guernsey and then went to work elsewhere. On their return they were refused permission to occupy the house they owned on the island and prosecuted for unlawful occupation.

Held: (ECtHR) The applicants' right to respect for their home had been interfered with. The housing authority had given insufficient weight to their particular circumstances. The interference was disproportionate to the legitimate aim of keeping the population within acceptable limits and promoting the well-being of the island. (1989) 11 E.H.R.R. 335

Key Principle: **Environmental pollution may constitute an interference with the physical well-being of a person and thus**

interfere with his private life. It may also deprive a person of the possibility of enjoying the amenities of his home.

Hatton v UK

The eight applicants all lived in properties near Heathrow Airport. Before 1993 the noise caused by night flying at the airport had been controlled through restrictions on the number of take-offs and landings. But after that date the scheme of control changed, effectively allowing more flights. The applicants claimed violations of Articles 8 and 13 on the ground that judicial review was not an effective remedy.

Held: (Grand Chamber) Reversing the decision of the court that there were violations of Articles 8 and 13, governments should consider the protection of the environment in acting within their margin of appreciation.

Commentary

The Grand Chamber clearly indicated that environmental rights did not merit special protection by the court. In *Guerra v Italy* (1998) 26 E.H.R.R. 357 pollution from a chemical factory a mile from the applicant's home provided grounds for a violation of Article 8 since the authorities had not provided relevant information about the risks to health. There is a positive obligation to inform local people about health matters. See also *McGinley and Egan v UK* (1999) 27 E.H.R.R. 1.

Lopez Ostra v Spain

Villagers living near an industrial plant which treated waste water complained of fumes and smells which made their lives intolerable. They claimed this was a violation of Article 8 as it it damaged their quality of life.

Held: (ECtHR) severe environmental pollution may affect individuals' well-being and prevent them from enjoying their homes in such a way as to affect their private and family life adversely without necessarily seriously damaging their health. (1995) 20 E.H.R.R. 277

Commentary

See also *S v France* (1990) 65 D.R. 250 where the noise caused by a nuclear power station affected the conditions in a Loire chateau. There was an interference under Article 8 but this was justified as having great benefit to the community.

Victims in Criminal Trials

Key Principle: **Principles of a fair trial may require that on occasions the interests of the defendant are balanced against those of the witnesses or victims under Article 8.**

Doorson v Netherlands
For facts see p.103.

Held: (ECtHR) The maintenance of the anonymity of the witnesses limited the ability of the defendant to question them. Although it would have been preferable for the applicant to have attended the questioning of the witnesses it was appropriate to consider that the applicant's interests were outweighed by the need to protect the witnesses. Their life, liberty or security of person may be at stake as may interests coming generally within the ambit of Article 8 of the Convention. There was no breach of Article 6. (1996) 22 E.H.R.R. 330

Commentary
This case, which arose from extreme circumstances, has been cited as illustrating that victims' rights may on occasion be balanced against those of defendants.

7. MARRIAGE AND PROPERTY

Key Principle: **Article 12 of the ECHR: "Men and women of marriageable age have the right to marry and to found a family, according to the national laws governing the exercise of this right."**

Right to Marry

Key Principle: **Transsexuals may have a right to marry.**

Goodwin v UK
A male-female transsexual complained that the UK was in breach of its obligations by not allowing her to register as a woman and by confining lawful marriage to a couple born respectively male and female. The case came via the British courts to Strasbourg.

Held: (ECtHR) The applicant's right to respect for private life under Article 8 and her right to marry and found a family under Article 12 had been infringed. There were no significant factors of public interest to weigh against the Article 8 infringement and there was no justification for a blanket bar to the marriage of transsexuals in their acquired gender. (2002) 35 E.H.R.R. 18

Commentary

This case illustrates the evolving nature of the Strasbourg jurisprudence. Governments could no longer rely on a margin of appreciation in view of changes in attitudes to transsexuals. Much of the earlier jurisprudence relating to the status of transsexuals has been superseded by *Goodwin v UK.*

The case dramatically restricted the margin of appreciation allowed to national governments in their treatment of transsexuals' right to marry in their acquired gender, and required the putting in place of effective remedies for transsexuals whose Convention rights were infringed. The trend in this direction is clear from the earlier cases in which the Strasbourg Court repeatedly affirmed the need to keep under review the law relating to transsexuals and to take account of changing social attitudes. The UK's refusal to amend a transsexual's birth certificate was held in *Rees v UK* (1987) 9 E.H.R.R. 56 to be within the state's margin of appreciation.

The court noted that domestic law gave UK transsexuals an advantage in comparison with states which required all official documents to comply with the records held by the registry office.

In *Cossey v UK* (1990) the Strasbourg Court upheld the 1973 Matrimonial Causes Act which makes marriage void unless the parties are respectively male and female. Citing *Rees*, the court said provision for transsexuals should be kept under constant review. *B v France* (1993) 16 E.H.R.R. 1 involved a complaint by a transsexual that the authorities would not alter her birth certificate to reflect her adopted gender. Upholding her complaint, the Strasbourg Court distinguished *Rees* and referred to the fact that law and practice were different in England and France on this issue.

The absence of a generally shared approach by member states was acknowledged in *Sheffield and Horsham v UK* (1999) 27 E.H.R.R. 163, where one of two joined cases was brought by a person registered at birth as male who had been married as a man but had subsequently undergone gender reassignment surgery. The applicant's former wife had obtained a court order terminating contact between the applicant and their daughter. This involved no violation of the Convention, the court held, since the aetiology of transsexualism was still unclear. However the court did affirm that Article 8 imposed a positive duty on the state to protect its citizens' private life, not merely a duty not to interfere with it.

Key Principle: **The right to marry does not necessarily include the right to divorce.**

Johnston v Ireland
For facts and holding see p.135.

Commentary
This case illustrates the extent of the margin of appreciation afforded to national states in this sensitive area. The approach to divorce illustrated here is tempered by the provision in Protocol 7, Article 5 that spouses within marriage should be treated equally "in the event of a dissolution".

Key Principle: **The qualifications on the right to respect for family life recognised by Article 8.2 applied equally to Article 12 rights.**

R. (Mellor) v Secretary of State for the Home Department
A prisoner serving a life sentence for murder married a member of the prison staff who he had met in prison. When they married he was 31 years old and given the tariff for his offence expected to spend at least another nine years behind bars. He asked for permission to be allowed to inseminate his wife artificially. The request was refused on the grounds that there was no medical need for artificial insemination and that the marriage had not been tested under normal circumstances and might not last. He was refused leave to seek judicial review and appealed.

Held: (CA) A prisoner who wished to start a family with his wife had no right to access to facilities for artificial insemination in the absence of exceptional circumstances. Appeal dismissed. [2001] 3 W.L.R. 533

Commentary
The Court of Appeal declared here that imprisonment was incompatible with the exercise of conjugal rights and consequently involved an interference with rights under Article 12 as well as those under Article 8. Leave to appeal to the House of Lords was refused. In exceptional circumstances it could be necessary to relax the imposition of detention in order to avoid a disproportionate interference with a human right but there was no case which indicated that a prisoner was entitled to assert the right to found a family by artificially inseminating his wife. The court referred to *R. v Secretary of State for the Home Department Ex p. Simms* [2000] 2 A.C. 115 where the House of Lords was expressly interpreting English law in accordance with the Convention on the premise that the relevant principles formed part of the domestic law. It declared that the approach under the Strasbourg jurisprudence and domestic law was the same. The consequences that the punishment of imprisonment had on the exercise of human rights were justifiable providing that they were not disproportionate to the aim of maintaining a penal system designed both to punish and deter. A policy which accorded to prisoners in general the right to beget children by artificial insemination would raise difficult ethical questions and give rise to legitimate public concern.

Peaceful Enjoyment of Possessions

Key Principle: **Protocol 1, Article 1—Protection of property: "Every natural or legal person is entitled to the peaceful enjoyment of his possessions. No one shall be deprived of his possessions except in the public interest and subject to the conditions provided for by law and by the general principles of international law."**

Key Principle: **A balance must be struck between the interests of the community in general and the protection of the individual's right to peaceful enjoyment of his home.**

Sporrong and Lönnroth v Sweden
In the first case the applicants' property was subject to an expropriation permit which was repeatedly extended until it was finally cancelled since the planned development no longer

affected the applicants' building. In the second case an expropriation permit in respect of the applicant's property was set to be valid for 10 years but the project was postponed. The request to have the permit withdrawn was refused and the expropriation permit and a ban on construction ran for eight and 10 years. The applicants claimed a violation of of Protocol 1, Article 1, and Articles 13 and 14.

Held: (ECtHR) There had been an interference with the applicants' properties since they had lost the possibilities of selling them at market prices. There should have been some possibility of review of the permits. The interference was disproportionate and violated Protocol 1, Article 1. (1983) 5 E.H.R.R. 35

Commentary

The court identified three rules in Protocol 1, Article 1. First peaceful enjoyment of property; secondly deprivation of possession only where certain conditions are met; and thirdly state control of use of property by law. Logically the court should establish whether the second and third applied before it could determine if the first was violated. Eight judges issued a dissenting judgment stating there had been no violation of Protocol 1, Article 1 since "the very essence of city planning is to control the use of property including private property in the general interest".

Key Principle: **The right to peaceful enjoyment of possessions may include a right to receive state benefits.**

Cornwell v UK; Leary v UK

Mr Cornwell was a widower with a young son who claimed that the lack of benefits for his status and the British social security legislation breached Article 14, Article 8 and Protocol 1 Article 1. Mr Leary was a widower with three young daughters who was also denied state benefits on these grounds.

Held: (Commission) The cases were admissible on grounds of violation of Protocol 1, Article 1 and Article 14. *The Times*, May 10, 2000

Commentary

Friendly settlements were reached on the basis that the applicants should receive benefit as if they were widows until the Welfare

Reform and Pensions Bill was in force. It appears that this principle applies to compulsory pension schemes (see *Muller v Austria* (1975) 3 D.R. 75) as well as those based on employment. In *Muller*, however, the Commission stressed the differences between a social security system and the management of a private pensions system. The operation of the former must include taking account of political and financial considerations. There have been a number of challenges to Strasbourg on the basis that some benefits under United Kingdom law are available to widows but not widowers.

Key Principle: **The right to enjoyment of possessions may be infringed in the public interest.**

Mellacher v Austria
The applicants claimed that legislation reducing the rental income they could charge on their properties interfered with freedom of contract and was a breach of Protocol 1, Article 1.

Held: (ECtHR): The rent control legislation pursued legitimate aims namely reducing disparities between rents for equivalent flats and controlling property speculation. The legislature was permitted to interfere with contracts in the public interest. There was no violation. (1990) 12 E.H.R.R. 391

Commentary
The court followed the case of *James v UK* (1986) 8 E.H.R.R. 123 which held that the leasehold enfranchisement, namely the right side of a long leaseholders to purchase their landlords' interests was legitimate. The court would not interfere unless the national parliament was acting without reasonable foundation. Here since Austria's policy of rent control was within its margin of appreciation there was no violation of the right to property. The court has also held that deprivation of a licence is an interference with property rights (*Traktorer Aktiebolag v Sweden*) as is deprivation of "goodwill" (*Van Marle v Netherlands* (1986)). The meaning attached to the "public interest" seems to be more generous than that of "necessary in a democratic society". In *James* the court commented:

> "the notion of 'public interest' is necessarily extensive. The court, finding it natural that the margin of appreciation available to the

legislature in implementing social and economic policies should be a wide one, will respect the legislature's judgment as to what is 'in the public interest' even if the community at large has no direct use or enjoyment of the property."

Key Principle: **The state has a right to enforce such laws as it deems necessary to control the use of property in accordance with the general interest or to secure the payment of taxes or other contributions or penalties.**

Lithgow v UK

The applicants had their assets nationalised and contended that the compensation was inadequate and a violation of Protocol 1, Article 1.

Held: (ECtHR) The standard of compensation for nationalisation was not necessarily to be based on the same criteria as that for compulsory acquisition of land. The Government had acted within its margin of appreciation in setting the compensation rates. (1986) 8 E.H.R.R. 329

Commentary

A number of cases have examined whether the extent of compensation by the state achieves a fair balance between the general interest and that of property owners. See *Holy Monasteries v Greece* (1995). In *Lithgow*, referring to the level of compensation for the nationalisation of the aircraft and shipbuilding industries, the court declared that it would "respect a national legislature's judgment in this respect unless manifestly without reasonable foundation".

Key Principle: **Natural or legal persons may only be deprived of property subject to the conditions provided for by law and by the general principles of international law.**

Hentrich v France

After the applicant had bought some land the Commissioner of Revenue exercised the right of pre-emption because he considered that the sale price was too low and suspected tax evasion.

The applicant failed in a challenge to the pre-emption and complained that her right under Protocol 1, Article 1 and Articles 6(1) and (2) of the Convention had been infringed. She also alleged breaches of Articles 13 and 14.

Held: (ECtHR) There had been a breach of Protocol 1, Article 1 and Article 6(1). (1994) 18 E.H.R.R. 440

Commentary
The court recognised that the prevention of tax evasion was a legitimate objective but while the system of the right of pre-emption does not lend itself to criticism as an attribute of the state's sovereignty, the same was not true when its exercise was discretionary and the procedure was unfair. The applicant here bore "an individual and excessive burden" and "the fair balance which should be struck between the protection of the right of property and the requirements of the general interest" was upset. The court has taken quite a passive stance in relation to a state's taxation policy. In *National and Provincial Building Society v UK* (1998) 25 E.H.R.R. 127 it upheld retrospective laws which amended a technical defect whereby applicants were attempting to recover tax they had paid.

Environment

Key Principle: **Environmental damage may affect the right to enjoyment of possessions.**

Powell and Rayner v UK
The applicants, who lived near Heathrow airport, complained among other things that noise nuisance had affected their property in violation of Protocol 1, Article 1.

Held: (Commission) This was not an arguable claim since there was no evidence that the value of the applicants' property had been substantially diminished or that aircraft noise had rendered it unsaleable. (1990) 12 E.H.R.R. 355

Commentary
There was a friendly settlement in the case of one applicant whose case was found to be admissible as to violations of Articles 8 and 13 and Protocol 1, Article 1. The Commission forwarded the other

two applications to the court with jurisdiction only as to Article 13. It found no violations since there was the possibility of civil action for trespass or nuisance. (For other cases on environmental damage see also p.44).

8. RELIGIOUS RIGHTS

Key Principle: **Article 9 of the ECHR—Freedom of thought, conscience and religion:**

"1 Everyone has the right to freedom of thought, conscience and religion; this right includes freedom to change his religion or belief and freedom, either alone or in community with others and in public or private, to manifest his religion or belief, in worship, teaching, practice and observance.

2 Freedom to manifest one's religion or beliefs shall be subject only to such limitations as are prescribed by law and are necessary in a democratic society in the interests of public safety, for the protection of public order, health or morals, or for the protection of the rights and freedoms of others."

Range of Beliefs

Key Principle: **Article 9 rights protect a broad range of beliefs and religions.**

Kokkinakis v Greece
The applicant and his wife were Jehovah's Witnesses sentenced to imprisonment, with a fine in lieu, for proselytising. He complained that this was a breach of his rights under Articles 7, 9 and 10. He argued that no clear dividing-line could be drawn between proselytism and freedom to change one's religion or belief and to manifest it. Religious freedom implied a freedom to bear witness.

Held: The applicant's conviction was not justified by a pressing social need, proportionate to the legitimate aim of maintaining social order or "necessary in a democratic society . . . for the protection of the rights and freedoms of others". (1994) 17 E.H.R.R. 397

Commentary
The court stated in this case that Article 9 ". . . is in its religious dimension one of the most vital elements that go to make up the identity of believers and of their conception of life, but it is also a precious asset for atheists, agnostics, sceptics and the unconcerned." However some political views are not covered by this Article. It does not embrace the concept of a political prisoner. In *McFeeley v UK* it was held that freedom to manifest belief does not include the right of an IRA prisoner to wear his own clothes in prison (see p.65).

Key Principle: **Organisations as well as individuals may claim the protection of Article 9.**

Chappell v UK
The applicant was a practising druid who complained that the ban on the summer solstice ceremony which had taken place at Stonehenge every year since 1917 was a breach of his right under Article 9 to freedom of religion.

Held: (Commission) The ban was lawful and necessary in a democratic society in the interests of public safety, for the protection of public order or for the protection of the rights and freedoms of others. (1990) 12 E.H.R.R. 1

Commentary
In *Church of X v UK* (1968) 12 Y.B. 306 the Commission indicated that it might be difficult for an organisation to demonstrate a violation of its rights.

Actions

Key Principle: **Actions influenced by a belief are not necessarily manifestations of that belief.**

Arrowsmith v UK
The applicant was imprisoned for incitement to disaffection after distributing pacifist leaflets to soldiers and complained that

her right to liberty under Article 5, her right to manifest her pacifist beliefs and her right to freedom of expression had been interfered with.

Held: (Commission) The application was rejected. The applicant's conviction had not violated her Convention rights. (1981) 3 E.H.R.R. 218

Commentary
The court considered that pacifism was a belief and therefore as such entitled to protection under Article 9. Here Article 10 was not violated either, because the state had a legitimate interest in national security. Again in *Kalac v Turkey* (1997) App. No. 20704/92 the court found no violation in the removal of a soldier from the military because in fact it was based on his conduct and attitude rather than being a manifestation of his religious belief.

Key Principle: **Conscientious objectors may be afforded protection under Article 9.**

Autio v Finland
The applicant had done non-combatant national service as a conscientious objector. The law required non-combatant servicemen to spend 240 days more in service than their military counterparts. The applicant complained that requiring him to spend longer in service amounted to discrimination in the enjoyment of his right to freedom of thought, conscience and religion. He further complained that there was no objective or reasonable basis for law, since it was the deliberate intention of the Government to make substitute service more burdensome than military service.

Held: (Commission) The extra length of service was found to be legitimate and proportionate.

Commentary
This issue of conscientious objectors also engages Article 4(3)(b) (see p.73).

Contractual Status

Key Principle: **An individual in claiming his rights under Article 9 may have to take into account his professional or contractual position.**

Stedman v UK
The applicant, a travel agency worker, was dismissed after 22 months' employment because she refused to accept an amendment to her contract of employment requiring that she work on Sundays. She complained to an industrial tribunal, which declined jurisdiction on the basis that she had been less than two years in the job. The dismissal was upheld by the Court of Appeal. She complained that the exercise of her Christian faith had been interfered with and there were violations of Articles 8, 9, 14 and 6.

Held: (Commission) The requirement that the applicant work a five day week to include Sundays on a rota basis, was not an interference with any of her Convention rights. Her dismissal was not based on her religious convictions. (1997) 23 E.H.R.R. CD 169

Commentary
These two cases illustrate that the European Court of Human Rights is slow to accept the concept of indirect discrimination. It could be argued that insofar as discrimination on religious grounds impacts on a particular racial group it is protected by existing United Kingdom race relations legislation. However some religious groups, such as Rastafarians, are not so protected.

Proportionality

Key Principle: **Any acceptable restrictions on the manifestation of a belief must be in accordance with law, pursuing a legitimate aim as set out in Article 9(2) and be necessary and proportionate.**

R. v Taylor (Paul Simon)
The appellant was convicted on a guilty plea of possessing cannabis with intent to supply. He was a Rastafarian who claimed he had had the cannabis for distribution and use in a

regular act of worship in the temple. Before his guilty plea he had submitted that the prosecution infringed his rights under Articles 8 and 9. In the alternative he argued that the Crown had to prove that the prosecution was a necessary and appropriate response in fulfilment of a legitimate aim. The prosecution accepted that Rastafarianism was a religion. The judge ruled that the drugs had been in use for religious purposes but that although the Convention was engaged, the appellant's rights were qualified by Article 9(2). The appellant appealed against conviction and sentence.

Held: (CA) Convention rights were engaged but the judge's ruling was correct. The jury was not required to examine the issues of proportionality and necessity. The 12-month prison sentence was excessive and was reduced to five months. (2001) *The Times*, November 15

Commentary
Kokkinakis v Greece (see above) illustrates the importance of the concept of proportionality in the Strasbourg jurisprudence. Its prominence in the Strasbourg cases means proportionality will have increasing importance in English law under the HRA.

Christianity

Key Principle: **By uniquely protecting the Christian religion the English blasphemy laws infringe Article 9.**

Choudhury v UK
The applicant had sought unsuccessfully to prosecute the publisher of Salman Rushdie's Satanic Verses for blasphemy. The English courts ruled that the offence applied only to attacks on Christianity and did not protect Islam. The applicant complained under Article 9 of the Convention that this limited his enjoyment of the right to freedom of religion. He also complained of discrimination under Article 14.

Held: On the Article 9 point, the Commission found no link between freedom from interference with Article 9 rights and the applicant's complaints. Accordingly the discrimination complaint was also rejected.

Commentary
It is arguable that in a pluralist society a criminal law which protects just one religion is not acceptable. An alternative approach is to criminalise attacks on all religions but this could in turn be condemned as an unacceptable infringement of freedom of expression in situations where there was no risk to public order. On the law concerning blasphemy see also *Gay News and Lemon v UK* (1982) 5 E.H.R.R. 123.

9. POLITICAL RIGHTS

Freedom of Expression

Key Principle: **Article 10 of the ECHR—Freedom of expression:**

"1 Everyone has the right to freedom of expression. This right shall include freedom to hold opinions and to receive and impart information and ideas without interference by public authority and regardless of frontiers. This article shall not prevent States from requiring the licensing of broadcasting, television or cinema enterprises.

2 The exercise of these freedoms, since it carries with it duties and responsibilities, may be subject to such formalities, conditions, restrictions or penalties as are prescribed by law and are necessary in a democratic society, in the interests of national security, territorial integrity or public safety, for the prevention of disorder or crime, for the protection of health or morals, for the protection of the reputation or rights of others, for preventing the disclosure of information received in confidence, or for maintaining the authority and impartiality of the judiciary."

Key Principle: **Government bodies should be open to uninhibited public criticism.**

Derbyshire County Council v Times Newspapers
A local authority brought a libel action against a newspaper which had questioned the propriety of its handling of a super-

annuation fund. On a preliminary point the judge held that the council could sue for libel in respect of its governmental and administrative functions. The decision was reversed in the Court of Appeal and the council appealed.

Held: (HL) Uninhibited public criticism of an elected body was vital in a democracy. The threat of libel actions would inhibit legitimate criticism. It was contrary to the public interest for central or local government institutions to have a common law right to sue for libel. The action would be struck out. [1993] A.C. 534

Commentary
The Court of Appeal applied Article 10 of the ECHR. in finding a local authority cannot sue for libel. The House of Lords held that the common law could determine the issue in favour of protecting free speech.

Key Principle: **Newspapers may have a qualified privilege defence to libel claims where an article, even if it turns out to be untrue, is in the public interest and the product of responsible journalism.**

Reynolds v Times Newspapers Ltd
The plaintiff, a prominent Irish politician, began proceedings for defamation against the defendants, the publishers of an article about the political crisis in Ireland in 1994. The plaintiff claimed that the article bore the meaning that he had deliberately and dishonestly misled the Dáil. The defendants pleaded qualified privilege. At the trial the jury decided in the plaintiff's favour and he was awarded one penny damages. The Court of Appeal ordered a retrial on the grounds of misdirections to the jury and that the publication was not covered by qualified privilege. The defendants appealed claiming that the law should recognise a generic qualified privilege encompassing the publication by a newspaper of political matters affecting the people of the United Kingdom.

Held: (HL) The common law should not develop a new subject matter category of qualified privilege for all political information. Qualified privilege was available in respect of political information by applying the common law test of whether there had been a duty to publish the material to the recipients and whether they had an interest in receiving it. In the circumstances the publication was not one which should be protected by privilege in the absence of malice. [1999] 3 W.L.R. 1010

Commentary

The paper here failed to benefit from the new defence since the key source had an axe to grant. The case has been hailed as a landmark of press freedom but it has not succeeded often in practice (see *Loutchansky v Times Newspapers* [2001] 3 W.L.R. 404). Both these cases were decided before the HRA came into effect and show differing approaches to Article 10. In the Court of Appeal judgment in *Derbyshire* Article 10 was involved to resolve uncertainty in the common law but the House of Lords in the same case took the view that the common law rules should reflect the principle that citizens should be exposed to news stories criticising government bodies and politicians. In *Reynolds* the House rejected a defence argument that a new category of qualified privilege "political information" should be created. By contrast, the Strasbourg Court has recognised that the position of a politician is different from that of a private individual (see *Lingens v Austria* (1986) 8 E.H.R.R. 407). In a case heard after the implementation of the HRA (*Turkington v Times Newspapers*, *The Times*, November 3, 2000) the House of Lords held that a press conference was a public meeting and thus protected by qualified privilege under the Defamation Act 1952. The judgment in *Turkington* was not based predominantly on Article 10 or the HRA. Lord Steyn in his judgment invoked the First Amendment to the United States constitution.

Key Principle: **Freedom of expression should be overridden only in extreme circumstances.**

R. v Secretary of State for the Home Department Ex p. Simms

There was a prohibition on visits to serving prisoners by journalists seeking to investigate whether prisoners had been wrongly convicted save on terms which precluded the journalists from making professional use of the material they collected. The applicant challenged the lawfulness of the ban.

Held: (HL) The more substantial the interference with fundamental rights the more the court would require by way of justification before it could be satisfied that the interference was reasonable in a public law sense. [1999] Q.B. 349

Commentary
The speeches, particularly that of Lord Steyn, assigned great importance to freedom of political speech and drew on American constitutional texts as well as Article 10. Lord Steyn stated:

> "The starting point is freedom of expression. . . Freedom of expression is intrinsically important. It is valued for its own sake. But it is well recognised that it is also instrumentally important. . . It acts as a brake upon the abuse of power by public officials. It facilitates the exposure of errors in the governance and administration of justice of the country."

Key Principle: **Any restrictions on freedom of expression must be prescribed by law and satisfy a pressing social need.**

Sunday Times v UK
The Sunday Times brought the action claiming an injunction upheld by the House of Lords ([1974] A.C. 273) infringed Article 10.

Held: (ECtHR) The interference with the applicants' freedom of expression was not justified under Article 10(2). There was no pressing social need for the injunction. (1979) 2 E.H.R.R. 245

Commentary
This case led to the passing of the Contempt of Court Act 1981.

Key Principle: **Freedom of expression may be restricted if other interests require it and the response is proportionate.**

Arrowsmith v UK
The applicant was a pacifist who distributed a leaflet to soldiers at an army camp urging them to go absent without leave rather than serve in Ireland. She refused to stop after a police warning and was arrested for conduct likely to cause a breach of the

peace. She was convicted under the Incitement to Disaffection Act 1934 and sentenced to prison. She alleged breaches of Articles 5, 9, 10(2) and 14.

Held: (Commission) The applicant's pacifism was a belief protected by the Convention but the distribution of leaflets was not a manifestation of belief in the sense of Article 9(1). Her freedom of expression was interfered with but this was justified under Article 10(2). The decision to prosecute her was necessary for the protection of national security and the prevention of disorder in the army. (1978) 3 E.H.R.R. 218

Ahmed v UK

Regulations under the Local Government and Housing Act 1989 restricted the political activities of certain categories of senior local government officers. The applicants were therefore required under the terms of their employment to refrain from engaging in certain political activities. They claimed violations of Articles 10, 11 and Protocol 1, Article 3.

Held: (ECtHR) The regulations pursued the legitimate aim of maintaining the political neutrality of local government officers. There were no violations of the ECHR. (1998) *The Times*, October 2

Commentary

By contrast there was a violation in *Bowman v UK* (1998) 26 E.H.R.R. 1 where the applicant had been prosecuted for distributing views on abortion and embryo experimentation which was in breach of the requirements on election expenses under the Representation of the People Act 1983. The aim of influencing others who are themselves responsible for their actions was an essential and legitimate aspect of the exercise of freedom of expression and opinion, in political and other matters.

National Security

Key Principle: **In cases of national security necessity and public interest disclosure cannot be argued as defences.**

R. v Shayler

The defendant was charged with offences under s.1(1) of the Official Secrets Act 1989. A preliminary issue was whether there was a defence of disclosure in the public interest or of necessity open to him. He argued that if there were not there would be a breach of Article 10.

Held: (CA) There were no such defences because the fact that the defendant could have disclosed the information to a Crown servant allowed him sufficient freedom. The statutory requirement that damage did not need to be proved when disclosure was by a security service member was justified since, *inter alia*, the lives of operatives were in danger and the United Kingdom might be in breach of its obligations under Articles 2 and 3. [2001] 1 W.L.R. 2206

Commentary
In *R. v Central Criminal Court Ex p. Bright, Alton and Rusbridger* [2001] 1 W.L.R. 662 the court quashed Special Branch orders made under the PACE to produce material against newspaper editors who had published articles based on revelations by Shayler. It stated that "inconvenient or embarrassing revelations whether for the security services or for public authorities, should not be suppressed".

Protest and Freedom of Expression

Key Principle: **Freedom of expression can encompass actions also.**

Steel v UK
For facts and holding see p.3.

Hashman and Harrup v UK
For facts and holding see p.3.

Commentary
In *Steel* the court took the view that the actions of two of the demonstrators constituted "expression" even though they were disrupting the activities of others. In their case the legal action taken against them was a proportionate interference with their freedom of expression. These cases illustrate the close connection between rights under Articles 10 and 11.

Obscenity

Key Principle: **Freedom of expression may include protection of ideas that offend, shock or disturb the state or any sector of the population.**

Handyside v UK
For facts and holding see p.6.

Commentary
The court maintained that protecting offensive ideas derived from the demands of "that pluralism tolerance and broadmindedness without which there is no democratic society". However how a state operated "the protection of morals" was within its margin of appreciation. In other cases religious sensibilities might be rightfully protected even though this might limit the exercise of artistic freedom (see *Wingrove v UK*).

Libel

Key Principle: **Damages in a libel suit must not be so high as to be a breach of Article 10.**

Tolstoy-Miroslavsky v UK
For facts and holding see p.130.

Commentary
The court has considered defamation in a number of cases. In *Lingens v Austria* (1986) the court held that successful private defamation actions brought by prominent politicians were a violation of Article 10. It stated: "Freedom of the press . . . affords the public one of the best means of discovering and forming an opinion of the ideas and attitudes of political leaders. More generally freedom of political debate is at the very core of the concept of a democratic society which prevails throughout the Convention." In this case the court criticised the Austrian defamation law for placing the burden of proof on the defendant to establish the truth of his statement. English law of defamation also places the burden of proof on the defence.

Balancing Rights

Key Principle: **Section 12 of the HRA—Freedom of expression:**

"(1) This section applies if a court is considering whether to grant any relief which, if granted, might affect the exercise of the Convention right to freedom of expression.

(2) If the person against whom the application for relief is made ('the respondent') is neither present nor represented, no such relief is to be granted unless the court is satisfied—

    (a) that the applicant has taken all practicable steps to notify the respondent; or

    (b) that there are compelling reasons why the respondent should not be notified.

(3) No such relief is to be granted so as to restrain publication before trial unless the court is satisfied that the applicant is likely to establish that publication should not be allowed.

(4) The court must have particular regard to the importance of the Convention right to freedom of expression and, where the proceedings relate to material which the respondent claims, or which appears to the courts, to be journalistic, literary or artistic material (or to conduct connected with such material), to—

    (a) the extent to which—

        (i) the material has, or is about to, become available to the public; or

        (ii) it is, or would be, in the public interest for the material to be published;

    (b) any relevant privacy code.

(5) In this section—

    'Court' includes a tribunal; and 'relief' includes any remedy or order (other than in criminal proceedings)."

Key Principle: **Restraints on publication referred in s.12 may be necessary to protect rights under Articles 2 and 3.**

Venables v News Group Newspapers Ltd

Two boys at the age of 10 had killed the two year old James Bulger. They had been convicted of murder and sentenced to be detained for life. At their original trial the trial judge had made an injunction for an unlimited period forbidding the publication of any information about the two other than their names. In 2001 when they reached 18 years a number of newspapers had applied for clarification. The boys claimed that their rights under Articles 2, 3, and 8 would be at risk if their whereabouts were published.

Held: (Fam. Div.) The protection of confidentiality and the placing of restrictions on the press was correct where not to do so would be likely to lead to serious physical injury or death. [2001] 2 W.L.R. 1038

Commentary

This was an extreme one but it made it clear that the courts can now protect privacy by court order in such cases. Another legitimate basis for press restraint is the protection of national security as the cases arising out of the *Spycatcher* saga showed, see *Observer and The Guardian v UK* (1991) 14 E.H.R.R. 153. The temporary injunctions fell within the state's margin of appreciation in assessing the possible threat to national security. However the confirmation of the injunction after the material was in the public domain because of overseas publication was a violation of Article 10. The specific protection afforded to freedom of expression in s.12 of the HRA will make it more difficult for a pre-trial injunction to be awarded against the press.

Copyright

Key Principle: **Restriction of the right to freedom of expression in Article 10 could be justified where necessary in a democratic society to protect copyright.**

Ashdown v Telegraph Group Ltd

The Sunday Telegraph published extracts from Lord Ashdown's *Diaries* including a direct quotation of a minute between Paddy Ashdown and the Prime Minister. The quoted part was 20 per cent of the whole minute. Ashdown claimed breach of copyright. Summary judgment was granted. *The Sunday Telegraph* appealed.

Held: (CA) Rare circumstances could arise where the right of freedom of expression came into conflict with the protection to copyright holders in the Copyright, Designs and Patents Act 1988 despite that Act's express exceptions. The court was obliged to apply the Act so as to give effect to the right to freedom of expression in Article 10. This required the court to look closely at the facts of individual cases. There was no justification for the extent of the reproduction of Lord Ashdown's own words. Article 10 did not mean that *The Sunday Telegraph* could make money out of this without compensating Lord Ashdown. *The Times*, August 1, 2001

Commentary
The court in this case was concerned with balancing the public interest and the need for commercial confidentiality. It considered it would be rare for the public interest to demand that the form of the work was reproduced. The case is an example of the impact the Human Rights Act on private litigants.

Protection of Sources

Key Principle: **Freedom of expression may require the protection of journalists' sources of information.**

Goodwin v UK
The applicant, a journalist, had received from a source whose identity he agreed not to disclose, a document about the financial affairs of two private companies. The companies obtained an injunction against publication and an order that the journalist disclose the source. He refused to comply with the order. He also refused to comply when the Court of Appeal varied the order to allow him to place the required information in a sealed envelope lodged with the court. He was found guilty of contempt and was refused a hearing at the Court of Appeal because of his refusal to comply with the order. The publishers and the journalist appealed. The House of Lords held that the Court of Appeal had erred in refusing to hear the journalist since the plaintiff did not oppose his being heard and his appeal was based on an alleged lack of jurisdiction of the court to make the order. The court had power to order disclosure notwithstanding that the plaintiff's object in seeking it was to identify the source. The potential damage to the complainants' business was great and there was no public interest in publication. The applicant claimed a violation of Article 10.

Held: (ECtHR) The order for discovery was an interference with freedom of expression which was prescribed by law and pursued a legitimate aim. The disclosure order, which merely served to reinforce the injunction, was not supported by sufficient reasons for the purposes of Article 10(2). (1996) 22 E.H.R.R. 123

Commentary
Significantly in *Goodwin* the protection of the commercial interests of the company was a legitimate aim but the measures to achieve them were disproportionate. On protection of commercial interests, see also *Ashdown v Telegraph Group* (2001) and *Markt Intern GmbH and Klaus Beermann v Germany* (1990). The growing importance of the protection of "whistleblowers" is now subject to legislation in the Protection of Disclosure Act, and may well raise Article 10 issues.

Extremism

Jersild v Denmark
The applicant was a television journalist who interviewed some racist youth for a documentary programme. The transmitted programme contained racist and offensive words. The youths were convicted of making racist statements and the applicant was convicted of aiding and abetting their offences. The applicant claimed a violation of Article 10.

Held: (ECtHR) Although the media must not overstep the boundaries which protected others when information and ideas were of public interest the press have a duty to impart them and the public a right to receive them. The documentary had an anti-racist message. Criminal sanctions were not justified and Article 10 was violated. (1995) 19 E.H.R.R. 1

Commentary
Article 10(2) lists the protection of others as a legitimate basis for restricting freedom of expression. This is more specifically cited in Article 17 which reads: "Nothing in this convention may be interpreted as implying for any State, group or person any right to engage in any activity or perform any act aimed at the destruction of any of the rights and freedoms set forth herein or at their limitation to a greater extent than is provided for in the Convention."

Access to information

Key Principle: **The right to receive information prohibited a government from restricting a person from receiving information that others wished or might be willing to impart to him. It does not give a right of access to secret information.**

Gaskin v UK
The applicant had been placed in the care of the local authority and was boarded with various foster-parents. After he reached the age of 18 the applicant tried to get access to his case records. Some but not all were disclosed. He claimed violations of Articles 8 and 10.

Held: (ECtHR) Persons in the situation of the applicant had an interest in receiving information necessary to know and understand their childhood and an independent authority should finally decide whether access was to be granted where a contributor does not give consent. There was no violation of Article 10 since it does not embody an obligation on the state to impart the information in question. (1990) 12 E.H.R.R. 36

Commentary
United Kingdom governments and authorities wishing to protect information may find support in *Leander v Sweden* (1987) 9 E.H.R.R. 433. The Swedish Government had refused to give his file to an applicant whom they had turned down for a job on security grounds. It was held that there was no violation since "freedom to receive information contained in article 10 prohibits a government from restricting a person from receiving information that others wish or may be willing to impart to him". It did not confer on an individual right of access to a register containing information on him nor did it embody an obligation on the government to impart such information. See also *Open Door Counselling and Dublin Well Women v Ireland* (1993) 15 E.H.R.R. 244. The United Kingdom has now passed a Freedom of Information Act which does not come into force before 2005.

Freedom of Assembly

Key Principle: **Article 11 of the ECHR—Freedom of assembly and association:**

"1 Everyone has the right to freedom of peaceful assembly and to freedom of association with others, including the right to form and to join trade unions for the protection of his interests.

2 No restrictions shall be placed on the exercise of these rights other than such as are prescribed by law and are necessary in a democratic society in the interests of national security or public safety, for the prevention of disorder or crime, for the protection of health or morals or for the protection of the rights and freedoms of others. This article shall not prevent the imposition of lawful restrictions on the exercise of these rights by members of the armed forces, of the police or of the administration of the State."

Key Principle: **Prior authorisation or bans for public assemblies is not necessarily a breach of Article 11.**

Plattform Artze für das Leben v Austria

The applicant association comprise the group of doctors who advocate abortion reform. Cancer demonstrators disrupted their demonstration. Violations of Articles 9, 10, 11 and 13 were claimed. The Commission allowed the application on the grounds of Article 13 only.

Held: (ECtHR) In a democracy the right to counter demonstrate cannot extend to inhibiting the exercise of the right to demonstrate. The state had a positive duty to ensure that the right to peaceful demonstration and assembly can be exercised. The Government had taken positive steps to protect assemblies and these measures are not in that the quote. There was no violation of Article 11 and therefore no violation of Article 13. (1991) 13 E.H.R.R. 204

Commentary

A broad margin of appreciation is allowed in considering the positive obligations on states but the court was clearly placing the responsibility for any harm that may be provoked on the counter-demonstrators. This case adopts the *Beatty v Gillbanks* (1881–82) L.R. 9 Q.B.D. 308 robust approach of the common law which was not followed in *Duncan v Jones* [1936] 1 K.B. 218. However, more recently in *Redmond-Bate v DPP* [1999] Crim.L.R. 998 a more trenchant rights based approach was adopted. The officer had no right to call upon a citizen to desist from lawful conduct because of a perceived threat from others.

Key Principle: **Prior bans or conditions may be imposed on rallies if they are proportionate to their legitimate aim.**

Rai, Allmond and "Negotiate Now" v UK

The proposed rally was banned by the Department of National Heritage on the advice of the Commissioner of the Metropolitan Police in accordance with government policy that no demonstrations should be allowed in Trafalgar Square if they concerned Northern Ireland. The applicants alleged breaches of Articles 9, 10, and 11.

Held: (Commission) The right to freedom of peaceful assembly is fundamental in any democratic society. There was an interference with rights under Article 11. With regard to the argument that the ban was not based on public order considerations but because it was controversial the Commission considered that there was a legitimate aim involved since the issues were sensitive and complex. The Government had not acted arbitrarily. There were other possible venues. Article 11 was not violated since the restrictions were prescribed by law and necessary in a democratic society. There was no evidence of political discrimination to found the violation on grounds of political opinion. (1995) 19 E.H.R.R. CD 93

Commentary

In finding that the ban was sufficient as prescribed by law the Commission stated: "it is compatible with the requirements of force the ability that terms which are on their face general and unlimited are explained by executive or administrative statements, since it is the provision of sufficiently precise guidance to individuals . . . rather than the source of that guidance which is of relevance". See also *Steel v UK* (p.3), *Hashman and Harrup v UK* (p.3) on the varying application of the "prescribed by law" requirement.

Key Principle: **Sanctions against demonstrators must pass the** test of proportionality and be necessary in a democratic society.

Ezelin v France

The applicant (a lawyer) had been charged with a criminal offence after taking part in a demonstration. The charges were dropped and the Bar Council found no reason to discipline him. However the Court of Appeal imposed a reprimand since he had refused to leave the demonstration or disassociate himself from the offensive and insulting acts which occurred. The applicant alleged breaches of Articles 10 and 11.

Held: (ECtHR) The assembly was lawful; there was an interference with his freedom of assembly which was disproportionate to the legitimate aim of preventing public disorder. (1992) 14 E.H.R.R. 362

Commentary

This is to date the only decision of the court finding a violation of the freedom of assembly guarantee of Article 11. Two judges considered that the interference fell within the state's margin of appreciation. A number of applications have not reached the court since the Commission considered them inadmissible.

Trade Unions

Key Principle: **The right to join a trade union may encompass the right not to join.**

Young, James and Webster v UK

For facts and holding see p.1.

Held: (ECtHR) The state was responsible under Article 1 for securing Convention rights to its citizens. Article 11 has as one of its purposes the protection of personal opinion and effectively coercing someone to join strikes at its substance. The harm suffered by the applicants was greater than that which was permitted by the aims of closed shop agreements. There was a violation of Article 11; it was not necessary to consider the violations of Articles 9, 10 and 13. (1981) 4 E.H.R.R. 38

Commentary

By contrast in *Sibson v UK* (1994) 17 E.H.R.R. 193 there was no violation of Article 11 after an employer transferred a worker to another place of work because he left one union to join another and other workers would not accept him. There was no risk to his job. In *Young, James and Webster* the court stopped short of completely endorsing the negative right of association which the applicants had advocated but they held that threats of dismissal were a very serious form of compulsion. This judgment has been controversial, trade union protagonists have argued that it shows the preference of the Convention for individualism over collective rights and its lack of regard for the social and economic implications of undermining trade union membership. Such cases illustrate the court's treatment of the complex issue of the closed shop which is no longer protected under English employment law. The difference in the court's decision in the two cases is explained by the fact that in *Young, James and Webster* the workers were threatened with loss of employment because of their refusal to join a union, however in Sibson there was no risk to the applicant's job.

Key Principle: **Governments may not empty the right of association of all content.**

Wilson v UK; Palmer v UK

Two separate employers, Associated Newspapers and Associated British Ports, offered pay rises to all union members if they relinquished their union membership and engaged in individual rather than collective bargaining. Those employees that refused this offer were denied the pay rise and lost future opportunity to benefit from enhanced terms and conditions. All the domestic courts except the House of Lords held that this was unlawful discrimination contrary to ss.146–148 of the Trade Union and Labour Relations (Consolidation) Act 1992. The House of Lords held that there was no violation since the real purpose behind the employers' actions was not to persuade employees to abandon union representation. It was rather to enable a change in the employment relationship to be made in the interests of efficiency.

Held: (ECtHR) There was a violation of Article 11 which enshrines the right of an individual to join a trade union for the protection of his/her interests. An individual was entitled not just to join a trade union but also to enjoy some minimum rights as a consequence, otherwise membership was worthless. The

United Kingdom had failed in its positive obligation to secure the enjoyment of rights under Article 11. [2002] I.R.L.R. 568

Commentary
This case shows that the ECHR is capable of defending collective as well as individual rights.

Key Principle: **The right to form and join a union does not include the right to strike.**

Schmidt and Dahlstrom v Sweden

The applicants were members of trade unions affiliated to one of the main federations representing Swedish state employees. The applicants' unions had called selective strikes not affecting the sectors in which worked the applicants who did not come out on strike. The applicant complained that on the conclusion of new agreements they as members of what were considered "belligerent" unions were denied certain retroactive benefits paid to members of other trade unions and to non-union employees who had not participated in the strike.

Held: (ECtHR) The Convention makes no express distinction between the functions of a contracting state as holder of public power and its responsibilities as employer. Article 11 is binding on the state as employer. Article 11 para.1 presents trade union freedom as one form or special aspect of freedom of association such as the right to retroactivity of benefits. The applicants had retained their personal freedom of association. The Convention safeguards freedom to protect the occupational interests of trade union members by trade union action which must be permitted by Member States. The right to strike is one of the most important of the means available but there are others. Such a right is not expressly enshrined in Article 11 and may be subject under national law to regulation of a kind that limited exercise in certain instances. There was no violation of Article 11 or Article 14. (1976) 1 E.H.R.R. 632

Commentary
The Court noted that the 1961 Social Charter only guarantees the right to strike subject to state regulations. In declaring that there was no violation of Article 14 it stated that the principle adopted

by the Swedish Government that "a strike destroys retroactivity" was legitimate and it was entitled therefore to pay only those who had not been on strike or supported the strike. In this case the court accepted that the state may regulate the use of industrial action by trade unionists. Thus in *Natfhe v UK* (1998) 25 E.H.R.R. 122 it found no violation of Article 11 in the statutory requirement to give an employer the names of trade union members before strike action was begun.

Key Principle: **Article 11 does not create a right to have a collective agreement concluded.**

Swedish Engine Drivers' Union v Sweden

The applicant union comprised between 20–25% of the eligible railway personnel. The majority of the personnel belonged to the railway men's section of the state employees union (the federations). The applicant complained that the Swedish national collective bargaining office (the Office) concluded it collective agreements only with the federations. The applicant alleged violations of Articles 11, 13 and 14.

Held: (ECtHR) While Article 11 para.1 presents trade union freedoms as one form of a special aspect of freedom of association, the Article does not secure any particular treatment of trade unions or their members by the state such as the right that the state should conclude any given collective agreement with them. The words in the article "for the protection of his interests" showed that the Convention safeguards freedom to protect the occupational interests of trade union members by trade union action the conduct and development of which the contracting states must both permit and make possible. Members of a trade union have a right that the trade union should be heard. The state is free to choose the means which may be by a collective agreement or by other means. There was no infringement of Article 11 para.1. It was not necessary to consider para.2. There was no violation of Article 14 since it was legitimate for the office to want to avoid having an excessive number of negotiating partners. There was no violation of Article 13. (1979) 1 E.H.R.R. 617

Commentary

In other cases the court has ruled that Article 11 does not guarantee any particular union the right to be consulted (*National*

Union of Belgian Police v Belgium (1979–80) 1 E.H.R.R. 578), nor does it create the right to join a particular union in certain circumstances (*Cheall v UK* (1985) 42 D.R. 178). The cases illustrate the limited protection offered to collective as opposed to individual rights in the Convention.

Prisoners

Key Principle: **Solitary confinement is not a violation of the right of association.**

McFeeley v UK
For facts see p.65.

Held: (Commission) Article 11 does not encompass the right of prisoners to associate with other prisoners in the sense of a right to be in their company.

Commentary
This case involved consideration of a number of Articles, including the nature of a criminal charge under Article 6 in relation to prison disciplinary hearings. The Commission also stated that Article 9 does not guarantee the right to special category status as a political prisoner. Freedom to manifest belief does not include the right of a prisoner to wear his own clothes.

Key Principle: **Convicted prisoners may be disenfranchised.**

R. (Pearson) v Secretary of State for the Home Department
Several prisoners sought judicial review of the authorities' refusal to register them to vote in parliamentary and local elections. They were disqualified from registering to vote by s.3(1) of the Representation of the People Act 1983. Another prisoner sought a declaration under s.4(2) of the HRA 1998 that s.3(1) of the 1983 Act was incompatible with Protocol 1, Article 3 and Article 14 of the Convention.

Held: (DC) Contracting states had a wide margin of appreciation in imposing conditions on the right to vote. But the conditions should not curtail the rights to such an extent as to impair their essence or remove their effectiveness, should be imposed in pursuit of a legitimate aim and the means employed should not be disproportionate or thwart the free expression of the opinion of the people in the choice of the legislative. Parliament had taken the view that convicted prisoners in custody had forfeited their right to have a say in the way the country was governed. (2001) *The Times*, April 17

Commentary

The Representation of the People Act 2000 gives remand prisoners and mentally ill patients, other than those convicted and in custody, the right to vote. In *Hirst v The UK (No. 2)* the applicant was a prisoner serving life for manslaughter who had brought an unsuccessful under s.4 of the Human Rights Act 1998 to challenge the compatibility of s.3 of the Representation of the People Act 1983, which barred convicted prisoners from voting in elections. The prisoner had served the tariff part of his sentence but had been denied parole as a public menace. He applied to Strasbourg firstly under Article 3 of the First Protocol which provides that "The High Contracting Parties undertake to hold free elections at reasonable intervals by secret ballot, under conditions which will ensure that the free expression of the opinion of the people in the choice of legislature". He also applied under Article 10 and Article 14, saying essentially that he had suffered discrimination which interfered with his right to expression. In response the Government claimed that prisoners were deprived of the vote so as to prevent crime, punish offenders and enhance respect for the rule of law. The court held that the provision indiscriminately stripped 70,000 people of their Convention right to vote. There was no logical reason to continue to punish the applicant whose detention was entirely for reasons of public safety. Insofar as a disqualification from voting was to be seen as part of a prisoner's punishment, there was no logical justification for it to continue in his case. There was no evidence that parliament had ever sought to assess the proportionality of the voting ban. An absolute ban was too sweeping and there had been a breach of Article 3 of the First Protocol.

These decisions illustrate the differing approaches of the domestic and Strasbourg courts. Kennedy L.J. had found that given the wide margin of appreciation to member states by the case law the exclusion of convicted prisoners from the right to vote was not in violation of the Convention. He took a restrictive view of the role of the courts stating that "there is a broad spectrum of approaches among democratic societies and the United Kingdom falls into the middle of the spectrum". He continued, "[i]n course of time this position may move, either by way of further fine tuning, as was recently done in relation to remand prisoners and others or more radically but its position in the spectrum is plainly a matter for parliament nor for the courts." Legislation to change the law is now likely.

Limitations

Key Principle: **Article 11 rights may be restricted in their application to the armed forces, the police, and civil servants.**

CCSU v UK
Mrs Thatcher as Minister for the Civil Service issued an order in Council withdrawing from employees at the Government Communications Headquarters (GCHQ) the right to belong to a trade union. There had been no prior consultation with the unions or the employees. The Civil Service unions and six employees sought judicial review on the ground that the minister was under a duty to act fairly by consulting those affected. The single judge granted a declaration that the order was invalid, the Court of Appeal found for the minister and the applicants appealed. The House of Lords held that merely because the minister was exercising a prerogative power she was not immune from judicial review or freed from the duty to act fairly. However the Government had shown that the decision was based on considerations of national security which outweighed fairness. The unions complained to the Commission.

Held: (Commission) The complaint was manifestly ill-founded. There had been an interference with the applicants rights under Article 11 para.1 but this was justified by the exceptions provided for under para.2. The employees at GCHQ were "members of . . . the administration of the state". The measures taken were in accordance with national law and the restriction could be interpreted as covering a complete prohibition of the right under Article 11. It was not clear whether the restriction in this area had to be proportional but even if this were so in cases of national security a wide margin of appreciation was allowed to contracting states. GCHQ was vulnerable to industrial action and given its vital functions the drastic measures taken were not arbitrary. (1987) 50 D.R. 228

Commentary

The Commission considered that it could get no guidance on this issue from the international instruments. The International Covenant on Civil and Political Rights 1966 did not restrict the rights of employees in state administration whilst the International Covenant on Economic Social and Cultural Rights 1966 did do so. The International Labour Organisation (ILO) however did find the United Kingdom to be in breach of the relevant Article of the ILO treaty on freedom of association. The judgment was controversial since it approved outlawing membership of a union, not just the right to take industrial action. The Blair Government has restored the right to join a union to the GCHQ employees.

Key Principle: **Discrimination against public sector employees on political grounds may be a violation of Articles 10 and 1.**

Vogt v Germany

A teacher had been sacked from her post because her active membership of the Communist Party was considered incompatible with her duties. She claimed violations of Articles 10 and 11.

Held: (ECtHR) Articles 10 and 11 were violated. (1996) 21 E.H.R.R. 205

Commentary

This was a landmark decision. In the earlier cases of *Glasenapp v Germany* (1987) 9 E.H.R.R. 25 and *Kosiek v Germany* (1987) 9 E.H.R.R. 328 the court had held that a condition that applicants for civil service jobs uphold the constitution was not a violation of the Convention. They were distinguished because the court considered there that the applicants had not been qualified whereas here the applicant had been a teacher for seven years before the dismissal. There were no security considerations and the ban was disproportionate. The ban made no distinction according to rank. There was no right of recruitment to the civil service in the Convention but "this does not mean . . . that a person who has been appointed as a civil servant cannot complain on being dismissed if that dismissal violates one of his or her rights under the Convention". The court also considered that German schoolteachers were "not members of the administration of the State", see also *Devlin v UK* p.134.

Professional Bodies

Key Principle: **Professional bodies do not necessarily fulfil the "common goal" requirements of voluntary association.**

Le Compte, Van Leuvan and de Meyere v Belgium
The first applicant, a doctor, was struck off the medical register; he did not comply with the order and was sentenced in a criminal court to imprisonment and a fine. The second and third applicants were also doctors who were suspended from practice by the relevant professional body. All three applicants alleged violations of Article 6(1) in that the hearings were not public, and Article 11.

Held: (ECtHR) The word "association" presupposes a voluntary grouping with a common goal. The non-voluntary and public nature of most professional regulatory bodies excludes them from Article 11. There were violations of Article 6(1) in that the cases were not heard publicly by a tribunal competent to determine all aspects of the matter. (1982) 4 E.H.R.R. 1

Commentary
The court noted that totalitarian regimes have resorted to the compulsory regimentation of the professions by means of closed and exclusive organisations taking the place of the professional associations and the traditional trade unions. The authors of the Convention intended to prevent such abuses. There were in Belgium several associations formed to to protect the interests of medical practitioners and which they were completely free to join or not. This safeguards rights under Article 11.

Free Elections

Key Principle: **Protocol 1, Article 3—Right to free elections: "The High Contracting Parties undertake to hold free elections at reasonable intervals by secret ballot, under conditions which will ensure the free expression of the opinion of the people in the choice of the legislature."**

Mattieu-Mohin and Clerfayt v Belgium
The French-speaking applicants complained that as voters living in Flemish administrative districts they could not elect French-

speaking representatives to the regional assembly and that as elected representatives they could not sit in that assembly whereas Dutch-speaking voters and elected representatives in the same municipalities could. They alleged violations of Protocol 1, Article 3 and Article 14.

Held: (ECtHR) There were no violations of either article. The state had a positive obligation to ensure free elections. Protocol 1, Article 3 protected the right to vote and the right to stand for election but these rights were not absolute and could be subject to implied limitations. Such limitations must not impair the very essence of the right. (1988) 10 E.H.R.R. 1

Commentary

This is to date the only case considered under Protocol 1, Article 3. Referring to the rights to vote and to stand for election the court stated that "since article 3 recognises them without setting forth in express terms, let alone defining them, there is room for implied limitations". See also *Ahmed v UK* (p.182). The court made it clear in *Mathieu-Mohin and Clerfayt v Belgium* (1987) that states enjoy a considerable margin of appreciation in this area and the courts will only interfere if the essence of the protected rights is interfered with. In *R. (Robertson) v Wakefield Metropolitan Council, The Times,* November 27, 2001, the applicant complained that the electoral registration officer had failed to respect his wish that his name and address should not be sold on to commercial organisations. The Administrative Court held that the officer had acted contrary to the Data Protection Directive and to Article 8 and to Protocol 1 Article 3 of the European Convention on Human Rights. The claimant had established an unjustified, disproportionate restriction on his right to vote.

10. SOCIAL RIGHTS— DISCRIMINATION

Education

Key Principle: **Protocol 1 Article 2—Right to Education: "No person shall be denied the right to education. In the exercise of any functions which it assumes in relation to education and** to teaching, the State shall respect the right of parents to ensure such education and teaching in conformity with their own religious and philosophical convictions."

Key Principle: The state's respect for the right of parents to ensure education and teaching in conformity with their own religious and philosophical convictions should be accepted in so far as it is compatible with the provision of efficient instruction and the avoidance of unreasonable public expenditure.

Campbell and Cosans v UK

The applicants had no realistic alternative but to send their children to Roman Catholic Schools where children were beaten. Following a minor disciplinary infraction the son of one of the applicants refused with his parents' support to accept a beating and was suspended. The school refused to readmit him until the parents accepted that in future he could be beaten . Both parents claimed breaches of Article 3 and Protocol 1, Article 2.

Held: The duty to respect parental convictions cannot be overrriden by the alleged necessity of striking a balance between differing viewpoints. The state's policy to move gradually towards abolition of corporal punishment was not in itself sufficient to comply with its duty. There were violations of both sentences of Protocol 1, Article 2. (1982) 4 E.H.R.R. 293

Commentary

The case illustrates that state must respect the religious and philosophical convictions of parents although there are limits to this respect. The state may satisfy the Article by a pluralist approach to education and it may claim financial restraint. The parents had to demonstrate that there was a demonstrable causal connection between their belief and the reason they object to what the state is doing. Opposing corporal punishment did amount to philosophical convictions. (See also pp.133–134).

Key Principle: The right to education encompasses the development and moulding of the character and mental powers of pupils.

Campbell and Cosans v UK
For facts see above.

Commentary
Here the court also acknowledged the importance of taking a broad view of the meaning of education in a pluralist society. It referred to ". . . a weighty and substantial aspect of human life and behaviour, namely the integrity of the person, the propriety or otherwise of the infliction of corporal punishment and the exclusion of the distress which the risk of such punishment entails."

Key Principle: **There is no positive obligation on a state to provide education in a minority language.**

Belgian Linguistic Case (No. 2)
French speaking parents living in Flemish speaking regions of Belgium wanted their children educated in French. However no state schools in the area taught in French. The parents alleged that their rights under Articles 8, 9, 10 and 14 of the Convention and under Protocol 1, Article 2 had been violated.

Held: (ECtHR) In principle a law which appears to comply with a Convention Article might in fact constitute a breach when that Article is read together with Article 14, if the law is discriminatory. Article 14 is an integral part of every other Article. It does not prohibit all differential treatment, only that differential treatment which is not objectively and reasonably justified. Protocol 1, Article 2 and Article 14 did not require the state to deliver education in the language of the parents' choice. (1979–80) 1 E.H.R.R. 252

Commentary
It is significant that the wording of the Articles is restrictive. It requires that the state shall not deny rather than that it should positively guarantee or respect the right to education. The burden is on the individual to prove interference not the state to defend non-provision. The Article gives the state discretion on the scope of its provision since it refers to "the exercise of any function which it assumed in relation to education and to teaching". Similarly the Article is primarily concerned with elementary education. There is no obligation to ensure that certain groups such as

prisoners or foreigners are given access to more specialist education such as university education. Nor is the state required to fund home or private education, though it may regulate them. *H v UK* (1984) 6 E.H.R.R. 606

Key Principle: **Although the state must not pursue an aim of indoctrination that does not respect parents' religious and philosophical convictions it may impart knowledge of an indirectly or directly religious or philosophical kind.**

Kjeldsen, Busk Madsen and Pedersen v Denmark
The applicants alleged violations of Protocol 1, Article 2 and Articles 8, 9 and 14 on the grounds that the compulsory sex education introduced by statute in Danish state schools was contrary to their beliefs as Christian parents.

Held: (ECtHR) Parents are not permitted to object to the imparting of information of a religious or philosophical kind because otherwise all institutionalised teaching could be impracticable. Information must be conveyed in an objective, critical and pluralist manner and must not amount to indoctrination which did not respect parents' religious and philosophical convictions. The legislation did not affect the right of parents to enlighten and advise their children. There were no violations of the Convention. (1979–80) 1 E.H.R.R. 711

Commentary
A key feature of this case was that the state could not avoid its responsibilities by referring to the legality of private schools. If it did so this would lead to the position that only the rights of wealthy parents were "respected".

Discrimination

Key Principle: **Article 14 of the ECHR—Prohibition of discrimination: "The enjoyment of the rights and freedoms set forth in this Convention shall be secured without discrimination on any ground such as sex, race, colour, language, religion, political or other opinion, national or social origin, association with a national minority, property, birth or other status."**

Ghaidan v Godin-Mendoza [2004] 2 All E.R. 411
For facts see p.18.

Commentary
The framework for addressing an Article 14 claim has been set out by the courts. In *Ghaidan*, Baroness Hale said (at paras.133 and 134):

> "It is common ground that five questions arise in an Article 14 inquiry, based on the approach of Brooke LJ in *Wandsworth London BC v Michalak* [2002] EWCA Civ 271 at [20], [2002] 4 E.R. 1136 at [20], [2003] 1 W.L.R. 617 as amplified in *R. (on the application of Carson) v Secretary of Sate for Work and Pensions* [2002] EWHC 978 (Admin) at [52], [2002] 3 All E.R. 994 at [52] affirmed [2003] EWCA Civ 797, [2003] 3 All E.R. 577. The original four questions were: (i) Do the facts fall within the ambit of one or more of the convention rights? (ii) Was there a difference in treatment in respect of that right between the complainant and others put forward for comparison? (iii) Were those others in an analogous situation? (iv) Was the difference in treatment objectively justifiable, ie did it have a legitimate aim and bear a reasonable relationship of proportionality to that aim? The additional question is whether the difference in treatment is based on one or more of the grounds proscribed—whether expressly or by inference—in Article 14. The appellant argued that that question should be asked after question (iv), the respondent that it should be asked after question (ii). In my view, the *Michalak* questions are a useful tool of analysis but there is a considerable overlap between them: in particular between whether the situations to be compared were truly analogous, whether the difference in treatment was based on a proscribed ground and whether it had an objective justification. If the situations were not truly analogous it may be easier to conclude that the difference was based on something other than a proscribed ground. The reasons why their situations are analogous but their treatment different will be relevant to whether the treatment is objectively justified. A rigidly formulaic approach is to be avoided."

Sex Discrimination

Key Principle: **The margin of appreciation accorded to states in relation to sex discrimination is very narrow.**

Schmidt v Germany
There was a requirement in the region where the applicant lived for all male but not female adults to perform local fire brigade duties or to pay a financial levy. The constitutional court held that there was an objective justification for the difference. In fact

women did serve in local fire brigade so it was the levy which constituted the difference of treatment on grounds of sex. The applicant alleged breaches of Articles 4 and 14 in relation to forced labour and with Protocol 1, Article 1 in relation to taxation.

Held: (ECtHR) There were violations of Article 14 in conjunction with the other two Convention rights. Reasons behind difference of treatment on grounds of sex must be very strong. As equality advances so the roles of the sexes must be re-addressed. (1994) 18 E.H.R.R. 513

Commentary
In this case the difference of treatment concerned a financial levy not physical activity so the court did not pronounce on whether there were intrinsic differences which made women less suited to certain kinds of work.

State benefits and discrimination

Key Principle: **Traditional practices and roles of men and women may not necessarily justify difference in treatment in relation to state benefits.**

Van Raalte v Netherlands
Unmarried childless women but not men over the age of 45 were exempted from having to pay contributions towards child benefit. The applicant, an unmarried childless man over the age of 45, claimed the exemption breached Protocol 1, Article 1 in conjunction with Article 14. The state claimed that the difference was because women over 45 rarely procreate but men do.

Held: (ECtHR) There was no objective reasonable justification for the different treatment. Women could claim child benefit by reason of adopting, fostering or becoming step mothers. There was a violation of Article 14 in conjunction with Protocol 1, Article 1. (1997) 24 E.H.R.R. 503

Commentary
By contrast, in *Petrovic v Austria* (1999) 4 B.H.R.C. 232 the court found no violation when a father was denied parental leave for a month. The court observed that such benefits originally applied only to mothers and have gradually been extended to fathers as

society's view changed. Here the difference (which had subsequently been removed by legislation) was within the state's margin of appreciation.

Homosexuals

Key Principle: **Discrimination cannot be justified by a fear that some members of society might draw misguided conclusions from its removal.**

Sutherland v UK
For facts see p.151.

Held: (Commission) There was a violation of Articles 8 and 14.

Commentary
See also pp.151 *et seq* for the protection afforded to homosexuals under ECHR.

Racial Discrimination

Key Principle: **Racial discrimination may amount to a type of degrading treatment under Article 3.**

East African Asians v UK
For facts see p.67.

Held: (Commission) The legislation which imposed immigration controls on most East African Asian citizens was racially motivated and amounted to degrading treatment under Article 3 in relation to the British subjects. In relation to the six applications by "protected persons" the legislation did not distinguish between categories of British protected persons on any racial basis and there was no violation. The refusal to grant residence to the applicants whose wives had already been granted permanent residence was a violation of Articles 8 and 14 since the applicants had been subjected to discrimination on the ground of sex in relation to their family lives. (1973) 3 E.H.R.R. 76

Commentary
By contrast in *Abdulaziz, Cabales and Balkandali v UK* (1985) 7 E.H.R.R. 471 the court disagreed with the Commission's finding

that there had been a violation of Article 3 when the husbands of three women immigrants who were lawfully and permanently settled in the United Kingdom were not allowed to join them. The rules then in place applied more strictly to men wishing to join their partners than to women or nationals of the EU Member States. It held that the difference of treatment complained of did not denote any contempt or lack of respect for the personality of the applicants and was not designed to, and did not humiliate or debase but was intended solely to achieve the aims of the policy. It could not therefore be regarded as "degrading" .There was accordingly no violation of Article 3. There had been a violation of Articles 8 and 14, along with Article 13, on the ground of sexual discrimination. However the rule was not racially discriminatory.

Under Article 14 there is a guarantee of freedom from "degrading treatment" which could apply to racial discrimination but in this case the Commission considered racial discrimination under Article 3. In 2000 the 12th Protocol was adopted providing a freestanding "equal treatment guarantee" under which discrimination by the state in any rule of conduct is prohibited. It will come into force when ratified by 10 states; the United Kingdom has not signed it. Article 13 of the treaty of Rome empowers the council, after consultation with the Parliament, to combat discrimination based on sex, racial or ethnic origin, religion or belief, disability, age or sexual orientation.

Disability Discrimination

Key Principle: **Article 14 has no independent existence if the facts of a case do not fall within another Convention right.**

Botta v Italy

The physically disabled applicant found there were no adequate facilities at his seaside holiday resort. Under Italian law private beaches are required to facilitate the access of disabled people. There were no proceedings against the local authorities for failing to enforce the relevant law. The applicant alleged violations of Articles 3, 5, 6(1), 13 and 14. The Commission declared admissible the applications in relation to Articles 3, 5, 8 and 14.

Held: (ECtHR) On the facts the case did not fall under any Convention right. Article 14 could not apply. (1998) 26 E.H.R.R. 241

Smith v UK

The applicant was a gypsy who argued that United Kingdom law criminalised her way of life such as her rejection of permanent accommodation. The offence of parking a caravan outside a designated area was discriminatory since it applied only to gypsies. She alleged breaches of Articles 8, 11 and 14.

Held: (Commission) The applicant had not proved that the law had a real and direct effect on her way of life so as to breach Articles 8 or 11. There was no violation therefore under Article 14. (1993) 18 E.H.R.R. CD 65

Commentary

In relation to some groups, such as the disabled and gypsies, the rights under the ECHR. are less comprehensive than those under national legislation, see for example the Disability Rights Commission Act 1999 and the Race Relations Act 1976 under which gypsies are protected as a minority group.

Political Opinions

Key Principle: **A difference of treatment in relation to political opinion may be justified if it pursues a legitimate aim.**

McLaughlin v UK

The applicant was a member of Sinn Fein. He complained that the directive issued by the Home Secretary in 1988 prohibiting the BBC and ITV to broadcast spoken words of any person who represented or appeared to support a proscribed organisation was a breach of Articles 10, 13 and 14. He was the victim of political discrimination since the ban did not apply to supporters of certain other political parties.

Held: (Commission) The interference with freedom of expression was prescribed by law and had a legitimate aim of combating terrorism. It was not disproportionate and although it would have little direct effect upon the amount of terrorism, it was legitimate to deny publicity to certain causes. There was no breach of Articles 10 or 14. The differential treatment was justified. (1994) 18 E.H.R.R. CD 84

Commentary

In *Arrowsmith v UK* (1978) 3 E.H.R.R. 218 the Commission found no violation of Article 14 since the difference of treatment with other protesters was justified. They had heeded police warnings to cease distribution of leaflets.

Jury Bias

Key Principle: **Racial discrimination by juries violates the ECHR.**

Sander v UK
For facts see p.91.

Held: (ECtHR) A tribunal must be impartial from a subjective as well as an objective point of view. Racial comments by jurors was a very serious matter in today's multi-cultural European societies. This was not redressed by the judge's redirection to the jury. The judge should have reacted in a more robust manner. There was a violation of Article 6(1). (2000) 8 B.H.R.C. 2791

Commentary
The case was distinguished from the earlier case concerning jury discrimination, *Gregory v UK* (1998) 25 E.H.R.R. 577. In the latter there had been no breach of the "impartial tribunal" guarantee in a trial of a black defendant when a jury member had passed a note to the trial judge that read "jury showing racial overtones. One member to be excused". It was considered in *Sander* that there were two grounds of distinction from *Gregory*. First in *Gregory* the complaint of bias was more vague and imprecise, and secondly in *Sander*, but not in *Gregory*, the applicant's counsel had insisted throughout the proceedings that the discharge of the jury was the only proper course.

11. REMEDIES

An Effective Remedy

Key Principle: **Article 13 of the ECHR—Right to an effective remedy: "Everyone whose rights and freedoms as set forth in this Convention are violated shall have an effective remedy before a national authority notwithstanding that the violation has been committed by persons acting in an official capacity."**

[N.B. This Article is not incorporated into English law by the HRA 1998.]

Key Principle: **In assessing whether to award damages and if so how much the court will take into account the seriousness of the violation of the victim's human rights.**

Aksoy v Turkey

The applicant was arrested as a suspected member of the Kurdish revolutionary movement, PKK. He was stripped naked, his hands were tied behind his back and he was strung up by his arms, a so-called "Palestinian hanging", while electrodes were applied to his genitals and water was thrown over him. He was severely beaten and tortured for four days. He made an application to the Commission but before it could be heard he was shot dead, allegedly by a government agent. His application was continued by his father, the prosecuting authority having failed to investigate the torture and murder of his son.

Held: (ECtHR) States were under a particular obligation to investigate incidence of torture. The prosecutor's decision to ignore the applicant's complaint was tantamount to undermining the effectiveness of any remedy available to the applicant. Since Turkish law did not provide proper compensation, the applicant would be awarded compensation consisting of medical expenses and loss of earnings, together with non-pecuniary damages, including an element to reflect the aggravated nature of the Convention breach. (1997) 23 E.H.R.R. 553

Commentary

This was an extreme case. Claims for punitive damages do not usually succeed apparently because they are not compatible with the aim of full restitution (see below).

Key Principle: **Article 41—Just satisfaction: "If the Court finds that there has been a violation of the Convention or the Protocols thereto, and if the internal law of the High Contracting Party concerned allows only partial reparation to be made, the Court shall, if necessary, afford just satisfaction to the injured party."**

Key Principle: **There must be a causal link between the violation and the loss.**

H v UK
The applicant had successfully claimed a violation of Article 6(1) over proceedings to obtain access to her child who was in local authority care lasting two and a half years. She now claimed damages for *inter alia* loss of the relationship with her daughter and loss of the opportunity to have children.

Held: (ECtHR) There was no identifiable causal connection between some aspects of the claim and the violation since it could not be said that a speedier conclusion would have led to a different relationship with her daughter. However it was not possible to exclude the possibility that speedier proceedings might have had a different outcome. There was therefore a loss of real opportunities and the court was prepared to award damages for this. (1988) App. No. 9580/81

Commentary
The United Kingdom Government had reached a settlement with the applicant over costs.

Damages and the Human Rights Act

Key Principle: **Limitation periods in civil claims must be interpreted in the light of Article 6.**

Cachia v Faluyi
A wife and mother had been killed in a road traffic accident in 1988 while the children were minors. At the time of the accident the husband sought damages and issued a writ both under the Fatal Accidents Act 1976 and on behalf of the estate under the Law Reform Miscellaneous Provisions Act 1934. The writ was never served. When the children were 21 in 1997 they commenced proceedings. The limitation period did not run till they reached majority but under s.2(3) of the Fatal Accidents Act 1976 not more than one action shall lie for and in respect of the same subject matter of complaint. It was submitted that Article 6 gave the children right of access to the court to claim compensation for their loss of dependency.

Held: (CA) It was necessary to construe the term "action" as meaning "served process". In this way the legislation was given effect in a way which was compatible with Convention rights. [2001] 1 W.L.R. 1966

Commentary

This case demonstrates the effect of the HRA in personal injury cases. To date there have been no awards of damages in an English court specifically under the Act. The Government had resisted including Article 13 in the HRA arguing that s.8 of the Act provides for effective remedies. During the passage of the Bill-through Parliament it was conceded that the courts may have regard to Article 13 when applying s.8(4) of the HRA 1998 which reads: "In determining (a) whether to award damages, or (b) the amount of an award, the court must take into account the principles applied by the European Court of Human Rights in relation to the award of compensation under Article 41 of the Convention." Section 8(4) refers only to the principles applied by the Strasbourg Court rather than their application to individual assessment of damages. In the Court of Appeal decision in *Heil v Rankin* [2001] Q.B. 272, a personal injury case, Lord Woolf viewed the court's task as "limited to providing fresh guidelines so as to give effect to well established principles as to the objective which should be achieved by an award of damages. Full compensation was the main objective, applying to non-pecuniary as well as to pecuniary loss. The use to which the claimant would put the money was irrelevant." The English law on this is undergoing development. The Law Commission has considered the application of the principle of full restitution under the HRA and concluded that the English courts were not bound in every case to follow Strasbourg precedents and would determine the majority of cases according to the normal common law rules for determining damages. Lord Woolf has commented that the absence of Strasbourg principles as to damages would allow the English courts to develop their own principles within the statutory framework.

Key Principle: **Damages under HRA are not recoverable as of right but only when it is just, appropriate and necessary to achieve just satisfaction.**

Anufrijeva v Southwark LBC

The claimants were asylum seekers whose benefit had been withdrawn by social security following an internal Home Office decision to reject their application for asylum. They were not informed of the decision until nearly six months after it was taken, and were without benefit for the whole of that period.

The issue arose as to the calculation of damages for the infringement of their Article 8 rights.

Held: (CA) The English courts should be at least as liberal in awarding damages as the Strasbourg Court. The basis of the award had to be just and equitable and necessary to afford just satisfaction. It had to be borne in mind in determining the level of damages that the award would deplete public resources for meeting other deserving cases. [2003] EWCA Civ 1406

Commentary
The court set out substantive and procedural guidance for the award of damages. The fundamental principle was to place the applicant in the same position as he would have been if his Convention rights had not been infringed, as far as was possible. There were difficulties in the case of non-pecuniary loss and the court felt the ECtHR had not followed a consistent approach in deciding whether to award damages for anxiety and stress resulting from the breach of Convention rights. The court was concerned that a claim for damages for maladministration under the HRA was likely to cost much more than the likely amount of damages. Alternative remedies such as use of the Ombudsman should be considered. If proceedings were brought they should be in the Administrative Court by way of judicial review. Guidance on the level of damages was available in Judicial Studies Board Guidelines.

The House of Lords in *R. (Greenfield) v Secretary of State for the Home Department* [2005] UKHL 14 held that a finding that there had been a violation of Article 6 was just satisfaction to the injured party and only in exceptional cases would damages be awarded.

Judicial Review

Key Principle: **Judicial Review may be an adequate remedy for the purposes of Article 13.**

Soering v UK
For facts see p.61.

Held: (ECtHR) The "death row phenomenon" constituted torture or inhuman or degrading treatment but the fact that a United Kingdom court would have jurisdiction to set aside a decision on these grounds was an effective remedy. (1989) 14 E.H.R.R. 248

Commentary

The Strasbourg Court has addressed this question in a number of cases and has come to differing decisions. For example in *Smith and Grady v UK* (2000) 29 E.H.R.R. 493 (p.7) it stated that in those circumstances judicial review was not an effective remedy and in fact the domestic courts had taken a similar position. See also *Chahal v UK* (1997) 23 E.H.R.R. 413 (p.60) where the court held there had been a violation of Article 13 and there were no effective remedies available since neither the advisory panel nor the courts had the power to review the Home Secretary's deportation decision. This was a case where national security was involved. There is a particular problem where private bodies are involved because they are not generally subject to judicial review. In a number of recent cases the court has questioned the effectiveness of judicial review. In *Peck v UK* (see p.137) the court commented that judicial review did not provide an effective remedy since the "irrationality" test set too high a threshold.

Inadequate Redress

Key Principle: **The Police Complaints Procedure is not an adequate remedy for the purposes of Article 13.**

Khan v UK
For facts see p.107.

Held: There had been a violation of the applicant's rights under Article 8 and since the Police Complaints Authority was not a sufficiently independent body to protect individuals from abuse by the authorities there was a breach of Article 13. (2000) 8 B.H.R.C. 310

Commentary

The case illustrates that even though there may be procedures for redress under national law they may not be acceptable under Article 13. In *Silver v UK* (1983) 5 E.H.R.R. 347 there was a violation of Article 8 in relation to a prisoner's correspondence. The court stated that neither the prison board of visitors, nor the Parliamentary Commissioner for Administration, nor judicial review nor the Home Secretary were able to supply effective remedies to comply with Article 13.

Key Principle: **Article 13 can be satisfied even where the domestic remedy is limited by statute.**

Powell and Rayner v UK
For facts see p.172.

Held: (ECtHR) Although liability for nuisance and trespass resulting from aircraft noise had been excluded by statute, the exclusion was not absolute and it was for a court to decide whether it applied. Unreasonable aircraft use and noise could still form the basis of a domestic action for trespass or nuisance so there was no violation of Article 13. (1990) 12 E.H.R.R. 355

Commentary
For treatment of exclusion of liability under the HRA where Convention rights are involved, see *Marcic*, p.44.

Responsibilities of Contracting States

Loizidou v Turkey
The European Court of Human Rights had awarded damages to the applicant, a Greek Cypriot, against the Turkish Government in respect of her claims relating to property in Kyrenia which had been seized by the Turkish administration in North Cyprus. The court found that the Turkish action had violated her Convention rights. The Turkish Government refused to pay the award, stating that it could be paid to the applicant in the context of a global settlement of all property cases in Cyprus. The committee of ministers in 1999 strongly urged Turkey to comply, but Turkey did not.

Resolution: (Committee of Ministers) Turkey's obligation to abide by judgments of the court is unconditional . . . Turkey has had ample time to fulfil in good faith in the present case its obligations. Failure on the part of a High Contracting Party to comply with a judgment of the Court is unprecedented. The refusal of Turkey to execute the judgment of the Court demonstrates a manifest disregard for its international obligations, both as a High Contracting Party to the Convention and as a member State of the Council of Europe. In view of the gravity of the matter, it is strongly insisted that Turkey comply fully and without any further delay. Resolution DH (2000) 105, July 24, 2000

Commentary
This case indicates the limitations of the enforcement procedures where a state is recalcitrant. Under Article 46 responsibility for

supervising the execution of the ECtHR's judgments rests with the Committee of Ministers. Decisions of the Committee of Ministers are published as resolutions. Defendant states can issue measures which include payment to the applicant, reopening of proceedings, reversing the verdict, discontinuing the expulsion proceedings and implementing changes to legislation. In a resolution issued in June 2001 the Committee noted that in order to give effect to the decision in *Jordan, Stephen v UK* (App. No. 30280/96) the Government had introduced amending legislation and made a payment to the applicant in respect of costs and expenses. It had thus addressed the violation that the Strasbourg Court identified when it had found faults in the courts-martial system.

Key Principle: **An application can be struck out of the list if the court is satisfied that the parties have reached a satisfactory agreement.**

Duyonov v UK

The applicants were Georgian refugees who had intended to seek asylum in Canada. Instead they were put ashore in Gibraltar, where they surrendered to the immigration authorities. The governor authorised their removal under a local immigration control ordinance. They brought habeas corpus proceedings on the basis that the section of the ordinance used against them applied only to people had been fined or imprisoned in the courts. The case was on its way to the Privy Council. There was no provision for legal aid before the Privy Council. The applicants claimed that was a breach of their rights under Article 6. Before the case reached Strasbourg the Government and the applicants reached a friendly settlement and legislation was introduced to allow legal aid in Privy Council proceedings. The Government applied for their action to be struck out.

Held: (ECtHR) The court was satisfied that the settlement was based on respect for human rights as defined in the Convention and the case should accordingly be struck out of the list. App. No. 36670/97

Commentary

The United Kingdom Government agreed to pay the applicants £5,000 to cover pecuniary and non-pecuniary damages and costs.

Account should be taken of the fact that damages would be paid out of public funds not out of a bottomless purse. Section 8(3) of the HRA makes it clear that damages should not be nominal since the purpose is to achieve "just satisfaction", nor for the same reason should they be exemplary or punitive. In a recent controversial decision, *Akman v Turkey* 2001 (App. No. 37453/97) the court struck out an application from a father who alleged his son had been unlawfully killed by the Turkish security services. He claimed violations of Articles 2 and 13. It was not in dispute the son had been killed by the security services but the authorities claimed he had opened fire. No investigation took place into the death. The Turkish Government had issued a declaration of regret at the death and an *ex gratia* payment of £85,000 was paid.

Key Principle: **Neither Article 13 nor the Convention in general requires that contracting states implement the provisions of the Convention in any particular manner.**

Swedish Engine Drivers' Union v Sweden
For facts see p.195.

Held: (ECtHR) The Swedish Labour Court examined the union's complaints and took into account Sweden's international obligations. Neither Article 13 nor the Convention lays down for contracting states any given manner for ensuring within their internal law the effective implementation of any of the provisions of the Convention. There was no violation of Article 13. (1976) 1 E.H.R.R. 617

Commentary
The court stated that in these circumstances it was not called upon to rule whether, as the Swedish Government had contended and the Commission affirmed, Article 13 is applicable only when a right guaranteed by another Article of the Convention has been violated. However in a later case, *Silver v UK* (1983) 5 E.H.R.R. 347 the court made it clear that it was not a precondition of Article 13 that there was an actual breach of another Convention right. It was necessary for the applicants to have "an arguable claim" to be entitled to seek an effective remedy. The court referred to the 1961 Social Charter of the Council of Europe. Article 6 para.2 of that document affirmed in the court's view the voluntary nature of collective bargaining.

Key Principle: **Article 5(5): "Everyone who has been the victim of arrest or detention in contravention of the provisions of this Article shall have an enforceable right to compensation."**

Benham v UK

The applicant, who was unemployed and not drawing benefit, failed to pay community charge. He was denied legal aid before the magistrates, who decided that his failure to pay was wilful and committed him to prison. The Queen's Bench Divisional Court later held that the magistrates were wrong to have done so because prison should only be used for non-payers who had the means to pay. The applicant complained that the denial of legal aid was a violation of Article 6.

Held: (ECtHR) In view of the severity of the penalty risked by the applicant and the complexity of the applicable law, the interests of justice demanded that, in order to receive a fair hearing, Mr Benham ought to have benefited from free legal representation during the proceedings before the magistrates. There was no breach of Article 5(1) and thus no right to compensation. (1996) 22 E.H.R.R. 293

Commentary

Article 5 is the only Article which gives a right to compensation where there is a breach. The key question here was whether the decisions of the magistates' court were within its jurisdiction or in excess of jurisdiction. The former were effective unless or until they were overturned by a superior court whereas the latter would be null and void from the outset. The court here felt able to distinguish *R. v Manchester City Magistrates' Court Ex p. Davies* (1989) on the basis that there the magistrates had failed altogether to carry out the inquiry required by law whereas in the present case the magistrates had addressed the question but had reached a finding which could not be sustained on the evidence. It should be noted that Article 13 has no application where Article 5(4) or Article 6(1) are in issue. These have specific requirements.

Exclusion of Evidence in Criminal Trials

Key Principle: **Police and Criminal Evidence Act, s.78:**

"(1) In any proceedings the court may refuse to allow evidence on which the prosecution proposes to rely to be given if it appears to the court that, having regard to all the circumstances, including the circumstances in which the evidence was obtained, the admission of the evidence would have such an adverse effect on the fairness of the proceedings that the court ought not to admit it.

(2) Nothing in this section shall prejudice any rule of law requiring a court to exclude evidence."

Key Principle: **Exclusion of evidence may result from breach of a Convention right.**

R. v Looseley
For facts see p.110.

Held: (HL) The court had to balance the need to uphold the rule of law by convicting and punishing criminals with the need to prevent the police from acting in a manner which constituted an affront to the public conscience or offended ordinary notions of fairness. It would be unfair and an abuse of process if a person had been lured, incited or pressurised into committing a crime which he would not otherwise have committed. [2001] 1 W.L.R. 2060

Commentary
In this case the House of Lords articulated the approach of the courts to the application of s.78 of the PACE. It made it clear the possible remedies for breach of the Convention in criminal proceedings, namely a stay of prosecution or exclusion of evidence. Human rights points should be raised in the criminal proceedings themselves not in parallel judicial review proceedings. Only the higher courts can issue a declaration of incompatibility as a species of remedy (see Chapter 2).

12. THE EUROPEAN UNION AND HUMAN RIGHTS

General Principles

Key Principle: **The general principles of European Union law enshrine fundamental human rights.**

Matthews v UK
A Gibraltar resident did not have the opportunity of voting in the elections for the European Parliament because of the limited scope of Annex 2 of the European Community Act on Direct Elections 1976. She claimed that the right to free election under Protocol 1, Article 3 of the ECHR had been infringed.

Held: (ECtHR) There was a breach of the Protocol. [1999] 28 E.H.R.R. 361

Commentary
Prior to this decision the Court of Human Rights had considered all cases concerning European Community law to be inadmissible. This decision paves the way for the intervention of the Court of Human Rights into areas previously thought to be within the jurisdiction of the European Court of Justice (ECJ). The Court of Human Rights accepted that the European Community could not be challenged because it was not one of the high contracting parties to the ECHR. (see *Re Accession of the Community to the European Human Rights Convention*, Opinion 2/94, below). However, the United Kingdom, since it had participated in making the council decision, had violated the ECHR. If the court had not acted the applicant would have lacked a remedy for a serious violation of the fundamental human right.

Key Principle: **The European Community could not accede directly to the ECHR.**

Re Accession of the Community to the European Human Rights Convention Opinion 2/94
The ECJ was asked to give its opinion of whether the Community could accede directly to the Convention.

Held: (ECJ) There was no legal basis in the Treaty of Rome to permit accession. [1996] 2 C.M.L.R. 265

Commentary
The European Community would have to amend the treaty of Rome in order to accede. Article 6 of the Treaty on European Union 1997 (The Treaty of Amsterdam) states that "the Union shall respect fundamental rights for the protection of Human

Rights and Fundamental Freedoms signed in Rome on November 4, 1950 and that they result from the constitutional traditions, common to the Member States, as general principles of Community law". However this is a non-justiciable Article. In the face of pressure for a more coherent human rights approach the heads of state and government decided at the Cologne summit in July 1999 that an E.U. charter of fundamental rights would be drawn up, including general rights of liberty and equality as well as economic and social rights. The Charter was proclaimed at the Nice Conference in December 2000 but was not made part of the subsequent treaty.

Key Principle: **The Convention is a source of Community law.**

Firma J Nold v Commission
The applicant's argued a violation of his property rights after a Commission decision, revising the terms of trading for coal wholesalers, meant that he could not meet the requirements.

Held: (ECJ) Property rights were protected by German constitutional provisions and the Convention. Such rights could be limited in the public interest and the applicant could not be protected in the absence of fundamental errors or flaws in procedure. [1974] 2 C.M.L.R. 338

Commentary
All Member States of the European Community had signed the Convention by 1974.

INDEX